Speculation and the Dollar

The Political Economy of Global Interdependence
Thomas D. Willett, Series Editor

Speculation and the Dollar

The Political Economy of Exchange Rates

Laurence A. Krause

Westview Press

BOULDER • SAN FRANCISCO • OXFORD

The Political Economy of Global Interdependence

Copyright © 1991 by Westview Press, Inc.

Published in 1991 in the United States of America by Westview Press, Inc., 5500 Central Avenue, Boulder, Colorado 80301, and in the United Kingdom by Westview Press, 36 Lonsdale Road, Summertown, Oxford OX2 7EW

Library of Congress Cataloging-in-Publication Data
Krause, Laurence A.
  Speculation and the dollar : the political economy of exchange
rates / Laurence A. Krause.
    p. cm. — (The political economy of global
interdependence)
  Bibliography: p.
  Includes index.
  ISBN 0-8133-7754-4
  1. Foreign exchange futures. I. Title. II. Series.
HG3853.K73 1991
332.4′560973—dc19   89-5652
                                                                        CIP

Printed and bound in the United States of America

      The paper used in this publication meets the requirements
 ∞   of the American National Standard for Permanence of Paper
      for Printed Library Materials Z39.48-1984.

10   9   8   7   6   5   4   3   2   1

Contents

Tables

Figures

Diagrams

Acknowledgments

I began serious consideration of the issues and subject matter that comprise this book as a graduate student at the University of Massachusetts at Amherst. In need of a dissertation topic and vaguely curious about international monetary economics, I decided to sit in on Leonard Rapping's undergraduate course on international finance. Needless to say, I was soon hooked. Within several months I was teaching my own course on international money and beginning to write an outline of what would become my doctoral dissertation on foreign exchange speculation. Once completed the dissertation thesis became this basis for this book.

In the process of starting and completing this research project, I learned and borrowed from many individuals. In this respect, my foremost intellectual and personal debt is to Leonard A. Rapping, who served through the process as my dissertation chairperson, informal guide to the academic world, and friend. If it were not for Leonard's advice, encouragement, and active support, I do not know how I would have completed the work.

Second in the list of contributors has to be my sister, Michele, who served as informal editor, friend, and writing advisor. I would also like to thank Fordham University for its generous grant, Thomas D. Willett for his many helpful suggestions, the patient workers at Fordham's computer center for their help, Craig Plunkett for doing such an admirable job with my data tape, and the I.C.P.S.R. for providing the tape of the IMF's *International Financial Statistics.*

Finally, I would like to thank all my friends, relatives, colleagues, and students for their encouragement and understanding, which provided a source of strength for completing the book. In this vein, my mother deserves special note because of her constant encouragement to finish what at times seemed to be a neverending project.

L. A. K.

About the Book and Author

The large swings in exchange rates that have characterized the free market exchange rate system since its inception in March 1973 have rekindled interest in the economics of exchange rates in general and the role of foreign exchange speculation in particular. Critics of the free market exchange rate system argue that currency speculators destabilize the market, producing swings in rates as well as increasing currency market volatility. Defenders claim that to some extent the ups and downs as well as the day-to-day volatility in currency rates are normal for asset markets like the foreign exchange market. And they believe that the only method of reducing instability is for policymakers to adopt more reasonable monetary and fiscal policies. As to the role of speculation, defenders of the system claim that speculators simply speed up needed adjustments of currency rates to their ever-changing equilibrium values.

In this book Dr. Krause argues that the currency system is plagued by destabilization because of the explosive combination of unstable economic fundamentals, destabilizing currency speculation, and relatively ineffective policing operations by the central banks of the principal industrial powers. In addition, he attempts to show that the effects of these currency swings are to reduce international trade, damage trade relations, and increase overall macroeconomic instability. To remedy the problem, he proposes a system of temporary taxes and subsidies on traded goods to shield the world's trading system from the consequences of currency bubbles.

Laurence A. Krause is an assistant professor of economics at State University of New York, College at Old Westbury, Old Westbury.

1

Exchange Rates

INTRODUCTION

Since the emergence of capitalism in the sixteenth century, the leading nation-states have been linked together economically by world markets in goods and finance. Over many centuries, the continuing development of these economic ties has required the creation of supporting markets, institutions, and government policies of ever more increasing sophistication. Economic historians claim that by around 1870, very similar economic "rules of the game" were adopted by all the leading industrial powers. Thus, it was deemed appropriate to refer to those principal rules governing international trade and finance as an international monetary system.

An international monetary system requires, at the very minimum, several key components which permit large volumes of trade and finance to flow between countries without disruption.[1] These key components include: (1) an adjustment mechanism to coordinate reductions in external surpluses and deficits in the world economy; (2) the provision of world money to serve as a unit of account, means of payment, and store of value for global trade and finance; (3) an exchange rate system to convert one domestic money into another; and (4) a global crisis manager to serve as an international lender

1

of last resort during financial crises and to manage world demand during global recessions and inflations.[2]

The metamorphosis of one international monetary order into another also has involved the disintegration of one or more of these four key components as well as the development of new "rules of the game." But in the intervening period between the breakup of one order and the emergence of another, international economic chaos seems to develop. The likely reasons for the emergence of international economic disorder are not hard to find. First, the transformational process itself has involved some alteration in the mix between market and public direction that forms the very foundation of the system. Second, this process also has been accompanied by significant shifts in the balance of political and economic power between competing nation-states. The combination of the dissolution of the existing "rules of the game," the alteration of the mix between private and public authority at the core of international economic relations, and shifts in the balance of power seems to weaken the foundations of the world economy, thus making the global economy, which intertwines the fortunes of all nations, prone to crisis.

Since 1870 several international monetary orders have come and gone. The first, the classical gold standard, reigned from 1870 to the eve of World War I. It consisted of fixed exchange rates, an "automatic" internal adjustment mechanism, and the use of the British pound and gold as world money with the Bank of England as the "conductor of the international orchestra."[3] The classical gold standard provided a firm international foundation for expanding trade and finance, and produced in the latter half of the period what is still known in European circles as "the beautiful era."[4] However, the rise of increasing international competition for markets, growing inter-state rivalries, militarism, and imperialism led the leading nation-states down the road to the Great War.[5] "[T]he very tendencies in the pre-1914 economy which made the era so golden for the middle classes," argues the noted historian Eric Hobsbawm, "drove it towards world war, revolution and disruptions, and precluded a return to the lost paradise."[6]

In the immediate post-World War I period, floating rates and near financial chaos prevailed, thus inducing the "great" powers to rush to stabilize their economies in preparation for a return to gold, which seemed then to symbolize a return also to "order, international law, security, international confidence, and discipline."[7] It is no great mystery why the leading powers were so eager to re-fix their currencies to gold. In Figure 1.1, the currency values as a percentage of the prewar parities are plotted for ten leading industrial nations-- Switzerland, the United States, Great Britain, Belgium, France, Japan, Germany, Sweden, the Netherlands, and Italy--from 1914-1925. It is noteworthy that only the United States was able to maintain the gold value of its currency at its prewar level throughout the period, while Germany, France, Sweden, and the Netherlands suffered depreciations in excess of fifty percent. The remaining countries experienced only "moderate" depreciations-- depreciations not exceeding twenty-five percent. To put this into perspective, it must be remembered that in the previous forty years industrial country currency rates remained relatively fixed. Thus currency depreciations of this magnitude must have seemed alarming and unacceptable to many contemporary policymakers.

By 1926 a gold exchange standard was erected that once again tied the key currencies of the world economy to gold. However, the resulting international monetary arrangements did not otherwise resemble the prewar system. Exchange rates were fixed, but the "automatic" internal adjustment mechanism ceased to function, the dollar began to rival the pound as world money, political leaders in Great Britain were no longer capable of stabilizing the world economy on their own, and the political elite in the U.S. were perhaps able but unwilling to assume the reins from Britain.[8] The beginning of the

4

Figure 1.1
Floating Exchange Rates: 1914 - 1925

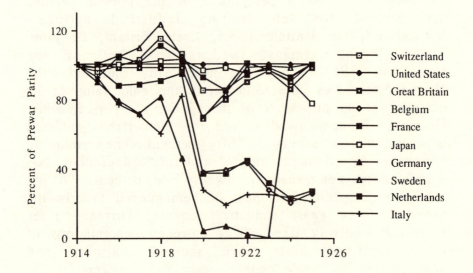

Source:
Melchior Palyi, *The Twilight of Gold* (Chicago: Henry Regnery Company, 1972), pp. 38-39.

collapse of the global order came in 1931 when Great Britain, under increasing financial stress, did the unthinkable--it severed the pound's link to gold and let the pound depreciate. International economic disorder, of course, followed. In the absence of a global manager, the multilateral trading and financial system disintegrated and in its place bilateral trading blocks were formed.[9] The breakup of the international monetary system and the Great Depression that followed helped produce the second "great" war of the twentieth century.

The first post-World War II monetary order was established at a conference in the resort town of Bretton Woods, New Hampshire, in 1944. The Bretton Woods agreements established a fixed but adjustable exchange rate system--a so-called adjustable peg--with an adjustment mechanism that emphasized internal adjustment but also permitted the use of controls, credit, and exchange rate adjustment, the dollar backed by gold as world money, and the U.S. as the global stabilizer. By 1973, however, several major components of the Bretton Woods arrangements were dismantled, creating the current monetary order known either as the dollar standard or, more disparagingly, as the nonsystem. A floating exchange rate system replaced the adjustable peg system, the dollar ceased to be backed by gold, several key currencies became substitutes for the dollar as world money, and the relative economic decline of the U.S. forced it to begin sharing its global management responsibilities.

Exchange Rate Flexibility

An important element in the evolution of international monetary systems since 1870 has been the nature of the exchange rate system and the degree to which exchange rates have been flexible. In the classical gold standard era, exchange rates among the leading industrial powers--England, France, Germany, and the

U.S., not to mention a host of smaller European powers--
were kept fixed throughout the period. Keeping exchange
rates fixed benefited mostly those who were engaged in
international trade and finance by reducing so-called
exchange risk, the risk of loss due to changes in the value
of foreign exchange.

In the classical gold standard era, the continued
adherence to fixed rates, *laissez-faire*, and the "rules of
the game" required that policymakers adjust their
monetary policies when faced with significant gold
outflows. This process worked as follows. If market forces
weaken one's currency, forcing it to depreciate beyond
the so-called gold points, then gold arbitragers could
profit by buying gold in the weak currency country and
exporting and selling in the strong currency country.
(Because there are large transactions costs for buying and
shipping gold from one country to the next, arbitragers
only would engage in these transactions if the price
difference between the two markets more than
compensated them for the transactions cost incurred--
thus, the existence of the so-called gold points.) To
maintain two-way convertibility between gold and
domestic money, each country's central bank had to hold
gold reserves against its outstanding currency liabilities.
At a certain point, therefore, the outflow of gold reserves
would force the central bank of the weak currency
country to act to protect its ability to convert currency
for gold. Usually this would require a tightening of
monetary policy, thus raising interest rates to the point
where pressure on a country's currency was removed.
The higher interest rates provided both a short-run and
long-run solution to the underlying problem--in the
former by attracting an inflow of finance and in the latter
by creating domestic deflation and increased
international competitiveness.

However willing or able governments were to follow
the rules before 1914, they were unwilling or perhaps
unable to do so in the post-World War I gold exchange
standard. In this period, stretching roughly from 1926 to

1931, governments agreed to fix their exchange rates but failed to carry through on the monetary adjustments needed to keep them fixed. As economic pressures mounted, government after government chose to de-link its currency from gold rather than adopt the policies needed to defend the fixed exchange rate system.

The subsequent collapse of the gold exchange standard ushered in a brief chaotic period of floating rates, much like that of the early 1920s, followed by a managed float. The process culminated in the Tripartite Agreement between the U.S., the U.K., and France in 1936, which set up a formal mechanism to manage exchange rates.[10]

In a similar vein, one of the more important consequences of the demise of the Bretton Woods agreements was the emergence of a chaotic floating exchange rate system in March 1973. Since then exchange rates in the core countries of the international monetary system have become almost a by-product of an increasingly unstable global currency market organized by money-center banks. Prior to the advent of generalized floating, the key currency rates in the world economy were pegged by central banks that permitted exchange rates to fluctuate only within narrow bands (plus or minus one percent). In principle, these pegs were adjustable whenever a country had a so-called "fundamental disequilibrium" in its balance of payments. In practice, however, adjusting the exchange rate pegs was a "policy of last resort," to be used only when external deficits and the resulting pressure on one's currency proved to be unmanageable.

Whether they were intended to do so or not, the Bretton Woods agreements prevented governments from using exchange rate policy as a method of solving their balance of payments problems and reducing exchange market pressures, except in dire emergencies. In fact, governments routinely had resorted to running down their foreign exchange reserves rather than implementing alternative economic policies (such as

controls or contractionary demand policies) in order to
shrink their external deficits. Towards the twilight of the
Bretton Woods era, the inability or unwillingness of
governments to adjust their exchange rates was an
important reason why the major central banks were
unable to fend off a series of exchange market crises,
which eventually undermined the adjustable peg
exchange rate system altogether.

This flaw in the Bretton Woods currency
arrangements was anticipated by John Maynard Keynes
in the 1940s. In developing a plan for international
monetary arrangements to be put in place after the war,
Keynes studied and critiqued the preexisting
international monetary arrangements. He discovered that
one of the lessons of the past was that some built-in
exchange rate inflexibility was needed to prevent
governments from using exchange rate policy to export
their unemployment problems through real currency
devaluations. However, he also noted that some exchange
rate flexibility was needed to reconcile the divergent
rates of wage and price inflation that were bound to
develop in the postwar era.[11]

Keynes therefore argued that exchange rate
inflexibility was needed because the competitive struggle
for markets between states would push government after
government into a destructive cycle of competitive
devaluations, which is exactly what happened when Great
Britain went off the gold standard in 1931. Thus to
prevent governments from giving in to the temptation to
undervalue their exchange rates (combined with the fact
that exchange rate policy had inherent spillover effects)
Keynes argued that *large real* exchange rate changes
needed to be internationally supervised.[12] Keynes
recognized, however, that changes in real exchange rates
had their place in adjusting chronic balance of payments
problems, but because such changes produced their
effects by zero sum reparcelizations of world markets, he
believed that they should be used sparingly and only
under international supervision.

However, Keynes was not against *nominal* exchange rate flexibility. He understood that if countries pursued full employment policies in the postwar period, then their differing political circumstances inevitably would produce divergent rates of wage and price inflation. Under these circumstances, if "high" inflation countries were forced to keep their nominal exchange rates fixed, they would suffer needlessly the consequences of currency overvaluation. The resulting currency overvaluation would produce declines in the price competitiveness of their traded goods sector. And more importantly, the loss of price competitiveness eventually would undermine either the existing exchange rate regime (as it did in 1931) or the political resolve needed to adhere to the goal of full employment (which Keynes considered the paramount policy goal). An inflexible, nominal exchange rate system like the one created at Bretton Woods was a complete anathema to the types of policies that Keynes desired for the postwar era. After all, a fixed nominal exchange rate system, like the "adjustable" peg system, would force high inflation countries to choose between opting out of the exchange rate system or adopting the harsh, deflationary medicine of the gold standard.[13]

Keynes was clear then that inflexible nominal exchange rates were undesirable. In his view, this was one of the fundamental flaws of the gold standard. The gold standard, in effect, fixed exchange rates in order to place an external constraint on domestic wage and credit policies. "The error of the gold-standard," Keynes noted, "lay in submitting national wage-policies to outside dictation. It is wiser to regard stability (or otherwise) of internal prices as a matter of internal policy and politics."[14] Thus he advocated that currency rates needed to be altered over the long run in accordance with differences in national efficiency wages: "Broadly speaking, the factor governing the exchanges in the long run is the level of money wages relatively to efficiency in one country as compared to another."[15] This implied that "[i]f money wage rates in a particular country have gotten thoroughly out of gear there is nothing to be done but to alter the exchanges."[16]

It is worth noting that Keynes' critique of exchange rate inflexibility did not lead him to advocate a free float --Keynes believed that free markets simply could not be trusted to get exchange rates right. Instead, he advocated that governments be coaxed into managing their nominal exchange rates in order to keep domestic efficiency wages in line with those of their foreign competitors. Government control, thought Keynes, would require central banks to monopolize currency dealings:

> We [the British Government] contemplate the central bank or similar institutions monopolizing dealings in foreign exchange for its own nationals. . . . That would get rid of the whole element of exchange speculation which caused so much trouble after the last war.[17]

In the 1950s, this particular flaw in the Bretton Woods system was rediscovered by Milton Friedman, one of the foremost advocates of the doctrine of *laissez-faire*.[18] He pointed out that if inflation rates differed across countries and exchange rates were kept fixed, currency rates in the "high" inflation countries must become overvalued and thus balance of payments deficits would develop. Like Keynes before him, Friedman argued that in order to maintain balance of payments equilibrium it would be infinitely easier and less costly to adjust one price, the exchange rate, rather than use deflationary demand policies to adjust all internal prices downward. Internal price adjustment is more costly because goods prices are highly inflexible. It is unfortunate, however, that Friedman and other conservative critics of the Bretton Woods exchange rate system used this insight to argue for a switch to a market-determined exchange rate regime rather than to advocate a system of government-managed flexibility.

But given their overriding ideological commitment to free markets, this was inevitable.

The early advocates of free market exchange rates also bolstered their argument by claiming that a whole spectrum of benefits would result from generalized floating. In retrospect, however, many of these claimed advantages of floating rates seem unrealistic and/or exaggerated today in light of our dismal experience with floating rates.[19] The most important of these supposed advantages of floating rates included: (1) In a floating rate system, exchange rates would adjust automatically and quickly to offset differences in national inflation rates, thereby preventing exchange rates from ever becoming overvalued or undervalued. (2) Nominal exchange rates would prove to be more stable under a floating rate system than under the crisis-prone Bretton Woods system. (3) The effects of business recessions would no longer be transmitted internationally because floating rates would shield countries from external monetary shocks, deemed by monetarists like Friedman to be the single most important cause of business fluctuations. (4) Floating rates would promote monetary autonomy, or the ability of each nation-state to control its own monetary policy *independently of the monetary policies adopted by other governments*. (5) Floating rates would permit and even encourage the world trading system to function without trade barriers. (6) Central banks would no longer need to hold large reserves of foreign currencies in order to intervene in the foreign exchange market to manage their own exchange rates. This would thus save taxpayers the additional expense of having their governments needlessly holding low interest-earning assets.

Economists have taken two different routes in coming to terms with the many "surprises" or "disappointments" which the floating exchange rate system has entailed. The majority of the profession has settled comfortably into a position which holds that the flaws in the arguments made by the early advocates of floating rates prevented

them from predicting accurately the actual course of
market events. More specifically, the chief culprit was
diagnosed to be the underlying model employed by the
advocates of free market exchange rates. Instead of
theorizing the exchange rate as an asset price (as
economists do now) and thus predicting that exchange
rates would behave as erratically and unpredictably as
stock and bond prices do, they argued mistakenly that
currency rates would behave much like goods prices.
Furthermore, it is argued, this mistaken belief resulted
from the idea that the exchange rate could be considered
as the relative price of *goods* traded in world markets
rather than as the relative price of *assets*. From this
perspective, once the required change in outlook is made,
it is possible to "explain" the stylized facts of the floating
period.

An alternative critique of the position argued by the
early advocates of floating rates stressed not only the
shortcomings of their commodity-trade model of the
exchange rate, but also the misrepresentation of the
important role that currency speculation played in the
foreign exchange market. In its modern form, this view
borrows and then develops further the long-standing
position that currency speculators destabilize market
prices by forcing rates to deviate from the market's
"fundamentals." From this perspective, the inherent flaw
in the arguments made by the early advocates of floating
rates revolved around their assumption that, for the most
part, speculation would be stabilizing. In fact, this
critique had been seen by the early advocates of the
floating rate system as the principal counter-argument in
their crusade to alter U.S. international monetary policy.

In its older guise, this debate centered upon whether
or not rational speculators would induce exchange rates
to move closer to underlying long-run equilibrium values,
as the advocates of floating rates argued, or whether
speculators would exaggerate deviations of exchange
rates away from their fundamentals, as the defenders of
continued government-managed exchange rates claimed.

The former type of speculation was labeled "stabilizing" while the latter was termed "destabilizing." The "stabilizing" versus "destabilizing" debate has continued to rage in the economics profession ever since, although now each side has a more sophisticated arsenal from which to defend its position.

Before proceeding further, I would like to define carefully the term foreign exchange speculation. The literature on *foreign exchange speculation* contains a number of distinct definitions.[20] The most common definition used is that foreign exchange speculation is the purchase (or sale) of foreign exchange with the intention of making a profit by reselling (or repurchasing) in the near future. According to this definition, speculators are traders who take open positions in a currency so that they can reap profits by anticipating short-run changes in exchange rates. Thus, this conventional view holds that speculation is motivated solely by anticipated profits. For the purposes of this study, however, a more inclusive definition is preferable. I define speculation as the purchase (or sale) of foreign exchange that is induced solely by expectations of future changes in exchange rates.[21] This broader definition of speculation not only includes speculation for profit but includes also the trading activity of agents who close their positions due to exchange rate expectations ("speculative" hedging), as well as the trading activity of agents who maintain open positions to avoid expected exchange losses (speculative flight).

The "stabilizing" versus "destabilizing" debate now centers upon the existence and empirical significance of speculative currency bubbles. Speculative bubbles arise when currency traders perceive that an exchange rate is deviating from its fundamental rate. They thus go on to bet that the deviation will continue to grow fast enough to provide them with lucrative returns that are expected to be high enough to compensate the traders for any perceived risk. A currency bubble can become self-feeding if the prospective returns lure enough new entrants into the market. These new investors bid up the value of a currency and insure that the underlying profit expectations that are driving the process are realized. Since such deviations are unsustainable over the long term, corrections are inevitable. However, over the medium run, large currency bubbles induce significant shifts in international price competitiveness which then produce sizeable macroeconomic disturbances.

On the surface at least, the vision of the exchange rate system as one dominated by large currency bubbles capable of magnifying exchange rate volatility and producing large self-reversing swings in exchange rates fits the stylized facts quite well. Regardless of how one measures currency rate instability, the floating rate era has been characterized by highly unstable exchange rates between the dollar and the major currencies of Western Europe and Japan. Over the years, exchange rate instability has manifested itself in several different ways. First, exchange rates have been very volatile on a day-to-day or week-to-week basis, varying by as much as six percent in a single trading day. Not surprisingly, compared to the Bretton Woods system, exchange rate volatility has been five-times greater since the era of generalized floating.[22]

Second, and more importantly, there have been several large seemingly self-reversing swings in nominal exchange rates. As illustrated in Figure 1.2, almost every significant change in the trade-weighed dollar has been subsequently reversed in the following period! It seems that if the dollar depreciates (or appreciates) for any length of time the one thing that can be relied upon is that the movement will be reversed sooner or later. Third, Figure 1.2 also shows that these large medium-term swings in nominal exchange rates have resulted in equally large changes in *real* (inflation adjusted) rates. This fact suggests that these medium-term swings potentially can produce substantial alterations in international price competitiveness between the U.S., Western Europe, and Japan. And finally, Figure 1.2 shows

Figure 1.2

The Nominal and Real Trade Weighted Dollar:
1973 - 1988

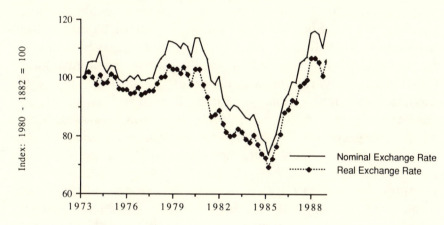

Source:
All data are from Morgan Guaranty Trust, *World Financial Markets*.

that the magnitude of these medium-term swings in both the nominal and real exchange rates have been increasing over time. Since exchange rate instability has proven to be problem that has worsened with time, it should be seen as an endemic problem rather than simply a passing phenomenon.

THE SCOPE OF THE BOOK

This book consists of a set of theoretical and empirical arguments in support of the hypothesis that speculation in the foreign exchange market during the floating era has been destabilizing. This destabilizing speculation has resulted in several large currency bubbles, each sparked by major economic and political disturbances, but thereafter reflecting a self-feeding speculative process. As a result, the core states in the world economy have experienced several large self-reversing swings in their nominal and real exchange rates that have had little, if anything, to do with the underlying market fundamentals which are thought by many to govern the behavior of currency rates. Moreover, the instability generated by currency speculation has forced the major central banks to intervene repeatedly in order to assure at least the semblance of stability in international monetary affairs. In effect, what has emerged is a "political exchange rate cycle."

This political exchange rate cycle has had three phases. First, large shocks to the international monetary system have created, by their effects upon market expectations, the foundations for large currency bubbles. Second, these induced shifts in market expectations then produced one-way speculative trading in the foreign exchange market, which enormously magnified the initial impact of the shock and thus transformed it into a self-feeding movement of currency rates away from their fundamentals. And finally, once these large bubbles began to threaten the stability of the dollar-based international monetary system, a temporary alliance was forged among the major central banks that intervened in order to contain the damage.

This study concludes with an assessment of the economic and political costs imposed by these currency bubbles on the international trading and monetary system, as well as a survey of options for international economic policy.

The guiding concern of this book is to contribute to the ongoing debate about the nature of foreign exchange speculation by establishing the theoretical and empirical foundations for the existence of destabilizing speculation in the form of large speculative currency bubbles. After careful evaluation, I conclude that foreign exchange speculation is destabilizing because it tends to increase market turbulence, generates substantial deviations away from "fundamentals," and magnifies political and economic instability. It is my sincere hope that my research will help contribute to the formation of a consensus that regulatory mechanisms are needed in order to combat the causes and effects of destabilizing foreign exchange speculation.

NOTES

1. On this subject, see John Williamson, *The Failure of World Monetary Reform, 1971-1974* (New York: New York University Press, 1977), Charles P. Kindleberger, *The World in Depression, 1929-1939* (Berkeley: University of California Press, 1986), and John Maynard Keynes, *The Collected Writings of John Maynard Keynes* vol. XXV (London: Cambridge University Press, 1980).

2. Kindleberger views the crisis manager as the agent, usually the dominant nation-state, which provides the public good of stability during periods of economic and financial distress. For an extended discussion, see Kindleberger, "International Public Goods Without International Government," in *The International Economic*

Order: Essays on Financial Crisis and International Public Goods (Cambridge: MIT Press, 1988), pp. 133-135.

3. There are two views about how the classical gold standard system operated. The traditional view was that it was a market-directed system. Market signals in the form of inflows and outflows of gold were believed responsible for orchestrating central bank policy. The central banks were seen as passive agents that simply followed the lead of the international currency and gold markets. The second view was first put forth by Keynes. He suggested that the system worked through the wise management of the Bank of England. "During the latter half of the nineteenth century the influence of London on credit conditions throughout the world was so predominant that the Bank of England could almost have claimed to be the conductor of the international orchestra." John Maynard Keynes, quoted by Kenneth W. Dam, *The Rules of the Game* (Chicago: University of Chicago Press, 1982), p. 18. For a discussion of these issues, see ibid., pp. 14-19.

4. "From the middle of the 1890s until the Great War, the global economic orchestra played in the major key of prosperity. . . . Affluence based on booming business formed the background to what is still known on the European continent as 'the beautiful era' *(belle epoque)*." See Eric Hobsbawm, *The Age of Empire, 1875-1914* (New York: Random House, 1987), p. 46.

5. No individual understood the profound changes that took place due to the war better than Keynes: "What an extraordinary episode in the economic progress of man that age was which came to an end in August, 1914! The greater part of the population, it was true, worked hard and lived at a low standard of comfort, yet were, to all appearances, reasonably contented with this lot. But escape was possible, for any man of capacity or character at all exceeding the average, into the middle and upper classes, for whom life offered, at a low cost and with the least trouble, conveniences, comforts, and amenities beyond the compass of the richest and most powerful

monarchs of other ages. The inhabitant of London could order by telephone, sipping his morning tea in bed, the various products of the whole earth, in such quantity as he might see fit, and reasonably expect their delivery upon his doorstep; he could at the same moment and by the same means adventure his wealth in the natural resources and new enterprises of any quarter of the world, and share, without exertion or even trouble, in their prospective fruits and advantages; or he could decide to couple the security of his fortunes with the good faith of the townspeople of any substantial municipality in any continent that fancy or information might recommend. He could secure forthwith, if he wished it, cheap and comfortable means of transit to any country or climate without passport or other formality, could dispatch his servant to the neighbouring office of a bank for such supply of the precious metals as might seem convenient, and could then proceed abroad in foreign quarters, without knowledge of their religion, language, or customs, bearing coined wealth upon his person, and would consider himself greatly aggrieved and much surprised at the least interference. But, most important of all, he regarded this state of affairs as normal, certain, and permanent, and any deviation from it as aberrant, scandalous, and avoidable. The projects and politics of militarism and imperialism, of racial and cultural rivalries, monopolies, restrictions, and exclusion, which were to play the serpent to this paradise, were little more than amusements of his daily newspaper and appeared to exercise almost almost no influence at all on the ordinary course of social and economic life, the internationalization of which was nearly complete in practice." See John Maynard Keynes, *The Economic Consequences of the Peace* (New York: Harcourt, Brace and Howe, 1920), pp. 10-12.

6. Hobsbawm, *The Age of Empire*, p. 55.

7. Robert Mundell, quoted by Dam, *The Rules of the Game*, p. 60.

8. This is, in brief, Kindleberger's explanation of the Great Depression. See *The World in Depression*, ch. 14.

9. Ibid., chs. 8-11.

10. Dam, *The Rules of the Game*, pp. 46-50.

11. To quote Keynes: "We should like to have some agreed system to prevent competitive exchange depreciations. Exchanges have to be altered from time to time because the social and wage policy of different countries do not keep step with one another necessarily but there should be no exchange depreciations which are merely passing on one country's perplexities to its neighbours. Some provision should be made against that." See Keynes, *The Collected Writings* vol. XXV, p. 208.

12. "There have to be provisions by which," wrote Keynes, "rates of exchange can be altered if circumstances indicate it to be necessary, but not altered by unilateral action. Only altered in accordance with the general principles of the system." Ibid., 212.

13. Keynes summarized his position as follows: "The primary aims of an international currency scheme should be . . . to prevent . . . those evils . . . which follow from countries failing to maintain stability of domestic efficiency costs and moving out of step with one another in their national wage policies without having at their disposal any means or orderly adjustment, and if orderly adjustment is allowed, that is another way of saying that countries may be allowed by the scheme, which is not the case with the gold standard, to pursue, if they choose, different wage policies and, therefore, different price policies." See John Maynard Keynes, *The Collected Writings of John Maynard Keynes* vol. XXVI (London: Cambridge University Press, 1980), p. 32.

14. Ibid., p. 33.

15. Keynes, *The Collected Writings* vol. XXV, p. 105.

16. Ibid., p. 106.

17. Ibid., p. 212.

18. Milton Friedman, "The Case for Flexible Exchange Rates," in *Essays in Positive Economics* (Chicago: University of Chicago Press, 1953), pp. 157-203.

19. See Ronald MacDonald, *Floating Exchange Rates: Theory and Evidence* (London: Unwin Hyman, 1988), pp. 1-4.

20. For a sample of the various definitions see Steven W. Kohlhagen, "The Identification of Destabilizing Foreign Exchange Speculation," *Journal of International Economics* 9 (1979), p. 325.

21. This is more or less the definition Kohlhagen adopts. Ibid., p. 325.

22. Jacob A. Frenkel and Morris Goldstein, "Exchange Rate Volatility and Misalignment: Evaluating Some Proposals for Reform," in Federal Reserve Bank of Kansas City *Financial Market Volatility*, a symposium sponsored by the Federal Reserve Bank of Kansas City (Jackson Hole, Wyoming: August 17-19, 1988), p. 186.

2

Foreign Exchange Speculation

In this chapter, I will explore the major theoretical issues which divide the economics profession into two opposing camps, each with a well-developed, diametrically opposed position about the nature of foreign exchange speculation. My review of this debate begins by examining the older literature, which focused on the issue of whether or not speculation was "stabilizing" or "destabilizing." Then, I will examine the recent literature on so-called rational speculative disturbances and integrate it with the older literature in order to create a cogent and rich framework for understanding and interpreting the events in the market for foreign exchange since the demise of the Bretton Woods agreements. The framework developed provides a basis for showing that economic theory suggests that currency speculation can be destabilizing by increasing exchange rate volatility, generating sharp deviations from "market fundamentals," and intensifying economic and political instability.

NURKSE AND THE INTERWAR EXPERIENCE

The modern literature, as well as all of the subsequent debates about the detrimental consequences of foreign exchange speculation, originated with the work of Ragnar

Nurkse.[1] Nurkse's contribution to the debate is found in his *International Currency Experience: Lessons of the Inter-war Period*, a review of the causes of disorder in the interwar monetary system, which made concrete recommendations for the reconstruction of a stable international monetary order in the post-World War II era. Part of his study focused on the short, chaotic floating exchange rate regime of post-World War I Europe.[2] In his study, Nurkse argued that the devastation of Europe after the war forced European governments to run large import surpluses in order to rebuild their war-torn economies.[3] The inadequacy of the European governments' foreign exchange reserves made foreign capital imports the only viable medium-term method of financing current account deficits at relatively stable exchange rates. In the absence of higher interest rates, private wealth holders were willing to provide the financing for the burgeoning deficits at first, because they anticipated that the then depreciated European currencies would return to their prewar parities as soon as Europe returned to "normal." (In the context of the era, the return to "normal" meant a stabilization of the war-time induced inflations to allow governments to return to the gold standard at the prewar parities.) In the early stages of the float, therefore, currency depreciation aided in the stabilization of currency values by attracting speculative capital inflows.

However, the era of stabilizing capital inflows ended after a brief period. The continuation of expansionary policies by the rebuilding European countries produced seemingly intractable inflation and budgetary problems that only encouraged the decline in currency values. The further depreciation of currencies had the effect of depleting speculators' optimistic expectations and produced instead speculative anticipations of continued weakness. Thus in the uncertain and volatile postwar environment, the bearish expectations of investors produced speculative flight from those currencies considered weak.[4] Furthermore, as investors' confidence weakened, flight from the "weak" currencies tended to spread to the "strong" currencies. In response, European governments were forced to adopt drastic policy measures in order to stem speculative flight.

There were some economists who argued that the large depreciations were primarily the result of inflationary monetary policies. However, Nurkse claimed that this view was only partially correct. Instead he argued that the initial currency depreciations may have had inflationary origins, but the sharp depreciations that followed were the result of speculative anticipations of continued currency weakness. Nurkse argued that as the ensuing capital flight gathered momentum, it generated large depreciations, which in turn had inflationary consequences:

> [T]he fall in the exchange rate became literally the leading factor in the mechanism of inflation, driving up the cost of living and creating an irresistible pressure for wage adjustments, which in turn called forth demands for additional currency on the part of the government as well as businessmen.[5]

Therefore, in Nurkse's view, the causal chain went from speculatively induced exchange depreciations to a cost-push inflation that was accommodated eventually by monetary expansion.

From this admittedly limited but suggestive experience, Nurkse drew several controversial conclusions about the nature of currency speculation. First, he argued that when speculative anticipations resulted in capital flight and currency depreciation, the process was likely to be self-fulfilling and self-feeding. Nurkse was very explicit on this matter:

> Such anticipations are apt to bring about their own realization. Anticipating purchases of foreign exchange tend to produce or at any rate hasten the anticipated fall in the exchange value of the national

currency, and the actual fall may set up or strengthen expectations of a further fall.[6]

Nurkse's second conclusion was that speculative disturbances were likely to produce a "highly unstable" environment in which "psychological factors may at times be overwhelming." Moreover, in turbulent times, he said, exchange rate movements were likely to have an "indeterminate character" which was "swayed by speculative anticipations."[7] All of these lessons convinced Nurkse, as well as a generation of economists, that floating exchange rate regimes were undesirable because of their inherent instability. "If there is anything that the inter-war experience has clearly demonstrated," concluded Nurkse, "it is that paper currency exchanges cannot be left free to fluctuate from day to day under the influence of market supply and demand."[8]

THE STABILIZING VERSUS DESTABILIZING DEBATE

Nurkse's work stimulated an intense debate in the 1950s and early 1960s on the nature of foreign exchange speculation. Economists who favored floating exchange rates argued that, on average, speculation would tend to be "stabilizing." On the other hand, those economists who defended continued currency regulation argued that speculation under a floating regime would tend to be "destabilizing." In the literature, destabilizing speculation has had three distinct meanings.[9] The conventional meaning was that speculation was destabilizing when the variance of the spot exchange rate increased as a result of speculation. A second definition interpreted speculation as destabilizing when it forced the exchange rate to deviate from its equilibrium rate consistent with underlying market fundamentals. And a third definition stated that speculation was destabilizing when it induced unwarranted alterations in the equilibrium rate.

Nurkse's main argument is interpreted best as an attempt to show that speculation was destabilizing because it induced a shift in the currency market's fundamentals path. Moreover, he also believed unambiguously that speculation could produce prolonged deviations from fundamentals, although he never developed an argument explaining this position. Finally, even though Nurkse never explicitly argued that speculation increased market volatility, it was still implicit in his argument. In other words, Nurkse's views strongly imply that speculation in the 1920s was destabilizing in all of the aforementioned ways.

The Friedman-Meade Counter-Revolution

In the immediate postwar period, Milton Friedman, the modern founder and spiritual leader of monetarism, and J. E. Meade, a Keynesian, led a counter-revolution in the economics profession.[10] They managed to restructure the debate on foreign exchange speculation that Nurkse had stimulated into an extremely narrow framework. Friedman and Meade believed that the issue was really whether currency speculation increased or decreased the volatility of the exchange rate itself.

In the Friedman-Meade view, traders in the foreign exchange market bought and sold foreign exchange in order to acquire goods and assets whose prices were quoted in foreign currencies. Moreover, these sales and purchases were said to be sensitive to the *current price* of foreign exchange, not the *expected future price*. Thus Friedman and Meade implicitly assumed that the foreign exchange market was dominated by nonspeculative trading. It was in this simplified view of the foreign exchange market that currency speculators were supposed to operate.

Friedman and Meade also assumed that the typical speculator was a trader with better than average insight and foresight into the market process. For speculators to be successful, according to this theory, they would sell foreign exchange when the market is "high" (when rates are overvalued), and buy foreign exchange when the market is "low" (when rates are undervalued). If speculators correctly anticipate changes in the market's equilibrium and follow the Friedman-Meade strategy, they act to stabilize the market, albeit unintentionally. In a market with this type of speculation, adjustments to equilibrium are hastened and market turbulence is kept to a minimum. Therefore, speculation of the Friedman-Meade variety would be considered stabilizing.

In the Friedman-Meade framework, destabilizing speculation could arise from expectational errors. For example, Meade claimed that destabilizing speculation was due either to "perverse" or "grossly excessive" market forecasts. In the first case, speculators erred in the direction of change in the market. Thus, if changes in equilibrium values caused the home currency to appreciate and speculators anticipated wrongly that the currency would depreciate, the speculators would end up purchasing depreciating foreign currencies. In the second case, speculators anticipated correctly the direction of a currency's change while at the same time overestimating the magnitude of the change. This induced speculators to continue buying and/or selling foreign exchange even when the market reached equilibrium. In both these cases, speculators' expectational errors "destabilized" the market by causing either temporary perverse adjustments, as in the first case, or temporary overshooting, as in the second case. Such speculation was deemed destabilizing because the exchange rate became more volatile than it would have been in the absence of such speculative trading.

Friedman took the argument several steps further in an attempt to argue that *rational, profit-seeking speculation had to be stabilizing*. First, he contended that while both stabilizing and destabilizing speculation were abstract possibilities, destabilizing speculation tended to be unprofitable for speculators as a group:

It is said that speculators will take a decline in the exchange rate as a signal for a further decline and will thus tend to make the movements in the exchange rate sharper than they would be in the absence of speculation. The special fear in this connection is of capital flight in response to political uncertainty or simply to movements in the exchange rate. . . . People who argue that speculation is generally destabilizing seldom realize that this is largely equivalent to saying that speculators lose money, since speculation can be destabilizing in general only if speculators on the average sell when the currency is low in price and buy when it is high.[11]

In contrast, Friedman argued, stabilizing speculation would be profitable, on average, for speculators as a group. Therefore, according to this view, the unfettered market penalized destabilizing speculation while at the same time rewarding stabilizing speculation. Over the long term then, "professional" speculators with better foresight and insight into market fundamentals would survive at the expense of their destabilizing counterparts. If for some reason the competitive pressure generated by the market was insufficient and left too many "amateurs" in the market, the government easily could step in and speculate against them. Thus, Friedman argued, the market's own internal selection mechanism would tend to eliminate destabilizing speculation. However, he also recognized that government intervention might be warranted if the market's own selection process proved inadequate, thus requiring it to play the role of stabilizer.

A second argument advanced by Friedman said that Nurkse was incorrect in claiming that speculative currency movements would cause induced monetary accommodation. Within the Friedman-Meade framework, Nurksian destabilizing speculation can be characterized as follows. If a speculative disturbance raises the value of foreign exchange above the market's equilibrium and creates an increase in the money supply via cost-push pressure, the demand for foreign exchange will shift up and to the right. Therefore, speculative anticipations can be self-fulfilling, as Nurkse argued. For Friedman though, inflation is ultimately a monetary phenomenon--only a weak government would allow the accommodation. From Friedman's perspective, speculators were "right" in the 1920s since they correctly anticipated that governments did not have any anti-inflationary backbone. A government strongly committed to an anti-inflationary monetary policy would not invite speculative flight from its currency.[12] Of course, if speculators did not believe in the government's position, they would lose money by challenging the government's resolve to refuse to accommodate the market.[13]

Both Friedman and Meade's contribution to the debate predated the postwar floating exchange rate system. It is interesting to note that they envisioned that a properly functioning, free market exchange rate system would operate much like an ideal fixed exchange rate system. For example, as noted earlier, Friedman and Meade took for granted that exchange rates would be stable from day to day, fluctuating only within narrow bands as they did under the Bretton Woods adjustable peg system. Moreover, they also noted that when balance of payments disequilibriums surfaced due to inconsistent economic policies, smart speculators would insure that exchange rates would adjust quickly to restore balance of payments equilibrium. Finally, they hinted that only if the international economy became unstable would the exchange rate system become disorderly.[14] Therefore, Friedman and Meade's simple and rarefied model of the foreign exchange market led them to believe that floating exchange rate regimes would behave much like a textbook adjustable peg system, although smart speculators would now replace the inept and politically motivated policymakers as the regulators of currency rates.

Profitable Destabilizing Speculation?

By the end of the Bretton Woods era, most economists had adopted Friedman's arguments along with his critique of Nurkse, but of course there were dissenters. At the theoretical level, the dissenters centered their attacks on Friedman's proposition that destabilizing speculation had to be unprofitable and consequently would not be reproduced by the profit-seeking traders in the foreign exchange market. A dissenting literature then developed, attempting to dispute the importance of, or finding counter-examples to, Friedman's famous proposition.

One argument against Friedman's position was that although he may have been right that destabilizing speculation was unprofitable for speculators *on average*, the claim may have been irrelevant. The dissenters argued that destabilizing speculation could occur in two stages. In the first stage, a group of "insiders" destabilize the exchange rate, and before the market crashes, sell out to a group of "outsiders" attracted into the market by the lure of high profits.[15] Speculation would then be destabilizing and unprofitable for speculators as a group, but a subgroup of insiders would profit. The market would reproduce destabilizing speculation as long as a periodic supply of outsiders was coaxed into the market by the success of the "insiders."

Three counter-examples were also produced by the anti-Friedman group, which disputed the claim that destabilizing speculation had to be unprofitable. The first counter-example was the least damaging and the least interesting of the three: If we assume nonlinear demand and supply curves for foreign exchange, destabilizing speculation could be profitable.[16] In this case, if the supply and demand schedules generated two stable equilibria and speculators bounce the exchange rate back and forth, speculation would have been destabilizing and profitable. Unfortunately for Friedman's opponents, this counter-example forces just a footnote in his argument and generally has been seen as irrelevant.[17] Why such nonlinearities should exist in the first place was left unexplained, and thus Friedman's position held in all but seemingly insignificant circumstances.[18]

A more interesting counter-example was put forth by William Baumol.[19] He argued that the problem with Friedman's rule was that it was based on a static view of the market. Friedman and Meade's hypothetical speculators adopted the strategy of buying when the price was low and selling when it was high. Baumol assumed that market fundamentals moved the exchange rate up and down in a cyclical manner. In the presence of sufficient uncertainty about when turning points occur, the strategy of trying to buy when the market hits bottom and selling when it peaks is extremely risky. However, if speculators could recognize the turning points *ex post* with more certainty, then they would be able to adopt the strategy of attempting to buy when the market is rising and sell when it begins falling. In other words, speculators could follow the rule: "Run your gains, cut your losses."[20] This stratagem could be profitable and would increase the amplitude of the market's swings. Therefore, Baumol managed to produce an interesting and relevant counter-example by introducing a few simple alterations in Friedman's analysis.[21]

An alternative method of getting around Friedman's claim that destabilizing speculation must be unprofitable for speculators as a group is to introduce other actors into the market--namely, the central banks.[22] Let us assume that central bankers wish to maintain an orderly market for foreign exchange. To avoid potential disorder, the central banks may purchase currencies from speculators when they appreciate above their equilibrium values (to prevent collapses) or buy currencies when they depreciate below equilibrium (to prevent rapid appreciations). In this policy environment, speculators as a group could profit at the expense of the central banks since the central bankers are assumed to be willing to swallow short-term losses to avoid sharp movements in exchange rates.

While the above counter-example has limited applicability, it does show that central bank intervention can change market outcomes and thus influence speculative behavior. In particular, the above example illustrates the possible paradoxical effect that a central bank "bailout" policy might have. In this case, the policy actually encourages destabilizing speculation by increasing the probability that it will be profitable.

Can Speculation Be Both Destabilizing and Stabilizing?

So far we have been assuming that speculation is either stabilizing or destabilizing. An alternative view, put forth by Nicholas Kaldor, says that both types of speculation coexist within highly speculative markets.[23] He argues that so-called "flex-price" markets are characterized by cycles of destabilizing and stabilizing speculation.[24] In Kaldor's view, speculators are assumed to follow a Baumol-like strategy of running their gains as long as prices are within a broad range of their equilibrium values. However, once an exchange rate is clearly overvalued, speculation becomes stabilizing as more and more investors turn bearish. Similarly, in the depreciation phase of the cycle, speculation turns destabilizing again as a bandwagon effect develops. When the depreciation phase ends, the exchange rate is clearly undervalued and, therefore, causes investors to turn bullish again.

Ironically, in this hybrid model, speculation becomes stabilizing only as a result of a bout of destabilizing speculation. For destabilizing speculation to check itself and produce the conditions necessary for stabilizing speculation, the exchange rate must become excessively overvalued or undervalued. In the process, however, exchange rates move up and down in a yo-yo-like fashion with each bull market planting the seeds for the next successive bear market.

SELF-FEEDING SPECULATION

For the most part, the challenges to the Friedman-Meade position I have discussed are essentially internal criticisms because they accept the basic framework in which the problem is posed.[25] The *sine qua non* of the Friedman-Meade position is that speculative trading is only a marginal part of market activity. Friedman and Meade's speculators are assumed to be able to alter the speed at which the market adjusts, but not its ultimate direction of change. However, if speculative trading is a large component of total trading, speculators can determine the direction in which the market moves, as Nurkse has claimed. This need not be true at every moment in time because speculative trading can dominate the market intermittently. The essential point, though, is that a change in the rules of the game can transform the behavior of speculators. In this environment, speculators *do not need to forecast the market's fundamentals to be successful because they can still profit by forecasting correctly the behavior of their fellow speculators*. To speculate successfully then, the individual trader can attempt to beat the crowd by forecasting the speculative psychology of the market. More specifically, a speculator profits by forecasting correctly what other speculators will do. This is the position articulated so elegantly by Maynard Keynes:

[P]rofessional investment may be likened to those newspaper competitions in which the competitors have to pick out the six prettiest faces from a hundred photographs, the prize being awarded to the competitors whose choice most nearly corresponds to the average preferences of the competitors as a whole; so that each competitor has to pick, not those faces which he himself finds prettiest, but those faces which he thinks likeliest to catch the fancy of the other competitors, all of whom are looking at the problem from the same point of view.[26]

In highly speculative market conditions, speculation becomes a game that is played out between speculators. It is not necessary (as pointed out previously) for speculators as a group to profit in order to keep speculative activity going. As long as a subgroup of speculators reaps profits, new generations of speculators can be attracted into the market, thus assuring the continuation of destabilizing speculative activity.

In a market where self-feeding speculation is important, it is possible that destabilizing speculation can be profitable for speculators on average. There is no doubt that when speculators' expectations are heterogeneous, speculation for profit resembles a zero sum game. Here, the object of the game, as Keynes noted, is to profit at the expense of other players:

> For it is, so to speak, a game of Snap, of Old Maid, of Musical Chairs--a pastime in which he is victor who says Snap neither too soon nor too late, who passes the Old Maid to his neigbour before the game is over, who secures a chair for himself when the music stops.[27]

However, when expectations are instead homogeneous, the pressure to buy or sell is tilted in one direction allowing all players to profit. For instance, a speculative rise in the value of the dollar inflates, temporarily, the paper wealth of all traders who join the bandwagon. Their net worth increases relative to those who do not play the currency game. As long as the bubble lasts, most speculators will profit despite the fact that speculation is clearly destabilizing. Whether these paper profits are realized before a crash is immaterial to the continuity of ongoing bouts of destabilizing speculation.

The roots of this alternative statement of the problem go back to the work of Keynes and Kaldor in the 1930s, yet it is only recently that it has been taken seriously in a new guise. The probable reason that their position has all but been ignored was that formal statements of their arguments were almost nonexistent, and those formal statements which did exist were clearly inadequate. The typical mode of formalizing the idea of a self-feeding speculative process is to suppose that the elasticity of expectations is greater than one.[28] This assumption concerning the formation of expectations, combined with the assumption that trading volumes are very sensitive to expectations, can produce either an implosive or explosive exchange rate path resulting from some disturbance to market equilibrium. However, the advent of the "rational expectations revolution,"[29] has made possible more sophisticated models of speculative disturbances, while casting further doubt on the general applicability of the traditional Friedman-Meade perspective. These developments have revived the literature on speculative disturbances, and it is to this literature that I now turn.

RATIONAL SPECULATIVE DISTURBANCES

It is ironic that important recent developments in the theory of destabilizing speculation have been an outgrowth of the rational expectations literature, which itself originated in order to demonstrate the inevitability of stabilizing speculation. The contributions of the literature have been: (1) to show that speculation can create increased volatility, deviations from fundamentals, and feed political instability; (2) to provide a rudimentary typology of speculative disturbances; (3) to provide simple illustrations of speculative disturbances that have generated insights into "real life" speculation; and (4) to spawn a more sophisticated empirical literature to identify speculative disturbances. (This last contribution will be examined in Chapter 3.) The importance of this literature, however, should not be overestimated. I will argue that the most important finding of the rational speculative disturbances literature is to demonstrate that even under "pro-market" assumptions speculative disturbances are a theoretical possibility. However, since "real life" speculative disturbances have significant moments of irrationality, the rational expectations framework may be of fairly limited use.[30]

Bubbles

My review of this literature will begin with so-called rational bubbles. To introduce the concept of rational bubbles, I first will analyze a rational bubble in a perfectly arbitraged financial market. Then I will proceed to analyze a similar bubble in the foreign exchange market.

A simple model of a rational financial bubble has been developed by Olivier Blanchard and Mark Watson.[31] Their model employs the same assumptions that are made in the efficient financial markets literature. In the efficient markets literature, investors are assumed to rid markets of the possibility of profitable arbitrage opportunities. Assuming that investors are risk neutral, the "no profitable arbitrage" rule implies that speculators set the expected rate of return on an asset equal to a fixed interest rate. Furthermore, it is assumed that all investors have the same information. Thus, market equilibrium occurs when the expected capital gain plus the dividend on the asset is equal to the going rate of interest.[32] To close the model, Blanchard and Watson assume that expectations are formed rationally, or that traders make no systematic prediction errors when utilizing all existing information to forecast the future.[33]

In the rational expectations model, today's price depends on the path the market price is expected to follow in the future. In contrast to solutions using adaptive expectations, the rational expectations solutions are inherently forward looking. It is the assumed forward orientation of investors' expectations that produces the novel and interesting properties of the model. In most cases, the rational expectations solution is indeterminate --i.e., there is more than one solution.[34] The standard solution assumes that investors' expectations depend solely on the discounted expected future dividend stream of the asset which is the market fundamental.[35] Alternatively, today's market price can be made to be a function of the market fundamental, as well as a deviation (bubble) that has to grow exponentially to assure continued arbitrage.[36]

Several specifications of the bubble solution are possible. The simplest specification is the deterministic solution where the bubble must grow exponentially forever in order to be consistent with the no profitable arbitrage rule. However, outside of hyperinflations, a more interesting set of solutions is the so-called stochastic solutions. In stochastic solutions, a bubble is assumed to have a certain probability of continuing into the future and one minus that probability of crashing.[37] Moreover, while it lasts, a bubble usually is assumed to grow fast enough to provide above average returns to speculators in order to compensate them for the risk of a crash. (Although to be consistent with the rational expectations solution, stochastic bubbles need only grow exponentially while they last.)

Simple extensions can be made where the probability of a crash depends upon either how long the bubble lasts or how far the price of the asset is from its fundamentals. In an efficient market, if the probability of the bubble bursting rises as the bubble continues to grow, the deviation has to grow at an increasing exponential rate while the bubble lasts to compensate investors for the increased risk. This points out a major difficulty of bubbles--they are only self-correcting by crashing! Another possible extension is for a bubble to follow at least a third state between continuing to grow at its normal pace and crashing.[38] For instance, a bubble may grow at some reduced rate or even temporarily decline during a consolidation period as investors begin profit-taking.

Several observations are in order at this point. First, a growing bubble must attract new generations of investors to sustain it. Therefore, in their growing phase, rational bubbles resemble Ponzi games or pyramid schemes. In other words, the continuing deviation of market prices from fundamentals results from a self-sustaining speculative process fed by the attraction of new entrants into the gamble. For a bubble to grow at the micro level, would-be investors have to be tempted into the gamble by the lure of profits and with the hope of getting out before the bubble bursts. As Karl Marx observed over a hundred years ago:

> In every stock-jobbing swindle every one knows that some time or other the crash must come, but every one hopes that it may fall on the head of his neighbour, after he himself has caught the shower of gold and placed it in safety.[39]

Second, when there is a crash, the pyramiding phase of a bubble is superseded by a game of "musical chairs" as speculators race *en masse* out of the market to avoid capital losses.[40] Whatever forces the crash--disappointed expectations, unfavorable news, investor panic, etc.--it is assumed that the market price will drop immediately to its fundamental rate, thus wiping out investors' paper profits.

Third, if there is no cost in getting rid of the asset, a bubble cannot be negative. A negative bubble implies that a positive probability is assigned to the price of the asset being negative, thus violating the assumption of market rationality. Blanchard and Watson argue, however, that this is pushing rationality too far: It is possible for a bubble to be negative if investors consider that the possibility of the future price being negative is irrelevant.

Foreign Exchange Bubbles

Rudiger Dornbusch has extended Blanchard and Watson's analysis of rational bubbles to the foreign exchange market.[41] He assumes that with risk-neutral investors and perfectly mobile capital, the no profitable arbitrage rule implies that the uncovered interest parity condition holds. So:

$$E[e_{t+1}] - e_t = i - i^* \qquad (2.1)$$

where:

$E[e_{t+1}]$ = the log of expected exchange rate in the next
period
e_t = the log of the current exchange rate
i = domestic interest rate
i^* = foreign interest rate

Next, Dornbusch assumes there is a given probability of the bubble continuing into the future (b) and one minus that probability of the bubble crashing to the fundamental rate (1 - b). This allows the derivation of the following result: [42]

$$e_{t+1} - e_t = (i - i^*) / b + [(1 - b) / b] (e_t - e) \qquad (2.2)$$

where:

e_{t+1} = the log of the exchange rate in the next period
e = the log of the current fundamental rate which is
assumed constant

In the absence of a crash, the rate of change in the exchange rate depends upon (1) the interest differential;

(2) the probability of a crash; and (3) the degree of undervaluation of the exchange rate. In the above formulation, the greater the interest differential, the higher the probability of a crash, and the more undervalued the exchange rate, the more the exchange rate depreciates in the absence of a crash! This paradoxical conclusion results from the assumption that speculators need to be compensated by a faster rise in the exchange rate in order to make up for increased risk and lower interest paid on foreign assets. Dornbusch's model thus has the interesting characteristic that, as the desirability of foreign assets diminishes, a currency bubble must grow faster to maintain the needed portfolio shifts.

The presence of the interest differential also holds out the possibility that bubbles can result in sustained undervaluations or overvaluations. To illustrate this, let us assume that the rate of change in the exchange rate is zero. The preceding expression then becomes: [43]

$$e - e_t = (i - i^*) / (1 - b) \qquad (2.3)$$

As shown in this equation, a negative interest differential can sustain an undervaluation of the exchange rate. Dornbusch points out, for example, that a twenty percent probability of a crash combined with a five percent interest differential can sustain a twenty-five percent overvaluation. In other words, bubbles can create sustained overvaluations or undervaluations of exchange rates.

However, one shortcoming of Dornbusch's analysis is that it does not consider the role central bank currency operations play in the bubble process. If the central banks can affect the probability that the market assigns to the bubble continuing (b), then their currency market interventions can influence the path of the bubble. Paradoxically, in Dornbusch's model, if the central banks reduce the probability of the bubble continuing, they succeed only in increasing the investor's risk and thus forcing a more rapid rise in the bubble while it lasts!

This conclusion is more a reflection of the underdeveloped state of speculative bubble theory than any true insight into the underlying processes. In any case, the conclusion can be reversed easily if we assume that some potential entrants into the bubble will not join the bandwagon unless the probability of success is above a certain threshold level. Under these circumstances, the central banks can be successful in stopping a growing bubble when they reduce the probability of the bubble continuing. Such a policy could work because it would discourage prospective entrants and thus reduce the actual growth of the bubble. Once the actual growth of the bubble is reduced below the level which is necessary to compensate investors for their perceived risks, the necessary ingredients for a crash are in place. The above analysis highlights some of the inherent difficulties, as well as the possibilities for government-inspired, anti-bubble intervention measures.

In conclusion, we see that speculative bubbles can (1) increase market turbulence as long as the innovations in the fundamentals and in the bubbles are either uncorrelated or correlated; (2) produce deviations from fundamentals; and (3) develop into speculative traps that sustain prolonged undervaluations of exchange rates.[44]

Extraneous Beliefs

In the rational expectations literature, rational destabilizing speculation also can result from any extraneous belief that influences market trading.[45] For instance, let us assume that a group of investors begins to key in on an extraneous variable, a variable unrelated to the true underlying structure of the market. This extraneous variable could influence trading market-wide, since each trader would know that other traders were forming expectations and trading on the basis of actual and expected movements in the extraneous variable. The point is simple: Once the foreign exchange market fixates on extraneous events, traders can turn literally any variable into a leading indicator of exchange rate movements. And as Mathew Canzoneri claims, practically any extraneous news announcement is capable of generating exchange rate fluctuations.

> News of political or institutional change is often blamed, as is the reporting of new figures on inflation rates, trade balances, oil imports, etc. . . . [T]hese fluctuations are usually attributed to psychological or speculative factors. Instability in gold markets has also been identified as a possible source of instability in exchange markets.[46]

Dornbusch has also noted that the practical importance of extraneous beliefs influencing trading arises "because shifting from one irrelevant factor to another will precipitate major exchange rate collapses. The possibility that exchange rates are sometimes far out of line with the fundamentals cannot be discounted."[47]

The Peso Problem

Finally, another interesting category of rational speculative disturbances is a variation of the so-called peso problem.[48] Research on the peso problem originated when economists attempted to explain why there was a continuing forward discount on the Mexican peso, despite the apparent long-term success of the Mexican government in stabilizing the peso (at least prior to 1976). One possible answer that is consistent with rational expectations is that investors were assigning a high probability to the possibility that the Mexican government would devalue the peso.

A variation of the peso problem forms the basis of an analysis of speculative flight from currencies reminiscent of Nurkse's analysis. In the typical rational expectations model, today's exchange rate is dependent upon the market's anticipation of the future path of fundamentals. Given that traders do not really know which path the fundamentals will follow, they must assign probabilities to each possible path. The probabilities they assign can have a large effect on the current spot exchange rate. For example, the greater the weight that traders assign to a government following an adverse path, the more its currency will depreciate today. On the other hand, the higher the probablity that traders assign to a favorable path, the stronger the currency will be. Furthermore, if the market adjusts its assessments on the basis of momentary whims and fears, the exchange rate will move with every such alteration. Ironically, traders are acting the way textbooks claim they should by trying to forecast future policy in order to avoid exchange losses or to reap exchange gains. However, in doing so, traders fears of the future in an uncertain world can force large, unwarranted exchange rate movements.

The problem becomes even more complicated when considering a Nurkse-like situation because the market can induce policy accommodation. In this case, traders attempt to anticipate future policy, and if the market becomes convinced that there is a high probability of a government following an adverse policy path, traders can induce such a path by their own anticipations! Under such circumstances, in Dornbusch's words, the exchange rate system is "without an anchor." Market anticipations are bound to become self-fulfilling, generating cycles of large exchange rate changes followed by accommodating changes in policy. Of course, as Friedman has argued, a government always can resist such pressures, although it may do so only at substantial costs if the market readjusts its assessments slowly. In either case, speculative flight by investors in the foreign exchange market can contribute to market volatility and instability, as well as to political instability.

Even though bubbles, extraneous beliefs and the peso problem have been presented as separate alternatives in reality their boundaries are not distinct. As an empirical matter, it is virtually impossible to distinguish the three. This is so because all three predict that exchange rates can detach themselves from current fundamentals and take on a life of their own. And all three can explain plunges, crashes, etc., in exchange rates. Therefore, it is impossible to pinpoint the origin of such patterns without an intimate knowledge of agents' collective reasons for their behavior. In the absence of such information, it is reasonable to label all sustained departures from current fundamentals as "bubbles," whether the suspected cause is in truth a bubble, or traders' betting on the latest fads, or the result of the market's reassessments of the probabilities it assigns to different policy paths.

From a theoretical perspective, labeling the three varieties of speculative disturbances bubbles may not be far off the mark. Stochastic bubbles require continuous innovations to precipitate their growing phases. Therefore, it is not inconceivable that extraneous beliefs or reassessments of future policy would provide the trigger mechanism for large bubbles. For example, news concerning extraneous variables or news that forces the market to shift its future policy bets can cause large depreciations or appreciations in currency rates. The initial deviation from current fundamentals can develop into a bubble if the market anticipates and bets that the deviation will continue to grow. Moreover, news concerning extraneous variables and shifts in assessments about future fundamentals also can figure in the collapse of exchange rate bubbles. In short, there may be good reasons to believe that extraneous beliefs and the peso problem play the role of triggering the start as well as the collapse of large bubbles.

Rational Expectations and Stabilizing Speculation

The previous discussions demonstrate that there need be no link between agents' expectations being formed rationally and speculation being stabilizing. Of course, rational expectations can also be consistent with stabilizing speculation.[49] If circumstances are such that (1) the equilibrium is unique, (2) agents have enough information to recognize the equilibrium value, and (3) agents also *believe* that the actual rate will adjust toward its equilibrium rate, then speculation will be stabilizing. It is important to emphasize that it takes all three assumptions to produce Friedman and Meade's conclusion that speculation is stabilizing. In other words, for traders to force the current market rate towards its equilibrium rate, it is not sufficient that there be a unique equilibrium known to traders. As the discussions of bubbles and extraneous beliefs have shown, traders need to be able to assume that the current market rate will adjust to its equilibrium rate so that they can speculate in a stabilizing manner. In general, as Oliver Hart and David Kreps claim, rational "[s]peculators will buy when chances of price appreciation are high; which may or may not be when prices are low."[50] Speculation can be both rational and destabilizing if traders believe that a currency is likely to appreciate because it is following a bubble path or because of extraneous beliefs.

A separate set of issues arises when there are multiple equilibria in the model.[51] If there are several possible equilibria, then it is impossible for traders to form rational expectations. Multiple equilibria cases can exist with rational expectations when there is Nurkse-like policy accommodation. For instance, if a government accommodates any equilibrium generated by market traders, and if market traders believe that policymakers will accommodate them, then traders must realize that the exchange rate is indeterminate. Whatever speculators do--maintain the current rate, weaken the currency, or strengthen it--will be ratified by the government and create an unlimited set of possible future equilibrium values. In this context, expectations can become unglued from expected equilibrium values and thus become unstable. As Brian Hillier notes:

> [M]ultiple equilibria pose serious problems, since, if more than one outcome can be consistent with rational expectations, then how are economic agents to know which one to expect? This raises interesting questions of agents' expectations depending on other agents' expectations, and may make expectations susceptible to manipulation and volatile changes. Such problems are reminiscent of Keynes's views on the difficulties of formally modelling expectations.[52]

IRRATIONALITY AND SPECULATIVE DISTURBANCES

The examples of rational destabilizing speculation considered in the previous section are not only highly suggestive but serve to demonstrate also that speculative disturbances are possible, theoretically, in a world where all agents are rational. The strength of these models though is also their weakness: the assumption that all agents act rationally leaves the irrational elements unexplored. In a study on financial crises, Charles Kindleberger has shown that most large "real life" financial disturbances do have irrational aspects.[53] Kindleberger's study confirms the popular belief that speculators may act irrationally at times by either ignoring or heavily discounting relevant information due to the market's crowd psychology. This irrational behavior can produce biased forecasts which also create the possibility of large unanticipated mistakes.

Moreover, Kindleberger presents an interesting descriptive model of large bubbles which incorporates the effects of irrational crowd psychology.[54] The Kindleberger model is a restatement of Hyman Minsky's financial instability thesis.[55] According to Kindleberger, large speculative disturbances begin with a displacement or "some exogenous outside shock to the macroeconomic system."[56] The nature of this displacement varies across time and place and can be either economic or political in origin. What the displacement does is create large profit opportunities for speculators. This opening of a "window of opportunity" attracts an influx of funds, while at the same time it creates enormous paper profits which stimulate further rounds of speculative activity. The market is poised then for the second stage in the bubble process--namely, euphoria.

As the name suggests, a euphoric stage creates the illusion that speculative gains are never-ending and virtually riskless. Whereas the initial stage in the bubble is dominated by rational speculators, in the euphoric stage a collective irrational optimism takes hold of the market. This euphoria is self-limiting, though, since it creates unsustainable expectations and positions on the part of speculators. At a certain point, distress begins to take hold as a subgroup of speculators starts to withdraw its money from the market. At first, new entries may continue and thus offset flight from the market. However, sooner or later market prices cease to grow at their anticipated pace and thus create disappointed expectations which weaken the propensity to gamble. The onset of the market's distress signals the beginning of the end of the euphoric stage.

The euphoric stage may cease due to either an endogenous run from the market, which develops because investors begin to panic, or because some "shock" alters dramatically investors' expectations and confidence. In either case, there is a collective realization that the market can crash with disastrous consequences for market prices and investor profits. Thus, market distress can transform itself into a raging stampede to withdraw. In this case, a panic or "revulsion" concludes the speculative bubble. In the panic phase, as in the euphoric phase, market expectations may become irrational. An irrational, excessive pessimism may develop that permeates the market and precipitates a large fall in market prices.

Thus, the Kindleberger model suggests that speculative markets react to shocks by creating a collective psychology that produces a market-wide "manic-depressive" syndrome as a bubble moves from its euphoric to panic stages. Looking further at Kindleberger's model, the irrational elements add two dimensions to the problem of bubbles that we have yet to consider. First, irrational investor behavior may contribute to both the growth of speculative bubbles and to their crash. In the growth phase, entrants who are unaware of or discount the possibility of a crash may "overfeed" the bubble. Likewise, a crash may be precipitated or made even more severe by those speculators who panic and "oversell" in a vain attempt to cut their losses. Second, the introduction of irrationality leads to the possibility of large, if not catastrophic, mistakes on the part of speculators. Such mistakes occur because speculators may take levered positions on the basis of beliefs that are unwarranted by objective circumstances. Jack Guttentag and Richard Herring categorize the systematic underestimation of the probability of adverse surprises as *disaster myopia*.[57] No doubt the combination of a market crash with the presence of disaster myopia on the part of large traders is a recipe for financial instability, both within and outside the market.[58]

The above analysis brings into question also an assumption that there are no profitable arbitrage opportunities. In the rational bubbles literature, one important assumption is that markets are efficient since no risk-adjusted excess profits are earned by traders. While growing bubbles must provide a premium above the risk-free rate of return, this premium is said to compensate investors for the risk of a crash in the asset's price and does not constitute a real excess profit opportunity. However, once it is conceded that groups of investors may underestimate systematically the probability of a bubble continuing to grow, returns will no longer be perfectly arbitraged. Moreover, common sense suggests that the greater the real excess returns generated by growing bubbles, the *more entrants* the bubble will attract, the *faster* the bubble will grow, and the *higher* will be returns in the next period! Therefore, the euphoric stage of bubbles serves as a powerful magnet by creating real excess returns which attract new investors into the bubble.[59]

SUMMARY AND CONCLUSIONS

In conclusion, I would like to outline a descriptive model of currency bubbles that incorporates all the relevant aspects of the models reviewed. The purpose of this descriptive model is to provide a basis for the empirical work found in the next three chapters.

One of my principal findings is that there are two contrasting visions of the impact of currency speculation on market stability. In the Friedman-Meade view, currency traders are assumed to pay close attention to market fundamentals. They buy foreign exchange when the price is low and sell foreign exchange when the price is high. By following this strategy, these smart speculators make money by cushioning the foreign exchange market from the effects of adverse shocks. The Friedman-Meade view, therefore, comes close to equating rational behavior on the part of speculators with price stabilizing strategies.

In the alternative vision, developed by Nurkse, Keynes, and Kaldor, and formalized in the rational destabilizing speculation literature, currency speculation can force exchange rates to make significant departures from their fundamentals. Unlike the Friedman-Meade tradition, this contrasting position argues that profit-seeking behavior on the part of traders does not insure that traders will adopt what are, in effect, price stabilizing strategies. In fact, destabilizing speculation can be profitable and consistent with traders who form their expectations rationally. Therefore, there is no necessary link between traders being rational, profit-seeking agents, and the adoption of stabilizing betting strategies.

In the presence of destabilizing speculation, shocks of an economic or political nature first will produce a magnification effect, since such shocks serve as the sparks that ignite growing bubbles. Moreover, theory suggests that the initial magnification effect created by speculators will tend to be self-limiting. In general, the more undervalued (or overvalued) currency rates become and the longer the bubble phase lasts, the more likely a crash will take place. In a simplified analysis of bubbles, the magnification effects of bubbles are reversible only through crashes. In a managed or "dirty float," central banks probably can alter a bubble path by affecting market expectations. In doing so, central banks may play an important role in influencing the extent and timing of the growing and bursting phases of large bubbles.

The preceding review of the theoretical literature warrants several conclusions. First, there are no *a priori* reasons for believing that currency speculation will be stabilizing. Second, on the contrary, speculation can force deviations from market fundamentals, thus creating large "bubbles." And third, these speculative bubbles can flourish even in a world where expectations are formed rationally, although I suspect that such disturbances do have large, irrational elements. Thus the conclusions reached from our excursion through economic theory support firmly the empirical search for speculative disturbances.

NOTES

1. Ragnar Nurkse, *International Currency Experience: Lessons of the Inter-war Period* (Princeton: League of Nations, 1944).

2. For an extensive review of the period see Robert Z. Aliber, "Speculation in the Foreign Exchanges: The European Experience 1919-1926," *Yale Economic Essays* (Spring 1962), pp. 171-245.

3. This section relies on Nurkse, *Currency Experience*, pp. 113-122.

4. Nurkse also claimed that once traders began to anticipate further currency depreciations, trade flows would also begin to act perversely: "As the exchange declined, import prices rose, traders began to expect a further rise and so reacted by importing more instead of less. Similarly, exporters, expecting the price rise for their products to continue, held back their sales so as to get better prices later." Ibid., p. 120.

5. Ibid., p. 115.

6. Ibid., p. 118.

7. Ibid., p. 118.

8. Quoted by Kenneth W. Dam, *The Rules of the Game* (Chicago: University of Chicago Press, 1982), p. 61.

9. Robert Z. Aliber, "Speculation in the Flexible Exchange Revisited," *Kyklos* 23 (1970), p. 304. Willett and Wihlborg point out that many economists incorrectly labeled speculation as destabilizing if it was deemed to be disruptive. See Thomas D. Willett and Clas Wihlborg, "International Capital Flows, the Dollar, and U.S. Financial Policies," in William Haraf and Thomas D. Willett, eds., *Monetary Policy in an Era of Change: The International Dilemma* (Washington DC: American Enterprise Institute, 1990), p. 76.

10. Milton Friedman, "The Case for Flexible Exchange Rates," in *Essays in Positive Economics* (Chicago: University of Chicago Press, 1953), pp. 157-203 and J. E. Meade, *The Balance of Payments* (London: Oxford University Press, 1952), ch. 17.

11. Friedman, "Flexible Exchange Rates," p. 175.

12. Friedman went so far with this point that he actually believed that the speculative runs of the 1930s which undid the gold exchange standard, were stabilizing because it turned out that the speculators were "right." Friedman, "Flexible Exchange Rates," pp. 176-177.

13. Friedman also argued that freely floating exchange rates had many advantages such as maximizing multilateral trade by avoiding the need for costly controls, assuring the monetary independence of each nation state, and preventing the need for internal adjustments to external imbalances. For a review and evaluation of these claims see Robert M. Dunn Jr., "The Many Disappointments of Flexible Exchange Rates," Princeton University *Essays in International Finance* no. 154 (Aug. 1983).

14. Friedman's explanation for the "many disappointments of flexible exchange rates" is that current problems are the product of a long transitional period from a gold-backed monetary system which ended in 1971 with the delinking of the dollar from gold, to a system anchored by central banks: "Ever since [1971], we have been in a transition period. The basic issue is not "flexible" versus "fixed" exchange rates . . . but the monetary regime or regimes that will finally emerge from the trial and error groping that has necessarily characterized this transition. As the shape of that regime or those regimes becomes reasonably definite, the determination of exchange rates will accommodate itself, uncertainty will decline, and markets will become routinized and less exciting." See Milton Friedman, "Introduction," in Leo Melamed, ed., *The Merits of Flexible Exchange Rates* (Fairfax, Virginia: George Mason University Press, 1988), p. xix.

15. See, for example, Charles P. Kindleberger, *Manias, Panics, and Crashes: A History of Financial Crises* (New York: Basic Books, 1978), pp. 32-35, and Nicholas Kaldor "Speculation and Economic Activity," in *Essays in Economic Stability and Growth* (London: Gerald

Duckworth and Co. Ltd., 1980), pp. 17-58. Friedman anticipated this argument: "[P]rofessional speculators might on the average make money while a changing body of amateurs regularly lost larger sums. But while this may happen, it is hard to see why there is any presumption that it will . . ." Friedman, "Flexible Exchange Rates," p. 175. For a review of the stabilizing versus destabilizing debate that is more sympathetic to Friedman's perspective see Leland B. Yeager, *International Monetary Relations* (New York: Harper and Row, 1966), pp. 189-208.

16. Murray C. Kemp, "Speculation, Profitability, and Stability," *Review of Economics and Statistics* 45 (1963), pp. 185-189.

17. See, for example, Susan Schadler, "Sources of Exchange Rate Volatility: Theory and Empirical Evidence," IMF *Staff Papers* (July 1977), p. 259.

18. For a dissenting opinion, see John Williamson, "Another Case of Profitable Destabilizing Speculation," *Journal of International Economics* 2 (1972), pp. 77-84.

19. William J. Baumol, "Speculation, Profitability, and Stability," *Review of Economics and Statistics* 39 (Aug. 1957), pp. 263-271.

20. Aliber, "Speculation in the Foreign Exchanges," p. 173.

21. For a critique of Baumol see Schadler, "Sources of Exchange Rate Volatility," pp. 261-262 and for the original critique see Lester G. Telser, "A Theory of Speculation Relating Profitability and Stability," *Review of Economics and Statistics* 41 (Aug. 1959), pp. 295-301.

22. This issue was first raised by Jerome L. Stein, "Destabilizing Speculative Activity Can be Profitable," *Review of Economics and Statistics* 43 (Aug. 1961), pp. 301-302.

23. This section relies heavily on Kaldor, "Speculation and Economic Activity," pp. 17-58, Nicholas Kaldor, "Limits on Growth," *Oxford Economic Papers* 38 (1987), pp. 187-198, and Stephan Schulmeister, "Exchange Rates, Prices, and Interest Rates: Reconsidering the Basic

Relationships of Exchange Rate Determination," C.V. Starr Center for Applied Economics *Economic Research Reports* (July 1983).

24. See John Hicks, *The Crisis of Keynesian Economics* (New York: Basic Books, 1974), ch. 3.

25. The vision of speculative activity presented in this section has its roots in Kaldor, "Speculation and Economic Activity," and John Maynard Keynes, *The General Theory of Employment, Interest, and Money* (New York: Harcourt, Brace and World, Inc., 1964), ch. 12.

26. Keynes, *General Theory*, p. 156.

27. Ibid., pp. 155-156.

28. The elasticity of expectations can be defined through the following adaptive expectations equation:

$$E[e_{t+1}] - e_t = b(e_t - e_{t-1})$$

where:

$E[e_{t+1}]$ = the expectation of the log of the exchange rate in period $t+1$

e_t = the log of the current exchange rate

e_{t-1} = the log of the exchange rate in period $t-1$

b = the elasticity of the expected depreciation of the home currency with respect to its depreciation in the last period.

When $b > 1$ expectations are said to be elastic because a X% rise or fall in the previous period creates the expectation that currency rates will rise or fall by more than X% in the next period. See, for instance, Kaldor, "Speculation and Economic Activity," Charles P. Kindleberger, "Flexible Exchange Rates," in *Europe and the Dollar* (Cambridge: MIT Press, 1966), pp. 112-136, and more recently, Paul Davidson, *International Money and the Real World* (New York: Wiley, 1982).

29. The phrase is borrowed from David K. H. Begg, *The Rational Expectations Revolution in Macroeconomics* (Baltimore: John Hopkins University Press, 1982).

30. This view is shared by Kindleberger, *Manias, Panics, and Crashes*, pp. 25-41.

31. Olivier J. Blanchard and Mark W. Watson, "Bubbles, Rational Expectations, and Financial Markets,"

National Bureau of Economic Research *Reprint* no. 374 (June 1983), pp. 296-301.

32. This can be stated formally as follows:

$Rt = (Pt+1 - Pt + Xt) / Pt$

where:

Rt = the rate of return on the asset
Xt = the dividend on the asset
$Pt+1$ = next period's price of the asset
Pt = this periods price of the asset.

Let:

$E[Rt+1:t]$ = the expectation of the rate of return on the asset given all the information available in period t
r = the going rate of interest.

The no arbitrage rule implies:

$E[Rt+1:t] = r$

Equivalently, let

$E[Pt+1:t]$ = the expectation of next periods price given all the information in period t.

The no profitable arbitrage rule then becomes:

$E[Pt+1:t] - Pt + Xt = rPt.$

33. This is the standard definition. See, for instance, Begg, *The Rational Expectations Revolution*, pp. 29-31.

34. "[T]he indeterminacy" of the rational expectations solution," explain Flood and Garber, "arises because only one market equilibrium condition exists; but the researcher requires solutions for two endogenous variables--market price and the expected rate of market-price change." In the model of the financial market in note 32, the two endogenous variables are the current price and the future expected price. See Robert P. Flood and Peter M. Garber, "Bubbles, Runs, and Gold Monetization," in Paul Wachtel, ed., *Crises in the Economic and Financial Structure* (Lexington, MA: Lexington Books, 1982), pp. 275-276 and also see Begg, *The Rational Expectations Revolution*, pp. 63-65.

35. The fundamentals solution can be derived by using forward iteration. It is:

$Zt = \sum n^{i+1} E[Xt+i:t]$
$\quad i=0$

where:

$n = (1+r)^{-1} < 1$

Z_t = the fundamental solution for this period's price of the asset

$E[X_{t+i}:t]$ = the expectation of the dividend in period $t+i$ given all the information available at period t.

36. The price bubble arises out of the indeterminacy problem. "A bubble can arise," write Flood and Garber, "when the actual market price depends positively on its own expected rate of change, as normally occurs in asset markets. Since agents forming rational expectations do not make systematic prediction errors, the positive relationship between price and its expected rate of change implies a similar relationship between price and its actual rate of change. In such conditions, the arbitrary, self-fulfilling expectation of price changes may drive actual price changes independently of market fundamentals; we refer to such a situation as a price bubble." Flood and Garber, "Bubbles, Runs, and Gold Monetization," p. 276. In our model, the bubble solution is:

$$P_t = \sum_{i=0} n^{i+1} E[X_{t+i}:t] + C_t = Z_t + C_t$$

Where:

$E[C_{t+i}:t] = n^{-1} C_t, n^{-1} > 0$

C_t = the deviation from fundamentals or the bubble

$E[C_{t+i}:t]$ = the expectation of the bubble in period $t+i$ given all the information in period t.

37. The stochastic solution is:

$C_t = (bn)^{-1} C_{t-1} + U_t$ with probability b and

$C_t = U_t$ with probability $1 - b$

$E[U_t:t-1] = 0$

where:

U_t = the error term or innovations in the bubble

$E[U_t:t-1]$ = the expectation of U_t in period t given all the information available in period t-1.

38. Olivier J. Blanchard, "Speculative Bubbles, Crashes and Rational Expectations," *Economic Letters* 3 (1979), p. 389.

39. Karl Marx, *Capital*, vol. I (London: Lawrence and Wishart, 1974), p. 257.

40. There are no formal models of a crash.

41. Rudiger Dornbusch, "Equilibrium and Disequilibrium Exchange Rates," National Bureau of Economic Research *Reprint* no. 388 (July 1983), pp. 583-585.

42. The results are derived as follows:

et+1 - et = (E[et+1] - et) / b + [(1 - b) / b] (et - e)

From the above it can be seen that as the bubble grows larger the more it is expected to grow, the more undervalued the exchange rate is, and the higher the probability of a crash. By substituting the uncovered interest rate parity relationship the expression becomes:

et+1 - et = (i - i*) / b + [(1 - b) / b] (et - e)

43. The original expression was:

et+1 - et = (i - i*) / b + [(1 - b) / b] (et - e)

It becomes:

0 = (i - i*) / b + [(1 - b) / b] (et - e)

Or:

e - et = (i - i*) / (1 - b).

44. Dornbusch's model does not show explicitly the fundamental process. This can be rectified by considering the flexible-price monetary model as representing the fundamentals. The model is depicted in the following equations where all foreign variables are considered exogenously fixed.

1]p = p* + e (purchasing power parity)

2]E[et+1] - et = i - i* (uncovered interest rate parity)

3]L = p + y - hi (money demand)

4]M = m (exogenous money supply)

5]M = L (money market equilibrium)

Where:

p = the log of the domestic price level

p* = the log of the foreign price level

e = the log of the exchange rate

i = the domestic interest rate
i* = the foreign interest rate
E[et+1] = the log of the expected exchange rate
et = the log of the current exchange rate
L = money demand
y = log of real income
h = a coefficient
M = money supply
m = the log of the exogenous money supply.

If we solve the system for the exchange rate we get:

et = m - p* - y + hi* + h(E[et+1] - et)

or

et = [1 /(1 + h)] (m - p* - y + hi*) + [h /(1 + h)] (E[et+1])

Letting:

wt = m - p - y + hi*, we get:

et = [1 /(1 + h)] (wt) + [h /(1 + h)] (E[et+1])

Notice that the model suffers from the indeterminacy problem since we have one equation and two unknowns, i.e., the current exchange rate and the expected exchange rate. By forward iteration we can solve for the fundamentals solution:

$$e = [1 /(1 + h)] \sum_{i=0} [(h /(1 + h))]^i E[wt+i]$$

The bubble solution is:

et = **et** + ct

where:

ct - h(E[ct+1] - ct) = 0

The deterministic bubble solution is:

ct+1 = [(1 + h) / h] (ct), [(1 + h) / h] > 0

The stochastic solution is:

ct+1 = ut+1 with probability 1 - b and
ct+1 = (1 / b) [(1 + h) / h] (ct) + ut+1 with probability b
and E[ut+i] = 0

Where:

b = the probability of the bubble continuing
1 - b = the probability of the bubble crashing
ct = the bubble in period t
ut+1 = the innovation in the bubble in period t+1.

45. See Dornbusch, "Equilibrium and Disequilibrium Exchange Rates," pp. 587-589, Mathew B. Canzoneri, "Rational Destabilizing Speculation and Exchange Intervention Policy," *Journal of Macroeconomics* 5 (Winter 1983), pp. 75-90, and Kunio Okina, "Speculative Bubbles and Official Intervention," Unpublished, University of Chicago (May 1983), pp. 8-10.

46. Canzoneri, "Rational Destabilizing Speculation," p. 76.

47. Rudiger Dornbusch, "Flexible Exchange Rates and Independence," IMF *Staff Papers* 30 (1983), p. 44.

48. See Dornbusch, "Equilibrium and Disequilibrium Exchange Rates," pp. 585-587, and for an analysis of the peso problem in the gold market, see Stephen W. Salant and Dale W. Henderson, "Market Anticipations of Government Policies and the Price of Gold," *Journal of Political Economy* 86 (1978), pp. 627-648.

49. For a review of the issues raised here see Oliver D. Hart and David M. Kreps, "Price Destabilizing Speculation," *Journal of Political Economy* 94 (1986), pp. 927-952.

50. Ibid., p. 928.

51. See Brian Hillier, *Macroeconomics: Models, Debates and Developments* (New York: Oxford University Press, 1986), p. 209.

52. Ibid., p. 209.

53. Kindleberger, *Manias, Panics, and Crashes*, pp. 28-41.

54. Ibid., pp. 14-24. It is interesting to note that Kindleberger believes that his model is appropriate for the foreign exchange market. "One place where the model surely applies today is foreign exchange markets, in which prices rise and fall in wide swings, despite sizeable intervention in the market by monetary authorities, and in which exchange speculation has brought large losses to some banks. Financial crisis has been avoided, but in the opinion of some observers, not by much." Ibid., p. 23.

55. Minsky's thesis is presented in Hyman Minsky, *John Maynard Keynes* (New York: Columbia University Press, 1975).

56. Kindleberger, *Manias, Panics, and Crashes*, p. 15.

57. Jack M. Guttentag and Richard J. Herring, "Disaster Myopia in International Banking," Princeton University *Essays in International Finance* no. 164 (Sept. 1986).

58. An interesting model has been developed which assumes portfolio managers elicit advice from forecasting services who use both fundamental and technical analysis. Portfolio managers are assumed to use a weighted average of the two types of forecasts, choosing the weights based on the past relative accuracy of their forecasts. In this model, an initial shock which moves the exchange rate away from its fundamental rate can cause portfolio managers to put less reliance on fundamental analysis and more reliance on chartist strategies. Once these portfolio shifts begin they are capable of producing large, irrational bubbles. This model was first developed by Frankel and Froot. See Charles Goodhart, "The Foreign Exchange Market: A Random Walk with a Dragging Anchor," *Economica* 55 (Nov. 1988), pp. 452-453.

59. This is in fact how Schulmeister defines bubbles. For him, large bubbles are evident in periods where for several consecutive months, returns average above twenty percent or more on an annualized basis. He documents several such periods: from the end of 1972 to mid-1973; 1978; and the early 1980s. See "Exchange Rates, Prices, and Interest Rates," p. 25.

3

The Foreign Exchange Market

The foreign exchange market has undergone many significant transformations since its rebirth under the Bretton Woods accords. Therefore, hypotheses concerning the role of speculation in the exchange rate system must be able to explain the market's principal historical developments as well as its modern day empirical regularities. In this chapter, I will outline first the principal institutional arrangements and historical forces which shaped the relationship between speculation and the "free market" currency system. Then I will show that the bubble hypothesis is consistent with the stylized facts (the empirical regularities which hold true on average) of the post-Bretton Woods float. To demonstrate the latter point, I will argue that the historical and time series evidence supports, uniformly, the bubble hypothesis over a popular rival null hypothesis--namely, the random walk-efficient markets hypothesis.[1] The conclusions reached in this chapter are intended to be a prelude to the examination of the relationship between large bubbles, market fundamentals, and central bank intervention--the subject matter of Chapters 4 and 5.

A SPECULATIVE MARKET IN FOREIGN EXCHANGE

The roots of the current speculative market in foreign exchange can be traced to the political compromises made in establishing a market-based convertible currency system after World War II.[2] The Bretton Woods agreements reestablished a convertible currency system in order to assure the resumption of uninhibited, multilateral trade, which had collapsed during the interwar period. The architects of the Bretton Woods system agreed that the restoration of an open, multilateral trading system necessitated that the key currencies in the world economy be made freely convertible. However, they disagreed over whether the postwar, convertible currency system should be based on the principle of market convertibility or official convertibility.[3] In a regime of market convertibility, private institutions would assume the role of market makers by acting as the primary brokers between the ultimate buyers and sellers of foreign currencies. On the other hand, in a regime of official convertibility, public institutions would serve as these key intermediaries, thus enabling governments to control better the scope and nature of their international economic relations.

Prior to the Bretton Woods accords, there was a great deal of debate about which form of convertibility would work best. In fact, Keynes' alternative plan for restructuring international monetary relations included, as we have seen, a provision for all currency trading to be channelled through central banks.[4] In the end, however, the agreements forged were a compromise which created a regulated currency system based on the principle of market convertibility. Under the Bretton Woods agreements, the major foreign central banks were to peg their exchange rates to the dollar, although the peg was made adjustable in order to deal with so-called "fundamental disequilibriums" in a country's balance of payments.[5] Furthermore, in practice, the U.S. government was responsible for keeping the dollar value of gold at

$35 per ounce. This arrangement had the effect of establishing the dollar as the key world currency by making it the preferred international store of value, unit of account, and even medium of exchange for international trade and finance. Even to this day the overwhelming share of foreign exchange market operations are channelled through the dollar. Therefore, because the arena of international finance was built around the dollar after the war, the dollar has remained at the center of world finance ever since.

Moreover, to prevent the recurrence of destabilizing capital flows that undid the gold exchange standard of the 1930s, each country was allowed to place controls (or more to the point, allow existing war-time controls to remain in effect) on international capital flows. In the language of the accords, the principle of convertibility applied solely to current account transactions, which in effect allowed each member state to decide for itself the degree of convertibility in capital account transactions.[6] In essence, the Bretton Woods agreements permitted the reprivatization of the international capital and currency markets, but at the same time established a parallel regulatory apparatus which included an informal system of joint government management over currency rates complemented by direct controls on finance.

The underlying assumption guiding most Bretton Woods-era policymakers was that microeconomic liberalism, combined with exchange rate and financial regulation, together would prove to be a successful recipe by providing for a stable international financial system with a vibrant open trading system. This naive hope, however, was soon proven false. The principal reasons for the collapse of the Bretton Woods accords were (1) the internationalization of banking in the 1960s and (2) the decline of the U.S. as a hegemonic power.[7] These two developments eroded the potentially unstable balance between the Bretton Woods currency and capital regulations and the mainly private currency and capital markets. Eventually, these developments threatened the continued stability of the Bretton Woods international monetary arrangements.

In the first instance, the internationalization of banking increased the pressure on what can best be described as a dual system of domestic and international monetary controls by weakening the regulatory foundations for these controls. These Bretton Woods-era controls were intended to balkanize the major capital markets and financial centers in order to permit each nation-state to control its own financial affairs. This point and its implications were well understood by John Maynard Keynes, one of the principal architects of the accords:

> We intend to retain control of our domestic rate of interest, so that we can keep it as low as suits our own purposes, without interference from the ebb and flow of international capital movements or the flight of money. . . . Not merely as a feature of the transition, but as a permanent arrangement, the plan [Bretton Woods agreements] accords to every member government the explicit right to control all capital movements. What used to be heresy is now endorsed as orthodox. . . . Our right to control the domestic capital market is secured on firmer foundations than ever before, and is formally accepted as a proper part of agreed international arrangements.[8]

However, the internationalization of banking eroded the effectiveness of the regulatory barriers that had been erected between capital markets to slow international capital flows, thus loosening the grip of governmental control over the international financial system. Moreover, the regulations that had balkanized the leading financial centers were also an essential element needed for the continued survival of the adjustable peg currency system. Without these restrictions on capital flows, capital would be free to flow between financial centers generating large orders to buy or sell foreign exchange, thus making it extremely difficult for the central banks to control exchange rates as they wished.

Accompanying these important changes that were occurring at the microeconomic level were less dramatic but equally important political developments which further weakened the regulatory apparatus. Because of the key role of the dollar in the adjustable peg exchange rate system, stability in the international financial system was dependent, in part, upon the continued supremacy of the U.S. as an economic and political power. In effect, continued U.S. hegemony became one of the essential components of the political basis for continued stability in the international monetary system because it was anchored to the dollar-gold relationship. The slow but persistent economic and political decline of the U.S. over the postwar period created a structural balance of payments deficit in the U.S., putting the all-important dollar-gold relationship in constant jeopardy. In the end, the integration of the world's capital markets, combined with the erosion of U.S. power, proved too much for the adjustable peg exchange rate system. Thus, after repeated failed attempts to rescue the regulated currency system, the principal powers were forced to usher in a floating rate system by March 1973.[9]

As the above analysis suggests, even before the final demise of the Bretton Woods currency system, the foreign exchange market had already begun its transformation from a tightly regulated market into a full blown speculative market, in which expectations of future exchange rate changes were a principal factor in determining currency rates. This was precipitated, in part, because the foreign exchange market already had the necessary institutional characteristics needed to facilitate the predominance of speculative trading over nonspeculative activity.[10] To facilitate speculation, the objects of speculation need to have low carrying costs and small spreads between the dealers' bid (buying) and ask (selling) prices. In turn, these conditions require (1) that the objects of speculation be capable of being

standardized, (2) that the spot markets in which they are
traded be deep, (3) that the objects of speculation be
durable, and (4) that the objects of speculation be
valuable in proportion to their bulk. The first two
characteristics, along with low transactions costs (which is
itself a function of the volume of transactions and the
homogeneity of the asset), narrow the difference between
the purchase and the sale price. On the other hand, the
latter two characteristics determine an asset's carrying
cost, and given its yield, the net carrying cost of an asset.

The above organizational characteristics are the
essential institutional elements of speculative markets
because, potentially, they make prices extremely flexible
and thus responsive to every alteration in speculators'
portfolios which arises with changes in market
expectations and/or shifts in market confidence. In other
words, the effect of these institutional traits is to make
market prices *potentially* a by-product of market
psychology. Therefore, by permitting the establishment
of market convertibility and thereafter allowing the slow
but persistent erosion of the Bretton Woods financial
regulations, policymakers inadvertently were setting the
stage for exchange rates to become speculative prices.

In addition to these organizational traits, all
speculative markets require an array of market
specialists to fulfill functions that permit the normally
large volume of transactions to take place without
disruption. Among these specialists are the dealers who
serve in the role of market makers. The market makers'
primary function is to hold large inventories of foreign
exchange in order to allow retail customers to buy and
sell foreign exchange, even when no immediate offsetting
seller or buyer can be found. In performing this needed
function, dealers prevent temporary mismatches in
supply and demand from causing excessive price
volatility. From the perspective of the dealers, market
making is a lucrative activity because of the built-in fee
they receive in the form of the spread between their bid
and ask prices. In the market for foreign exchange, the

primary dealers are the large money-center banks that make up the global wholesale interbank currency market.

Nicholas Kaldor, a leading post-Keynesian scholar, has argued persuasively that dealers also speculate for profit in order to supplement their earnings as market makers.[11] As speculators, the dealers' privileged position provides them with a competitive edge over the competition who cannot buy and sell at wholesale and who do not have access to the same information. In addition, even if dealers prefer not to speculate for profit, they are forced in the normal course of their activities to take open positions and thus to "speculate."[12] In Kaldor's view, therefore, the existence of this interbank market of primary dealers served to institutionalize and professionalize foreign exchange speculation in the form of trading departments owned and operated by the large multinational banks.

The empirical evidence in support of these claims is well established. First, transactions costs for large buyers and sellers in the wholesale interbank market are extremely low. According to the best estimate available, transactions costs are .090 percent of the value of large wholesale transactions.[13] In comparison to other markets, the foreign exchange market is said to have perhaps the lowest transactions costs and thus is as close to being a "perfect" market (a market where the bid and ask prices are identical) as any in existence. Second, since foreign exchange speculators can purchase interest-bearing assets when holding foreign exchange, the carrying cost of foreign exchange for speculators is negative and thus highly competitive in relation to domestic assets.

According to the theory of speculative markets, these attributes should permit large trading volumes and make exchange rates potentially highly flexible prices. A 1986 survey of the big three trading centers--London, New York, and Tokyo--estimated that the combined daily turnover averaged nearly $200 billion.[14] Informal estimates place the entire market's daily volume at about $500 billion. Furthermore, many studies have confirmed that actual exchange rate volatility is closer to that of other speculative prices than to goods prices. Jacob Frenkel and Michael Mussa have shown, for example, that exchange rate volatility in the 1970s has been closer to that of stock prices than goods prices.[15]

Finally, the limited empirical evidence also confirms Kaldor's claim that dealers--namely, the large money-center banks--do most of the currency speculation. For example, the conclusion of a study by the U.S. Treasury of fifty-five multinational, nonfinancial corporations was that their "demand for sterling, like that for Deutschemarks, is a transactional demand associated with the conduct of business in that country."[16] In contrast, a different study concluded that the interbank market accounts for most of the trading and most of the speculation. The only other group of traders that speculate for profit as a matter of practice is the commodity dealers, particularly dealers of metals. However, commodity dealers as a group are responsible for only a small fraction of total currency trading.[17] Thus, Kaldor's hypothesis is consistent with the existing literature on the foreign exchange market.

To summarize my argument at this point: The market for foreign exchange has become a speculative market as a result of historical processes that transformed the Bretton Woods currency regime from a highly regulated market system into its current "free market" arrangement. However, the essential foundation for a speculative market in foreign exchange also was established inadvertently by the Bretton Woods accords. Furthermore, the formation of a speculative market in foreign exchange has institutionalized the importance of market psychology in determining exchange rates, as evidenced by the volatility of exchange rates. In addition, the foreign exchange market's institutional arrangements have created the conditions for the emergence of a professional class of currency speculators--namely the professional traders who speculate for profit for large multinational banks.

There are other institutional traits that influence the nature of speculative activity in the foreign exchange market. For instance, Olivier Blanchard and Mark Watson have argued that destabilizing speculation is more of a problem for some speculative markets than others.[18] In their view, speculative markets tend to develop destabilizing psychologies when it becomes difficult to predict market fundamentals. Thus, they claim that the gold market is more susceptible to bubble problems because of the inability of speculators in the gold market to forecast, with any certainty, the gold market's primary fundamental--the probability of a monetary collapse.

However, Blanchard and Watson restrict the scope of their claim unnecessarily by stating their argument is a market specific phenomenon. In contrast, John Maynard Keynes stated in the *General Theory* that the predominance of destabilizing betting strategies (which he characterized as an attempt to "beat the gun") was the direct result of the inability of agents to assess market fundamentals in the then chaotic and turbulent U.S. stock market of the late 1920s.[19] Keynes argued that such assessments depend upon conventional evaluations of the economic scene and that in chaotic and uncertain historical periods these evaluations tend to break down, leaving no acceptable means of assessing long-term fundamentals. Because of this, the decision making of agents becomes short-run, haphazard, and thus potentially unstable. As Keynes explains:

In abnormal times in particular, when the hypothesis of indefinite continuance of the existing state of affairs is less plausible than usual even though there are no express grounds to anticipate a definite change, the market will be subject to waves of optimistic and pessimistic sentiment, which are unreasoning and yet in a sense legitimate where no solid basis exists for reasonable calculation.[20]

A second interesting hypothesis has been suggested by Gardner Ackley, and by Nicholas Kaldor.[21] They have argued that deviations from fundamentals resulting from destabilizing speculative disturbances are more likely in markets where nonspeculative trading exerts little discipline over destabilizing speculation. In particular, Ackley and Kaldor claim that, in markets in which the flow supply and demand exert strong pressure on current trading, the growth of speculative bubbles will be inhibited. In a case where the flow supply and demand have a strong influence on market prices, a speculative rise in prices will lead to an increase in the flow supply and a decrease in the flow demand, which thus acts to dampen any bubble. Therefore, in such markets nonspeculative traders trade automatically so that they "lean against the wind" of destabilizing speculative price changes. Moreover, the further market prices veer from their equilibrium values, the stronger this pressure will be. In contrast, however, in those markets where the flow supply and demand do not exert strong and automatic counter-pressure to speculative bubbles, bubbles will develop unimpeded.

Undoubtedly, Milton Friedman and J. E. Meade assumed implicitly that the flow supply and demand for foreign exchange would discipline speculative activity, thus forcing speculation to be stabilizing. In the market for foreign exchange, a flow supply and demand for foreign exchange is created as a by-product of international trade. A country's exports create a flow demand for the home currency by the rest of the world, while its imports create a flow supply for foreign exchange by domestic purchasers of foreign products.

However, there are two good reasons for believing that the flow demand and supply for foreign exchange have not and will not discipline speculative currency bubbles in the foreign exchange market. In the first place, trade flows respond only with long and uncertain lags to changes in exchange rates. For the U.S., these lags have been estimated to be on the order of one to two

years or more. In fact, the flow supply and demand
responds in a perverse manner for at least the first year,
due to the so-called J-curve effect.[22] Second, many
observers have noted that trade flows are responsible for
a small and shrinking fraction of total currency trading.[23]
Estimates put the fraction of trading directly connected to
international trade at less than ten percent of the entire
market. Thus, unless the tail is wagging the dog, exchange
rate movements are not governed by trade flows.

Another interesting and related hypothesis has been
suggested by Kaldor.[24] Kaldor has claimed that
speculation becomes destabilizing when speculative
trading is a large component of total trading. In this
situation, speculators are more likely to attempt to
forecast future trends by forecasting the behavior of
their fellow speculators, rather than attempting to
forecast market fundamentals. As Kaldor explains:

> [The conventional argument] implies a state of affairs
> where speculative demand or supply amounts to a
> small proportion of total demand or supply, so that
> speculative activity, while it can influence the
> magnitude of the price-change, cannot any time
> change the direction of the price-change. If this
> condition is not satisfied, the argument breaks down.
> It still remains true that the speculator, in order to be
> permanently successful, must possess better than
> average foresight. But it will be quite sufficient for
> him to forecast correctly (or more correctly) the
> degree of foresight of other speculators, rather than
> the future course of the underlying non-speculative
> factors in the market. If the proportion of speculative
> transactions in the total is large, it may become, in
> fact, more profitable for the individual speculator to
> concentrate on forecasting the psychology of other
> speculators, rather than the trend of the non-
> speculative elements.[25]

Empirical support for these claims can be found in the evidence concerning the composition of trading activity, as well as by anecdotal evidence on how in fact traders do behave. In the first instance, the most complete study of the composition of trading suggests that the proportion of trading due to speculation and arbitrage accounts for roughly eighty-two percent of all interbank trading, which in itself accounts for ninety-five percent of all trading.[26] As Ian Giddy, the author of the above-mentioned study, concludes:

> We have learned that global foreign exchange activity consists largely of inter-bank trading for "speculative" and arbitrage purposes among a few currencies.[27]

And on the second point, there is much anecdotal evidence to suggest that traders in the market for foreign exchange trade in a Kaldorian fashion rather than in the manner suggested by Friedman and Meade. For instance, Charles Coombs, the former chief foreign exchange expert at the New York Federal Reserve Bank, has noted that

> Foreign exchange traders for better or worse, are not a bunch of scholarly Ph.D.s searching reams of statistical evidence for proof that a certain currency rate is becoming over or under valued and thereby triggering their decision to buy or sell. Anyone who has ever spent any time in a foreign exchange trading room knows only too well that traders focus primarily on short run developments. Foreign exchange traders have been taught by harsh experience that betting on the longer term fundamentals is an excellent way of losing your shirt. The name of the game is to anticipate market reactions to each new report coming off the ticker.[28]

Others have gone even further and have noted that, when traders focus on anticipating market reactions to "news," the result tends to produce bubbles:

Many market operators who follow exchange rates on a daily or hourly bases advance the view that exchange rates move in speculative runs, perhaps touched off by a change (or revision of expectations about) fundamental economic conditions, thereafter reflecting a self sustaining speculative mentality: "When the train is racing through the station at 90 miles an hour you don't think very long about where it is going to stop; you just try to get on board" (anonymous broker).[29]

Casino-Style Capitalism

In order to understand better the relationship between speculation and the foreign exchange market, we need to examine the institutional structure of the market for foreign exchange and its evolution within a broader framework. This will allow us to link larger macroeconomic dynamics with the changing character of the foreign exchange market. While providing such a framework is beyond the confines of this book, such considerations simply cannot be ignored. As a compromise, I will outline briefly several arguments that provide a broad, historical analysis of important trends which may have affected the nature and growing importance of speculation in the foreign exchange market in the 1970s and 1980s.

The emergence of the postwar international monetary order, as we have seen, was partially an outgrowth of the reorganization of capitalism prompted by the Great Depression and World War II. The depression and the war generated a series of regulations, both national and international in scope, designed to restore order and stability to financial affairs. The establishment of a stable monetary order became an important cornerstone for the long postwar boom, which lasted until the late 1960s. Subsequently, the demise of the postwar monetary order and the emergence of international economic disorder has characterized the world economy ever since. Our task is understand the dialectic between the rise and fall of the postwar international monetary order, the slowdown in economic growth, and the emergence of speculative fever in the foreign exchange market.

In this vein, some observers have argued that developments which originated in the real goods-producing sector may have influenced the relative importance of speculation throughout the world economy over the 1970-1980s, creating the foundations for what one observer has labeled aptly "casino capitalism."[30] For instance, Paul Sweezy and Harry Magdoff have argued that the emergence of economic stagnation has created powerful incentives for the growth of destabilizing speculation.[31] In their view, speculation for profit by financial institutions serves as a substitute for more traditional money making avenues. Therefore, during stagnant economic periods in which profit opportunities in the financing of the production and circulation of goods and services are limited, financial institutions tend to expand activities that they once considered ancillary--e.g. currency trading. Thus, Sweezy and Magdoff believe that, beginning around 1970 when the slowdown in economic growth with its accompanying fall in profit rates began, enormous incentives were unleashed for highly speculative, financial ventures, which stimulated a "financial explosion" alongside the stagnation in the real economy. Therefore, Sweezy and Magdoff's analysis suggests that the growth slowdown created irresistible incentives for the emergence of speculative fever that put an end to the stable, postwar financial order.

Alternatively, it can be argued that an important impetus for financial speculation in the 1970s and 1980s was the return of the "gambling spirit," or the increased willingness on the part of financial institutions to take risks in their never-ending search for higher returns. All market economies have rules and conventions which discourage high risk, speculative activities. However, the passage of time and the advent of new generations to positions of power may erode and ignore both of these constraints. If this is the case, once-effective constraints on the propensity to gamble (which, in our case, were a direct result of the Great Depression and its aftermath) wither away as social changes make these constraints obsolete because generational shifts produce corporate managers or government officials without first-hand experience of the events that bred respect, compliance, and political support for regulatory constraints.

Or perhaps large "exogenous" economic changes, such as changes in relative prices (energy prices, raw material prices, etc.), and/or the "exogenous" collapse of regulatory constraints (the Bretton Woods currency and capital controls) are to blame. Any of these rapid and pronounced economic changes may have created large potential profit opportunities in the financial sphere which were conducive to speculation.[32] Thus, reasonable arguments can be made that either the "endogenous" or "exogenous" collapse of the postwar international monetary order created the conditions for speculative fever by removing once-effective constraints on the propensity to gamble and/or by creating enormous profit opportunities in speculation.

The above suggestions provide several interesting reasons for the increased importance of currency speculation in the international banking community (which also happens to coincide chronologically with the advent of widespread floating). An eclectic view of this issue suggests that a number of factors may have been at work, providing both incentives and increased opportunities for highly speculative currency trading. These include (1) stagnation in the goods producing sector, (2) *de facto* deregulation of banking, (3) the collapse of the Bretton Woods currency accords, (4) an increased willingness of financial institutions to take on risk, (5) pronounced changes in the economic scene induced by the rise in oil and other commodity prices, (6) growing political and economic uncertainty which destroys the basis for reasonable calculation, and (7) institutional arrangements in the foreign exchange market which also have facilitated high-risk trading. Therefore, other than developments purely internal to the foreign exchange market, many external events may have contributed to the predominance of speculative tradings over what Keynes once referred to as enterprise.

THE STYLIZED FACTS

My main objective in the following sections is to explore and evaluate the empirical evidence obtained from historical information and time series analyses of spot exchange rates in order to establish the consistency of the bubble hypothesis with the empirical regularities of the foreign exchange market. Like the theoretical debates, the empirical debates about the nature of currency speculation originated with Milton Friedman's now famous "The Case for Flexible Exchange Rates," in which he asserted that the then existing empirical evidence generally had been misinterpreted.[33] "[T]his belief," that speculation has tended to be destabilizing, wrote Friedman, "does not seem to be founded on any systematic analysis of the available empirical evidence."[34] In a footnote, he went on to argue that Ragnar Nurkse's empirical work was the basis for the then popular belief that speculation was destabilizing, and that Nurkse's evidence was clearly inadequate:

[T]he evidence he cites is by itself inadequate to justify any conclusion. Nurkse examines only one episode in anything approaching the required detail, the depreciation of the French franc from 1922 to 1926. For the rest, he simply lists episodes during which exchange rates were flexible and asserts that in each case speculation was destabilizing. These episodes may or may not support his conclusion; it is impossible to tell from his discussion of them; and the list is clearly highly selective, including some cases that seem prima facie to point in the opposite direction.[35]

Friedman's sharp disagreement with Nurkse's work helped to spark the modern search for techniques and evidence to determine whether or not speculation tends to be stabilizing.

However, the mainstream position has changed with the emergence of widespread floating. The supporters of flexible exchange rates have been forced to move away from Friedman's position that free market currency regimes resemble optimally functioning adjustable peg regimes because the "facts" have made this position untenable. Instead, there is now widespread agreement from various theorists that exchange rates are potentially highly volatile speculative prices which respond immediately to changes in market psychology. Accordingly, the empirical disagreements among economists are focused on *alternative explanations* of market volatility and large swings in exchange rates. In the following sections, I will compare and contrast two competing explanations of the stylized facts--the bubble hypothesis and the efficient markets hypothesis.

Periodizing the Float

Since there are clear indications that there has been a strong ebb and flow in the propensity to gamble, as well as for central banks to intervene, a necessary first step in organizing the empirical evidence is to recognize these historically important delineations. From my perspective, the epoch of floating exchange rates can be usefully divided into six subperiods, each of which denotes a sharp change in either the dynamics of market speculation or a major shift in foreign exchange market policy. The subdivisions are illustrated in Figures 3.1, 3.2,

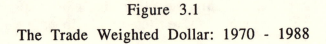

Figure 3.1

The Trade Weighted Dollar: 1970 - 1988

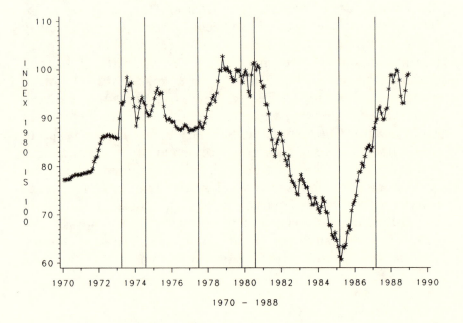

Legend:
Star = the trade weighted dollar, appreciation (-).
Source:
The trade weighted dollar is from the IMF, *International Financial Statistics*, U.S. MERM.

Figure 3.2

The Strong Currencies Against the Dollar: 1970 - 1988

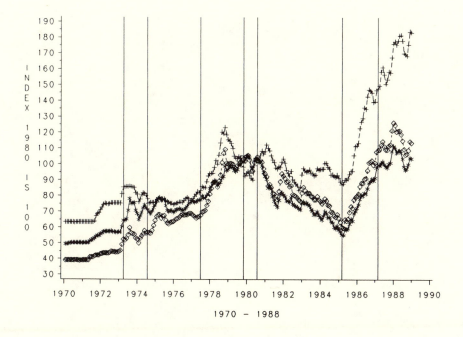

1970 – 1988

Legend:
Star = an index of the dollar price of the German mark..
Diamond = an index of the dollar price of the Swiss franc.
Plus = an index of the dollar price of the Japanese yen.
Source:
All data are from the IMF, *International Financial Statistics*, series AF.

80

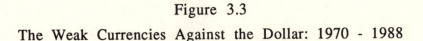

Figure 3.3

The Weak Currencies Against the Dollar: 1970 - 1988

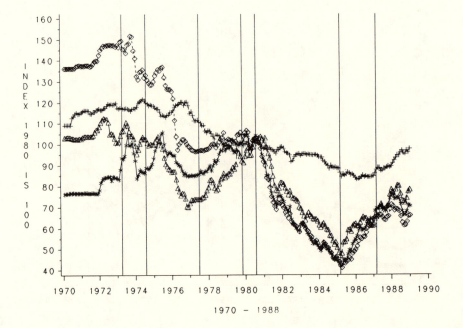

1970 – 1988

Legend:
Star = an index of the dollar price of the French franc.
Diamond = an index of the dollar price of the Italian lira.
Plus = an index of the dollar price of the Canadian dollar.
Triangle = an index of the dollar price of the British pound.
Source:
See Figure 3.2.

and 3.3. The first period extends from March 1973, the start of the floating rate era, to June 1974. In this period, currency rates became extremely volatile (see Table 3.1), the volume of trading was expanding rapidly, and, by many accounts, speculative betting in the interbank market was both significant and reckless. The second period, roughly stretching from July 1974 until May 1977, was ushered in by a near collapse of the currency market that was precipitated by the failure of two banks. This near collapse of the market created the conditions for a significant fall in trading volumes, a substantial reduction in market volatility (see Table 3.1), and ushered in a period of relative calm, at least for the then strong currencies--the dollar, the German mark, the Japanese yen, and the Swiss franc.

This period of relative calm came to an end when the Carter administration attempted to engineer a large depreciation of the dollar, which turned out to be more effective than the administration bargained for. In this third period, the markets once again became turbulent (see Table 3.1), trading volumes mushroomed, and speculation became rampant. Moreover, for the first time since the advent of floating exchange rates a sustained bout of one-way trading developed. The beginning of the end of speculative flight from the dollar came by January 1979 as a result of repeated attempts by the major central banks to stabilize the dollar-based currency system. A string of stabilization policies that began in January ended with the now famous shift in monetary policy in the U.S. beginning in October 1979.

After the October stabilization program, the foreign exchange markets stabilized. However, by July 1980, a series of events began to strengthen the dollar and transformed it into a vehicle for speculative gain. The strong dollar era began in earnest by the third quarter of 1980 and lasted until February 1985. In 1985, growing concern about the accumulating balance of payments deficits in the U.S. forged together a temporary alliance of

Table 3.1
Exchange Rate Volatility

Period	Trade Weighted Dollar	$/German Mark	$/Japanese Yen	$/Swiss Franc
1/70-12/70	.50	1.23	.23	.63
1/71-12/71	1.74	7.86	6.89	9.19
1/72-3/73	.98	5.10	4.05	11.32
4/73-12/73	1.58	10.15	2.74	7.81
1/74-6/74	1.83	6.12	3.54	8.04
7/74-12/74	.75	5.50	.77	10.78
1/75-12/75	2.13	7.77	2.39	6.29
1/76-12/76	.56	4.48	2.26	3.14
1/77-5/77	.19	1.48	2.30	1.15
6/77-10/79	3.39	9.99	11.32	16.39
11/79-12/80	1.47	4.45	6.95	1.43
1/81-12/81	3.68	6.69	4.82	7.15
1/82-12/82	3.73	4.51	6.52	6.99
1/83-12/83	2.71	6.31	1.74	3.40
1/84-12/84	4.20	10.19	3.78	9.04
1/85-12/85	6.14	15.59	9.62	15.63
1/86-12/86	3.42	7.94	5.21	8.19
1/87-12/87	2.34	4.69	3.73	4.95
1/88-12/88	1.78	4.46	1.90	4.91

Source:
Volatility is measured by the standard deviation of monthly exchange rate data. The trade weighted dollar is the IMF's MERM. All data are from the IMF, *International Financial Statistics*.

central banks in order to weaken the dollar, thus bringing an end to an extraordinary and unprecedented appreciation of the dollar.

The fifth period thus was ushered in as a result of the economic and political consequences of the soaring dollar. By the beginning of 1985, a consensus was developing among policymakers that the excessively overvalued dollar was a prime culprit behind the massive U.S. trade and current account deficits, which were being financed in this period by large private inflows of capital. The growing fear of protectionism aroused by these developments forced U.S. policymakers to join their European counterparts in engineering a depreciation of the dollar, mainly through central bank sales of dollars in the foreign exchange market. The dollar realignment policy was ratified formally at a Group of Five (England, France, Germany, Japan, and United States) meeting in New York's Plaza Hotel on September 22, 1985. The coordinated exchange market policy to realign the dollar was so successful that by early 1987, the dollar already had begun to reach new lows and the consensus among policymakers shifted from that of realignment to concern over maintaining stability at then current levels.

The shift towards the goal of stability and away from realignment marks the beginning of the sixth period in the ongoing political exchange rate cycle. The policy shift which delineates the sixth period was motivated by concerns that the fall in the dollar might go too far too quickly. The scenario that began to worry policymakers was the possibility of a "hard landing" for the dollar, which would engender problems similar to the speculative flight from the dollar in 1978-1979. This change in course was publicly announced at the Group of Five meeting in Paris on February 22, 1987. Since the so-called Louvre accord, the main thrust of policy has been to stabilize the dollar at existing levels to prevent both unwanted depreciations or appreciations of the dollar.

This periodization of the float is based on an assessment of spot exchange rate data and historical evidence. I will provide a more detailed analysis in support of this periodization below.

Ever since Friedman and Meade claimed that destabilizing speculation increases the volatility of spot exchange rates, periods of destabilizing speculation have been thought to be characterized by high variance.[36] In the rational bubbles literature, if the innovations in bubbles are either correlated or uncorrelated with the innovations in market fundamentals, then bubbles will increase volatility. It follows, therefore, that both literatures "agree" that speculative bubbles increase market turbulence. However, it is recognized that it is impossible to show that periods of "excess" volatility are necessarily the result of bubbles and not simply a by-product of unstable market fundamentals.[37] In fact, many authors have claimed that "newsy" periods give the false impression that exchange rates are "too" volatile.[38] (This alternative explanation of market volatility will be examined in detail and critiqued in Chapter 4.) Nevertheless, even though market volatility is not a clear indicator of the existence of bubbles, it can be a useful guide in periodizing the float in conjunction with other information.

Table 3.1 shows the ebb and flow of market volatility since the demise of the Bretton Woods accords.[39] The data indicate that currency market volatility, measured as the standard deviation of monthly exchange rate data, began during the breakup of the Bretton Woods system in 1971. Market volatility continued to be high with the advent of the floating exchange rate regime in March 1973. An explanation for this initial volatility can be found by examining the underlying forces at work in the foreign exchange market during this period. With the start of widespread floating, the large multinational banks saw what they considered an extraordinary opportunity to increase profits from their foreign exchange operations. Beginning in late 1972, banks' trading volumes increased in order to meet both growing retail demand and, more importantly, their own increased interest in speculating for profit.[40] According to one estimate, for example, foreign exchange trading by twelve large American banks increased from $15 billion in 1971 to over $42 billion in 1974.[41] This spectacular growth in trading volumes was accompanied by an equally spectacular growth in reckless currency speculation. Perhaps the best documented example of such reckless currency speculation was the case of the Franklin National Bank.

Franklin National was a growth-oriented, intermediate sized bank based in Long Island, New York, which, like its money-center competitors, was internationalizing its operations throughout the late 1960s and early 1970s. In Franklin National's case, currency speculation was seen, at first, as a potentially highly lucrative addition to their existing operations. Later on, however, Franklin National's management hoped to use profits garnered in currency speculation to offset losses in its other divisions. Unfortunately, like other large banks that were speculating heavily in this period, Franklin National's currency traders did not recognize nor prepare for the new risks associated with speculating in a floating exchange rate regime. Like other currency dealers, Franklin's traders were schooled in the art of currency speculation under the less risky, adjustable peg system.[42] As a result, institutional controls on position taking by traders were inadequate in preventing reckless betting by traders on very short-term movements in currencies. This combination proved to be extremely dangerous for many large multinational banks.

As with the banking industry as a whole, Franklin National's trading volumes exploded when the Bretton Woods currency accords began to wither. Accompanying this explosion in trading volumes was a dazzling and ultimately disastrous increase in currency speculation, as evidenced by Franklin National's spectacular profits and losses from currency trading.[43] Franklin National's traders were taking large, open positions by using the forward market to place their bets. Near the end, their activities became so alarming that other large banks refused to engage in normal interbank transactions with Franklin National. Morgan Guaranty officials even took the unusual step of reporting this decline in market confidence to Federal Reserve officers.[44] The end came when, in growing desperation, Franklin National's currency traders took large, short positions against foreign currencies in the mistaken belief that the dollar would continue to strengthen due to the ongoing energy crisis. This produced losses exceeding $36 million in February and March of 1974, which led ultimately to Franklin's demise.

Table 3.1 shows that an era of relative calm was ushered in after the near demise of currency trading that followed the previous period of reckless currency speculation. Prior to this near collapse of the foreign exchange market, many large banks were caught in the same vicious cycle that led to the failure of Franklin National--namely, attempting to place large risky bets in the currency markets in the hope of making up for declining profits elsewhere. As Joan Edelman Spero notes:

Virtually all important banks were heavily involved in foreign exchange trading. Many, tempted by the possibility of profits in a time when other divisions of banks were being squeezed, turned to foreign exchange speculation--and many suffered well-publicized losses. In April 1974 the Union Bank of Switzerland announced a "sizable loss" due to unauthorized trading. The loss was later estimated to have been $150 million. The Westdeutsche-Landesbank suffered foreign exchange losses of $105 million. Franklin's troubles were announced in mid-May. In late June in the midst of Franklin's prolonged crisis, the most serious incident occurred: the failure of Backhaus Herstatt. Revelations of other banks' foreign exchange losses continued throughout the year.[45]

The failure of Herstatt, in the uncertain and fragile environment that characterized the period, was the proverbial straw that nearly broke the camel's back. Like Franklin National, Herstatt was speculating in currency markets and losing. On June 26, 1974, at precisely four o'clock, Herstatt was ordered closed by German federal authorities. The closure was precipitated when the authorities discovered that Herstatt officials were falsifying their bookkeeping entries in order to hide large currency-related losses. The manner in which Herstatt was closed subsequently caused a disruption in the interbank settlement process, as explained by Andrew Brimmer, former governor of the Federal Reserve System:

Normally, in a foreign exchange trade, the buyer and seller of a currency promise to settle with each other within two days. In the Herstatt case, German marks were sold to Herstatt on June 24, 1974, by at least a dozen banks. Settlement was due--in dollars--on June 26.

On that date, the selling banks instructed their correspondent banks in Germany to debit their mark accounts and deposit the funds in the Landes-Central bank--the clearing house operated by the Bundesbank [the German central bank]. The funds were then credited to Herstatt. The selling banks expected to receive dollars on the same day through London or New York clearing houses.

However, Bankhaus Herstatt was officially declared bankrupt around 4 P.M. on June 26, 1974. This was after the market had closed in Germany-- but while foreign exchange was still being traded in New York. In the meantime, the Landes-Central Bank credited Herstatt with funds in Cologne, but the latter's doors were shut before Herstatt's dollars were credited to foreign banks.

This action triggered the disruption of the foreign exchange market--since it aborted the settlement process.[46]

The Herstatt episode made all the money-center banks participating in the interbank currency market keenly and painfully aware of the delivery risks associated with spot transactions.

As a result of the Herstatt incident, the foreign exchange market nearly collapsed. If it weren't for timely central bank intervention and reforms, the interbank currency and the related interbank Eurodollar market could have collapsed, bringing down with them the free market international monetary system established after Bretton Woods. While there are no precise estimates of trading volumes, one study found that trading volumes may have fallen by as much as two-thirds shortly after the Herstatt incident.[47] Moreover, three years later, trading volumes were estimated to be still twenty percent below the highs reached in the first half of 1974.[48]

An interpretation of these events which is consistent with the bubble hypothesis is that the dramatic, currency-related losses of 1974, combined with the resulting disruption in the market's settlement process, had the effect of discouraging currency speculation by reducing its profitability until its reemergence in June 1977. From this perspective, the temporary decline in the propensity to gamble by the large money-center banks was primarily responsible for the simultaneous reduction in currency trading volume and market volatility.

Some additional evidence for this interpretation of events is given in Figure 3.4. Figure 3.4 measures the average annualized return differences on a monthly basis from holding dollar denominated assets in the form of a long-term U.S. government bond versus a portfolio of foreign denominated assets consisting of equal weights of German, Swiss, and Japanese long-term government

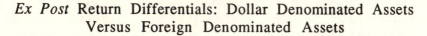

Figure 3.4

Ex Post Return Differentials: Dollar Denominated Assets
Versus Foreign Denominated Assets

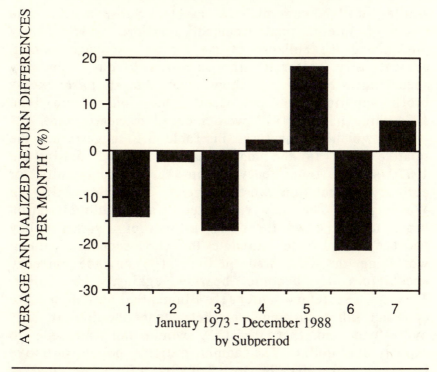

Legend:
Period 1 extends from January 1973 through May 1974.
Period 2 extends from June 1974 through May 1977.
Period 3 extends from June 1977 through January 1979.
Period 4 extends from February 1979 through June 1980.
Period 5 extends from July 1980 through February 1985.
Period 6 extends from March 1985 through February 1987.
Period 7 extends from March 1987 through December 1988.

Source:
The return differentials were computed by taking the long-term
U.S. government bond rate less a simple average of the long-term
German, Swiss, and Japanese government bond rates, plus the
annualized exchange gain from holding dollars against a simple
average of German marks, Swiss francs, and Japanese yen. All
data are from the IMF, *International Financial Statistics*.

bonds. A smart currency speculator who was lucky enough to purchase the foreign portfolio in January 1973 would have earned over fourteen percent on an annualized basis per month more than the holder of similar dollar denominated assets. Subsequently, the onset of international financial fragility, which nearly precipitated the collapse of the foreign exchange market, dramatically altered the returns from currency speculation. Figure 3.4 shows that the *ex post* excess profit opportunities from fleeing the dollar from June 1974 through May 1977 were reduced to nearly zero.

The volatility measures in Table 3.1 suggest that the relative calm in the marketplace continued until June 1977. At that time, renewed interest and opportunity for currency speculation were triggered by policy shifts in Washington. The newly elected Carter administration began to talk down the dollar as part of a larger policy package intended to stimulate the U.S. economy without worsening the U.S. trade deficit. To convince currency speculators to become bearish against the dollar, Treasury Secretary Michael Blumenthal attempted to convince the currency markets that the dollar was overvalued and that the U.S. would not intercede to support the dollar. The administration's policy initiative had quick results because of its effect on market expectations. As one trader put it "Blumenthal gave everybody the excuse to kick the hell out of the dollar."[49] Unfortunately, the policy was too effective. The administration was forced to reverse its policy stance only six months after the policy went into effect due to growing fears worldwide that currency speculation against the dollar was getting out of hand, thus jeopardizing the dollar-based international monetary system.

Much like the highly speculative period between January 1973 and July 1974, the period after June 1977 was characterized by a high degree of volatility in the key exchange rates (see Table 3.1) and by mushrooming trading volumes.[50] Furthermore, in the period from June

1977 through January 1979 when the bubble began to ebb, the German mark appreciated in fifteen out of twenty months over this span, the French franc appreciated in fourteen out of twenty months, and the Swiss franc appreciated in sixteen out of twenty months. In one stretch, the Swiss franc appreciated for ten months straight and fifteen out of seventeen months, thus yielding *ex post* monthly annualized exchange gains averaging above forty-three percent to speculators.[51] Furthermore, the return differential between a foreign portfolio of assets and dollar denominated assets averaged seventeen percent on an annualized basis per month over the period. (See Figure 3.4, period three.)

In addition, these "bubble like" returns to currency speculators occurred despite growing intervention by central banks to halt the process. By January 1979, however, the *ex post* excess returns from dumping dollar denominated assets and buying German, Swiss, and Japanese assets vanished. (See Figure 3.4, period four.) It is hard to avoid the conclusion that the concerted currency market interventions and the shifts in monetary policy that followed after January 1979 succeeded in eliminating the profitability of substituting one paper asset for another, at least until July 1980. With the decline of speculative flight from the dollar, moreover, currency market volatility declined substantially after the shift in monetary policy in October 1979. (See Table 3.1.)

The strong dollar era was ushered in as a result of the interaction of several economic and political factors. The most important of these were the stabilization policies initiated by the administration, which raised U.S. long-term real interest rates substantially above world rates; the election of a conservative president in the United States; the economic and political disintegration of Latin America due to the debt crisis; and a publicly announced policy by the Reagan administration that it would not intervene to prevent the dollar from appreciating because of its belief that the market knows best which rates are appropriate.

Much like the bubble in the Carter era, these "shocks" also created a large bubble as well by making the expectations of currency speculators homogeneous and thereby creating a one-way speculative trading in dollars. The Reagan-era bubble led also to an unprecedented string of positive *ex post* returns from holding dollar denominated assets.[52] Figure 3.4 shows that the *ex post* return differential from acquiring dollar denominated assets averaged over eighteen percent per month on an annualized basis from July 1980 to February 1985. And as in previous highly speculative periods, trading volumes mushroomed and currency market volatility escalated.[53] Eventually, the bubble which began in July 1980 was halted when the leading central banks began a concerted effort in early 1985 to bring down the value of the dollar in order to stabilize once again the dollar-based international monetary system.

The attempt to realign the dollar began on January 17, 1985, at a Group of Five meeting of finance ministers and central bank governors. This meeting launched concerted central bank policies to coordinate sales of dollars on the foreign exchange market to force the dollar down to more realistic levels. The object of this coordinated foreign exchange market intervention was to induce speculators to alter their expectations of the dollar, from being bullish to being bearish. The initial interventions were led by the Bundesbank (the German central bank) and "succeeded in restoring a two-way market" by February 1985, halting a five-year long appreciation cycle.[54] This set the stage for the wide-ranging agreements signed at the Group of Five meeting at the Plaza Hotel on September 22, 1985. The demonstrative show of unanimity by the Group of Five in New York had the immediate effect of pushing the dollar down by six percent, the largest daily fall in the dollar since March 1973.[55] After this point, the United States began to take a leading role in the interventions to reinforce its commitment to a weaker dollar. The resulting fall in the dollar was both dramatic and rapid, with the yen, Swiss franc, and German mark appreciating by over sixty percent from February 1985 to May 1986. Thus the corrections in 1985 and 1986 managed to restore the dollar in real terms to levels close to what it was in 1980, the year the dollar began its five-year long appreciation.[56]

What frightened policymakers into shifting course was that as the dollar continued to depreciate in 1986, the precipitous slide downward shifted from being a "managed correction" to becoming a "spontaneous decline."[57] The principal reason for this "spontaneous decline," according to astute observers at the Bank for International Settlements, "was that the longer the depreciation of the dollar lasted the more it bred expectations of further decline."[58] The source of this concern is not difficult to locate. Figure 3.4 shows that from March 1985 until February 1987 the policy of realigning the dollar produced return differentials averaging above twenty-one percent per month on an annualized basis. Furthermore, these "expectations of further decline" were reinforced by the fact that the policy consensus reached in early 1985 was eroding due to emerging differences in opinion as to whether realignment had gone far enough. The countries with appreciating currencies, eager to protect their export industries from a further loss in price competitiveness, began to argue that the dollar depreciation had gone far enough. On the other hand, U.S. policymakers were insisting that the dollar needed to depreciate further in order to enhance the prospects of shrinking the large and growing U.S. trade deficit. These sharp disagreements among policymakers left the market in doubt as to whether or not the central banks were still capable of controlling the dollar.

Eventually a new consensus was reached in Paris on February 22, 1987, with the so-called Louvre accord. To reach this new consensus, U.S. Treasury Secretary James

Baker III negotiated with the principal surplus countries, Japan and Germany, to stimulate their economies in return for U.S. support for stabilizing the dollar "around the current levels," which were stated to be "within ranges broadly consistent with underlying economic fundamentals."[59] From the perspective of U.S. policymakers, the economic stimulus promised in the accords by Japan and Germany would shrink the U.S. trade deficit without requiring a weaker dollar. This was acceptable for the U.S. because the whole purpose of weakening the dollar had been to bring about a needed correction in the U.S. balance of payments. Therefore, U.S. policymakers were willing to trade off further dollar depreciation for economic stimulus abroad.

The Louvre agreement successfully ended the dollar depreciation phase of the political exchange rate cycle and has so far worked to keep the dollar trading in a broad target zone around the rates agreed upon in February 1987. Once again, coordinated central bank intervention succeeded by taking the profit out of speculative flight from the dollar. (See Figure 3.4, period seven.) This dollar stabilization agreement has been generally labelled as "the most serious attempt to implement systematic currency stabilization . . . after more than a decade of uncharted floating exchange rates."[60] However, it is doubtful that the Louvre accord will be able to provide a long-term solution to current difficulties. It is only a matter of time before interstate conflicts of interest or conflicts over ideology will weaken the current policy consensus sufficiently, rendering the central banks helpless in the face of currency traders determined to move large sums from one leading currency to another.

Bubbles or a Random Walk?

In this section I will concentrate on testing the bubble hypothesis against a popular null hypothesis, the random walk hypothesis. To contrast the two, I will assume that in their growing phase bubbles produce a series of linked appreciations (or depreciations) which generate serial dependence between current and lagged exchange rates and that bursting bubbles also create periodic large jumps (or crashes) in exchange rates. Therefore, the bursting bubble hypothesis suggests that bubbles leave an "empirical legacy" that is in principle possible to detect.

To gauge the extent to which the bubble hypothesis is consistent with empirical reality, a null hypothesis is required. A popular null hypothesis is that exchange rate movements are a random walk.[61] In the efficient markets literature, it is argued that prices in speculative markets reflect fully all currently available information as well as all future developments which can be forecasted with any certainty.[62] Furthermore, changes in market prices are claimed to reflect new information released to the market, which forces a revision of expectations and, hence, prices. In speculative markets where expectations of the future are an important determinant of current prices, "news" announcements generate effects which potentially can force large price revisions. Therefore, from an efficient markets perspective, this period's price is related to the last period's price in the following manner:

$$e_t = e_{t-1} + \text{news, or } e_t - e_{t-1} = \text{news} \qquad (3.1)$$

where

e_t = the log of the exchange rate in period t

This equation shows that, in an efficient market, changes in the exchange rate are considered to be a news effect. Moreover, the news effect is said usually to be serially uncorrelated white noise. If serial dependence does exist, then it is possible for speculators to reap positive profits by using past news to predict future developments. This would violate a strict interpretation of an efficient market, which says that all available information is already reflected in current prices, making it impossible to use knowledge of past news to trade profitably in the market. The existence of such profit opportunities would imply that the market is not a fair game because it yields positive expected gains to speculators.

In contrast, the bubble hypothesis predicts some serial dependence during the growing phase of bubbles. In a growing bubble, the current change in the exchange rate reflects both the presence of a bubble and a random "news" element:

$$e_t - e_{t-1} = \text{bubble} + \text{"news"} \qquad (3.2)$$

It is important to note that the existence of large stochastic bubbles implies that changes in exchange rates will be correlated only when the bubble component assumes a positive value. At all other times, however, exchange rates may move randomly. In other words, the bubble hypothesis is consistent with the time series data having a large random element.

Using exchange rate data, several tests can be employed to detect the presence of serial dependence. First, following the work of William Poole, we can test for serial correlation in exchange rate data by using regression analysis to determine the relationship between what is in null hypothesis "news" and lagged "news."[63] Under the null hypothesis, which states that the market is a random walk, regression analysis can determine whether there is any correlation between today's "news" and yesterday's "news." To be consistent with the random walk hypothesis, regression results should confirm that both the intercept (which assumes there is no trend) and, more importantly, that the slope coefficients are zero. In contrast, the bubble hypothesis predicts serial dependence, although not necessarily a trend in the series.

In a previous study, I tested for serial dependence between current and lagged exchange rates using five daily spot exchange rates (the German mark, the French franc, the Swiss franc, the Japanese yen, and the British pound) over the time period March 1, 1973, through December 31, 1984.[64] In the tests, I assumed that changes in the current spot exchange rate were a polynomial distributed lag of changes in exchange rate in the preceding month (the previous twenty trading days). My results suggest that current changes in exchange rates are linked to previous changes in exchange rates. However, these lagged changes in exchange rates explain only a small fraction of current changes (the range was from one to four percent). The pattern of serial dependence revealed by the tests indicates that daily changes in the major spot exchange rates tested are negatively related to changes in the previous three trading days, but positively related to changes in the previous four through sixteen days (with little relationship thereafter). These results can be interpreted to suggest that speculators adopt short-run speculative strategies that combine running their gains and profit-taking. In this view, the dominance of profit-taking in the very short run accounts for the negative relationship during days one through three, while over the longer horizon, speculators tend to run their gain--which accounts for the positive serial dependence.

However, to get a better sense of the degree of serial dependence over longer time periods and to remove much of the statistical noise that permeates the data, it is best to employ monthly average exchange rate data. Table 3.2 shows the results of using Poole's procedure with lagged first differences in natural logs (which for small changes are approximately equivalent to percentage changes) to explain contemporaneous first differences for seven currencies--the British pound, the Canadian dollar, the French franc, the German mark, the Italian lira, the Japanese yen, the Swiss franc--relative to the dollar, from March 1973 to December 1988. In each

Table 3.2

Analysis of Serial Dependence in Monthly Exchange Rate Data:

March 1973 - December 1988

Dependent Variable: First Differences of the Natural Log of the Dollar/German Mark Rate

---

Lagged Dependent Variable	.30	R-Squared	.09
T-Value	(4.39)	*First-Order Rho	.06
Intercept:	.002	T-Value	(.25)
T-Value	(1.06)		

Dependent Variable: First Differences of the Natural Log of the Dollar/Swiss Franc Rate

---

Lagged Dependent Variable	.32	R-Squared	.10
T-Value	(4.59)	*First-Order Rho	.09
Intercept:	.003	T-Value	(.37)
T-Value	(1.43)		

(Continued)

Table 3.2 (Continued)
Dependent Variable: First Differences of the Natural Log
of the Dollar/Japanese Yen Rate

Lagged Dependent	.32	R-Squared	.10
Variable			
T-Value	(4.62)	*First-Order Rho	.36
Intercept:	.003	T-Value	(1.55)
T-Value	(1.59)		

Dependent Variable: First Differences of the Natural Log
of the Dollar/French Franc Rate

Lagged Dependent	.28	R-Squared	.10
Variable			
T-Value	(4.00)	*First-Order Rho	-.02
Intercept:	-.001	T-Value	(-.09)
T-Value	(-.31)		

Dependent Variable: First Differences of the Natural Log
of the Dollar/Italian Lira Rate

Lagged Dependent	.37	R-Squared	.14
Variable			
T-Value	(5.47)	*First-Order Rho	-.10
Intercept:	-.002	T-Value	(-.50)
T-Value	(-1.51)		

(Continued)

Table 3.2 (Continued)

Dependent Variable: First Differences of the Natural Log of the Dollar/Canadian Dollar Rate

Lagged Dependent Variable	.18	R-Squared	.03
T-Value	(2.46)	*First-Order Rho	.30
Intercept:	-.001	T-Value	(.74)
T-Value	(-1.04)		

Dependent Variable: First Differences of the Natural Log of the Dollar/British Pound Rate

Lagged Dependent Variable	.41	R-Squared	.17
T-Value	(6.15)	*First-Order Rho	.25
Intercept:	-.001	T-Value	(1.39)
T-Value	(-.45)		

Source:
All data are from the IMF, *International Financial Statistics*, series AF.
*The estimate of the first-order rho was obtained by using Durbin's method. Durbin's procedure is to estimate first-order rho in autoregressive models by regressing residuals on lagged residuals and the explanatory variables.

case, there is a statistically significant, positive relationship between this month's and last month's percentage changes. In addition, last month's percentage changes explain anywhere from three to seventeen percent of the percentage change in this month's exchange rate. In all, the results suggest a fairly strong and predictable relationship between what the dollar does on average one month to the next. The evidence presented in Table 3.2, however, cannot cast doubt upon the random walk hypothesis, since we intentionally used averaged data to suppress some of the statistical noise inherent in exchange rate data.

While the results from Poole's procedure are consistent with the bubble hypothesis, it is difficult to draw definite conclusions from the evidence. For example, in the tests employing daily data the estimated serial dependence accounts for only a small fraction of daily changes in exchange rates. Because of this fact, it becomes unclear that the random walk hypothesis cannot be rejected in favor of the bubble hypothesis. To appreciate this point, if we assume that either transactions costs are steep or that the expected speculative gains are sufficiently uncertain, then the observed serial dependence may be economically meaningless. Thus, the defenders of the efficient markets hypothesis may argue rightly that the market is "almost" a random walk and that the observed serial dependence is economically meaningless. We can thus conclude that the results from using regression procedures tend to confirm the bubble hypothesis, although it is difficult to claim with any certainty whether or not the observed serial dependence disproves the random walk hypothesis.

An alternative test for serial dependence is runs tests.[65] A run is said to occur when there is a series of changes of the same order. An example would be to flip a coin ten times with the following results: HHH TT H T H TT, where H = heads and T = tails. The number of runs in this example is six. If the sample data are truly independent, as suggested by the random walk hypothesis, the number of runs would be "large." On the other hand, if the number of runs is "small," this would demonstrate that sample values are not independent. Runs tests can be conducted on exchange rate data by dividing the data into the "growing" and/or the "bursting" side of a bubble by using the sign of either raw or detrended data. Under the null hypothesis that the exchange rate is a random walk, the expected number of runs are (N-1)/2 (when the mean is zero), where N = the number of observations. If the bubble hypothesis is valid, the number of runs should be significantly less than predicted under the null hypothesis. Statistically significant results from runs tests would demonstrate that the serial dependence found using regression procedures arises from a series of intermittent appreciations and/or depreciations. Such a finding would confirm further that the generating mechanism creating serial dependence is not that suggested by the null hypothesis.

Runs tests were conducted by Kunio Okina using weekly data starting from the seventeenth week in 1973 to the fifty-second week in 1980 on five currencies--the German mark, the French franc, the Japanese yen, the British pound, and the Canadian dollar.[66] Okina found that the number of runs in each case was less than those predicted by the null hypothesis. However, in the case of the French franc, the difference was not statistically significant at the ten percent level. Thus, Okina's results provide further evidence for the existence of speculative bubbles.

A third set of tests searches for the presence of serial dependence through the use of filter rules.[67] A filter rule is a trading rule that attempts to reproduce a simple buy and sell speculative strategy. The rule (or rules) usually assumes that speculators buy when the market rises by X percent, and sell when it falls by X percent. If the trading rule proves profitable, this is taken as an indication that existing serial dependence is consistent with the bubble hypothesis. It is possible for these trading rules to pick up some serial dependence that regression analysis and/or runs tests may not. Moreover, the existence of profitable trading rules suggests directly that the extent of serial correlation violates the random walk hypothesis. However, it is not yet possible to test for the statistical significance of such rules.

Empirical results from using filter rules to test for serial dependence have found nearly always that such rules yield positive profits. Critics note that the profits yielded are generally small and no one rule continuously yields profits. Thus, they claim that real world speculators could not profit from the existing serial dependence in exchange rate data. However, such criticisms are beside the point, since real world speculators can be infinitely more imaginative than any fixed rule.

Besides testing for serial dependence, which we take to be an indicator of the growing phase of bubbles, it is also possible to test for the existence of crashes.[68] If bubbles crash, they will produce a series of outliers in the sample distribution. Therefore, under the bursting bubble hypothesis, we expect to find fat tails (a high degree of kurtosis) in the sample distribution. The null hypothesis that asserts that the tails should be normal would represent the no bubble hypothesis if we assume the distribution of news announcements is not leptokurtic.[69]

To test for crashes, I examined the characteristics of the distributions of daily percentage changes in five currency rates--the German mark, the French franc, the Swiss franc, the Japanese yen, and the British pound.[70] Under the null hypothesis that the distribution of news announcements is normal, the distribution of percentage changes in exchange rates should be normal also--that is, the expected values for skewness and kurtosis in the sample distribution are expected to be zero. Four out of the five distributions exhibit some skewness, although they appear "near normal" in this respect. In each case, the significant departure from normality is due to a high degree of kurtosis. The high positive values of kurtosis indicate that the sample distribution has fat tails or too many outliers, as predicted by the bubble hypothesis. Therefore, the evidence from tail tests tends to support the bursting bubble hypothesis.

CONCLUSIONS

In this chapter I have argued four principal hypotheses concerning the evolution of the foreign exchange market and its relationship to speculative currency bubbles: (1) A speculative market in foreign exchange arose out of the shortcomings and contradictions of the Bretton Woods monetary accords and from subsequent economic and political developments that strained the regulatory apparatus controlling financial markets and exchange rates. (2) The institutional framework of the market, as well as larger historical trends that increased the propensity to gamble by financial institutions, created the foundation for destabilizing currency speculation (mainly by traders in the money-center banks who operated in the interbank market). (3) Since the advent of the float, there have been three major speculative periods. The first such episode began with the demise of the Bretton Woods accords and lasted through to the near collapse of the foreign exchange market in July 1974. The next major speculative episode began in June 1977 and ended in January 1979 when central bank intervention managed to put a temporary halt to speculation against the dollar. The latest speculative episode lasted from July 1980 until February 1985. This strong dollar era came to an end as a result of concerted central bank intervention to bring down the value of dollar. (4) Diagnostic tests of time series spot exchange rate data support the bubble hypothesis over the efficient markets hypothesis. In particular, these tests have shown that exchange rate data exhibits some serial dependence and that the sample distribution of percentage changes in exchange rates has an abnormally large number of outliers, both of which are predicted by the bursting bubble hypothesis.

NOTES

1. For a review of the efficient markets hypothesis and random walk model, see Eugene F. Fama, "Efficient Capital Markets: A Review of Theory and Empirical Work," *Journal of Finance: Papers and Proceedings* 25 (May 1970), pp. 383-417.

2. See Fred L. Block, *The Origins of International Economic Disorder: A Study of United States International Monetary Policy from World War II to the Present* (Berkeley: University of California Press, 1977), Michael Moffitt, *The World's Money* (New York: Simon and Schuster, 1983), John Williamson, *The Failure of World Monetary Reform, 1971-1974* (New York: New York University Press, 1977).

Williamson offers a brief but informative summary of this issue: "The question of 'market convertibility' concerns the circumstances under which the holder of one currency can sell it in order to acquire another. A multilateral system, which the architects of Bretton Woods aspired to create, requires that someone who is paid in one currency be able to convert that currency into any other currency that they need to make payments, since in the absence of such a right they are under pressure to spend their earnings on goods from the country in which the currency is acquired." Ibid., p. 2.

3. For the origin of this terminology, see Williamson, *The Failure of World Monetary Reform*, p. 2, note 1.

4. To quote from Keynes' alternative plan: "Many Central Banks have found great advantage in centralising with themselves or with an Exchange Control the supply and demand of all foreign exchange, thus dispensing with an outside exchange market . . . The further extension of such arrangements would be consonant with the general purposes of the Clearing Union . . ." See John Maynard

Keynes, "Keynes Plan," in J. Keith Horsefeld, ed., *The International Monetary Fund 1945-1965: Twenty Years of International Monetary Cooperation,* vol. III: Documents (Washington DC: International Monetary Fund, 1969), p. 29.

5. Officially, the articles of agreement fixed a gold price, not a dollar price, for each currency. See Williamson, *The Failure of World Monetary Reform,* p. 4. However, the parities could be expressed in the dollar equivalent of the fixed gold parity. "The par value of the currency of each member shall be expressed in terms of gold as a common denominator or in terms of the United States dollar of the weight . . .," in J. Keith Horsefeld, ed., *The International Monetary Fund,* p. 189.

As to altering the par values, the Articles of Agreement state: "A member shall not propose a change in the par value of its currency except to correct a fundamental disequilibrium." See "Articles of Agreement," ibid., p. 190.

6. To quote from the Articles of Agreement: "Members may exercise such controls as are necessary to regulate international capital movements, but no member may exercise these controls in a manner which will restrict payments for current account transactions . . ." Ibid., p. 194.

7. The importance of political hegemony for the stability of international monetary relations is stressed by Charles P. Kindleberger, *The World in Depression, 1929-1939* (Berkeley: University of California Press, 1986) and by Block, *The Origins of International Economic Disorder,* ch. 1. More recent contributions have noted also the important role of the internationalization of banking, see Moffitt, *The World's Money.*

8. Cited by Ralph C. Bryant, *International Financial Intermediation* (Washington DC: The Brookings Institution, 1987), pp. 61-62.

9. For accounts of the final demise of Bretton Woods, see Moffitt, *The World's Money* and Charles Coombs, *The*

Arena of International Finance (New York: John Wiley & Sons, 1976), ch. 12.

10. See Nicholas Kaldor, "Speculation and Economic Activity," in *Essays in Economic Stability and Growth* (London: Gerald Duckworth and Co. Ltd., 1960), pp. 20-22.

11. See Nicholas Kaldor, "Limits on Growth," *Oxford Economic Papers* 38 (1987), pp. 187-198.

12. See John Cooper, "How Foreign Exchange Operations can go Wrong," *Euromoney* (May 1974). Cooper argues there are three reasons why banks take open positions: "There are three main reasons why a bank might prefer not to undo or cover each deal as it is transacted. The first is deliberately to 'take a view'; that is, to go long or short of one currency against another currency on the assumption that rates of exchange would move in such a way before the deal had to be matched off that it could be so matched off at a profit. The other reasons are the usual, classic reasons for running a jobber's book in one currency against another: to refrain from matching off a lot of small 'retail' size deals until a position had been built up which was big enough to be matched off at wholesale--and therefore finer--rates; and to wait until one is approached by a counter-party-- either a commercial customer or a professional dealer in the market--who wanted to deal in such a way as to match one's book. . . . A point to be noticed about this is that whether or not a dealer is deliberately speculating or taking a view he is in fact laying himself open to the risks of speculation by running an unmatched position for either of the other two reasons." Ibid., p. 4.

13. This estimate comes from Frank McCormick, "Covered Interest Arbitrage: Unexploited Profits? Comment," *Journal of Political Economy* 87 (1979), pp. 411-417. Also see Jacob A. Frenkel and Richard M. Levich, "Transactions Costs and Interest Arbitrage: Tranquil Versus Turbulent Periods," *Journal of Political Economy* 85 (Nov.-Dec. 1977), pp. 1209-1226 for an analysis of the technique for estimating transactions costs and how transactions costs change in turbulent periods.

Furthermore, see Jacob A. Frenkel and Richard M. Levich, "Covered Interest Arbitrage and Unexploited Profits? Reply," *Journal of Political Economy* 87 (1979), pp. 418-422 for their reply to McCormick's critique of their estimates of transactions costs.

14. See the Bank for International Settlements, *Annual Report* (June 1987), p. 163.

15. Jacob A. Frenkel and Michael L. Mussa, "The Efficiency of Foreign Exchange Markets and Measures of Turbulence," *American Economic Review: Papers and Proceedings* 70 (May 1980), pp. 374-381.

16. Cited by Ian H. Giddy, "Measuring the World Foreign Exchange Market," *Columbia Journal of World Business* (Winter 1979), p. 42.

17. Ibid., pp. 41-43. Goodhart claims that foreign exchange speculation tends to be short term and that speculators are too risk-averse, creating "a shortage of (stabilizing) speculation." Charles Goodhart, "The Foreign Exchange Market: A Random Walk with a Dragging Anchor," *Economica* 55 (Nov. 1988), pp. 449-450.

18. See Olivier J. Blanchard and Mark W. Watson, "Bubbles, Rational Expectations and Financial Markets," National Bureau of Economic Research *Reprint* no. 374 (June 1983), pp. 300-301.

19. John Maynard Keynes, *The General Theory of Employment, Interest, and Money* (New York: Harcourt, Brace and World, Inc, 1964). To quote Keynes: "The actual private object of the most skilled investment to-day is 'to beat the gun', as the Americans so well express it, to outwit the crowd, and to pass the bad, or depreciating, half-crown to the other fellow." Ibid., p. 155.

20. Ibid., p. 154.

21. Gardner Ackley, "Commodities and Capital: Prices and Quantities," *American Economic Review: Papers and Proceedings* 73 (Mar. 1983), pp. 1-16 and Kaldor, "Speculation and Economic Activity," pp. 17-58.

22. For an explanation of the J-curve, see Rudiger Dornbusch and Paul Krugman, "Flexible Exchange Rates in

the Short Run," *Brookings Papers on Economic Activity* 3 (1976), pp. 537-575.

23. See Giddy, "Measuring the World Foreign Exchange Market," p. 41-43.

24. Kaldor, "Speculation and Economic Activity," pp. 17-19.

25. Ibid., pp. 18-19.

26. Giddy, "Measuring the World Foreign Exchange Market," p. 42. Goodhart claims that the volume of transactions is inflated (10 to 20 fold) by "natural market adjustments" in the interbank market which result from an initiating outside transaction. Goodhart, "The Foreign Exchange Market," p. 456.

27. Ibid., p. 43.

28. Cited by Moffitt, *The World's Money*, pp. 141-142.

29. Peter Isard, "Exchange Rate Determination: Survey of Popular Views and Recent Models," Princeton University *Princeton Studies in International Finance* no. 42 (May 1978), p. 16.

30. This thesis is argued by Susan Strange, *Casino Capitalism* (Oxford: Basil Blackwell, 1987).

31. See Paul M. Sweezy and Harry Magdoff, "The Financial Explosion," in *Stagnation and the Financial Explosion* (New York: Monthly Review Press, 1987), pp. 141-150.

32. See Leonard A. Rapping and Stephen Bennett, "Financial Deregulation, Speculation and the Interest Rate," in Leonard A. Rapping, *International Reorganization and American Economic Policy* (New York: Harvester, 1989), and Leonard A. Rapping and Lawrence B. Pully, "Speculation, Deregulation and the Interest Rate," *American Economic Review: Papers and Proceedings* 75 (May 1985), pp. 108-113.

33. Milton Friedman, "The Case for Flexible Exchange Rates," in *Essays in Positive Economics* (Chicago: University of Chicago Press, 1953), pp. 157-203.

34. Ibid., pp. 176.

35. Ibid., pp. 176, note 9.

36. There is an important literature that attempts to demonstrate that price volatility in speculative markets is greater than is warranted by observed volatility in market fundamentals. These tests require the specification of an explicit model of market fundamentals and the assumption that traders have rational expectations. Unfortunately, most of the literature focuses on the U.S. stock and bond markets because there is more agreement about the underlying fundamentals in these markets. See Stanford J. Grossman and Robert J. Shiller, "The Determinants of the Variability of Stock Prices," *American Economic Review: Papers and Proceedings* 71 (May 1981), pp. 222-227; Robert J. Shiller, "The Use of Volatility Measures in Assessing Market Efficiency," *Journal of Finance* (May 1981), pp. 291-304; and Robert J. Shiller, "Do Stock Prices Move Too Much to be Explained by Subsequent Changes in Dividends?" *American Economic Review* 71 (June 1981), pp. 421-436.

37. For a critical review of this literature, see Steven W. Kohlhagen, "The Identification of Destabilizing Foreign Exchange Speculation," *Journal of International Economics* 9 (1979), pp. 321-340.

38. Conservatives generally blame currency turbulence on instability in the underlying financial and trading system. For example, the following analysis is typical of their position: "The foreign exchange markets have been characterized by an unusually high degree of uncertainty [volatility] since the widespread adoption of floating rates in the early 1970s, but this has been due more to the underlying environment than to floating rates themselves. Exchange rate variability has not been greater than that in stock and bond prices. Establishment of greater exchange rate stability requires establishment of greater stability in the underlying economic and financial environment." Thomas D. Willett, "The Causes and Effects of Exchange Rate Volatility," in Jacob S. Dreyer, Gottfried Haberler, and Thomas D. Willett, eds., *The International Monetary System: A Time of*

Turbulence (Washington DC: American Enterprise Institute, 1982), p. 49.

Kohlhagen points out that in order to determine precisely the degree of excess volatility caused by speculators, one would need to know what volatility would be in the absence of speculation. This in turn requires knowledge of the "true" underlying model of exchange rate determination. See Kohlhagen, "The Identification of Destabilizing Foreign Exchange Speculation," p. 326.

39. See also Jeffrey R. Shafer and Bonnie E. Loopesto, "Floating Exchange Rates After 10 Years," *Brookings Papers on Economic Activity* 1 (1983), p. 36.

40. See Joan Edelman Spero, *The Failure of the Franklin National Bank* (New York: Columbia University Press, 1980), p. 21.

41. Ibid., p. 21.

42. The inherent difficulties of speculating in this early period have been noted by many observers. For instance, one author claims that: "Seasoned international investors of the late 1980s can well imagine that the dollar might rise or fall against the mark by as much as 50 per cent in two years or less. . . .

"The period from spring 1971 to the great recession of 1974-75 may be described as the 'infancy' of floating exchange rates. Investors were groping in a world of few known parameters. . . . In retrospect, some of the happenings in the currency markets during the early 1970s betray the inexperience of contemporary investors." Brendon Brown, *The Flight of International Capital* (London: Croom Helm, 1987), p. 298.

43. For a complete break down of Franklin National's trading volumes as well as their losses and gains from currency speculation, see Edelman Spero, *The Failure of the Franklin National Bank,* pp. 66 and 82.

44. Ibid., pp. 83-84.

45. Ibid., pp. 107-108.

46. Cited by Edelman Spero, ibid, p. 111.

47. Giddy, "Measuring the World Foreign Exchange Market," p. 37.

48. Ibid., p. 38.

49. This section relies heavily on Moffitt, *The World's Money,* chs. 5, 6, and 7. The quote from the trader is cited by ibid., p. 144.

50. See Giddy, "Measuring the World Foreign Exchange Market," p. 45.

51. These figures are from the *Federal Reserve Bulletin.*

52. See Stephan Schulmeister, "Exchange Rates, Prices, and Interest Rates: Reconsidering the Basic Relationships of Exchange Rate Determination," C.V. Starr Center for Applied Economics *Economic Research Reports* (July 1983), pp. 10 and 13 for estimates of the *ex post* returns to speculation.

53. The Bank for International Settlements reported that trading volumes in Tokyo quadrupled from 1983 to 1986 and over the same period trading volumes doubled in the New York market. See the Bank for International Settlements, *Annual Report* (June 1987), p. 163. In its *Annual Report* of 1985, the Bank for International Settlements presented figures on exchange market volatility. They noted that market volatility while high throughout the 1980s, was particularly high in September 1984 and from February through May 1985. See the Bank for International Settlements, *Annual Report* (June 1985), pp. 146-147. Frankel and Froot claim that between 1981 and 1985 the market switched from using forcasts based on fundamentals to that of chartists. See Jeffrey A. Frankel and Kenneth A. Froot, "Chartists, Fundamentalists, and Trading in the Foreign Exchange Market," *American Economic Review: Papers and Proceedings* 80 (May 1990) p184.

54. The Bank for International Settlements, *Annual Report* (June 1986), p. 142.

55. Ibid., p. 145.

56. Ibid., p. 147. An interesting side issue is whether or not the dollar fell far enough to restore balance of

payments equilibrium. Martin Feldstein has argued persuasively that the dollar did not fall enough to restore balance of payments equilibrium. He argued that the yen/dollar rate needed to fall to 100 yen per dollar, and that subsequent plans to stabilize the yen at 140-150 to a dollar was misguided.

57. The Bank for International Settlements, *Annual Report* (1987), p. 152.

58. Ibid., 152.

59. For an account of the political maneuvering which led to the Louvre accord, see Yoichi Funabashi, *Managing the Dollar: From the Plaza to the Louvre* (Washington DC: Institute for International Economics, 1988), pp. 177-187. The quotes are from ibid., p. 177.

60. Ibid., p. 177.

61. Paul Samuelson provides an informative yet highly intuitive explanation of a random walk and its relationship to the efficient markets hypothesis with respect to the stock market: "Plot the score of the random walk of a drunken sailor. If the coin comes up heads, the sailor moves up 1 yard; if it comes up tails, he moves down 1 yard. Draw a curve showing the sailor's position at each 100 coin tosses. next to the diagram, plot the drunken wandering IBM stock.

"Why the resemblance of speculative prices to a random walk? Merely a coincidence? Nothing but science fiction? No. Economists, on reflection, have come to realize the following truths: What looks much like a random walk is just how stock or commodity prices *should* look in an *efficient* market. Competitors discount in advance all that can be confidently foreseen and anticipated. So any good news is *already* in the IBM stock. And so too is any anticipated bad news ahead.

"What then, makes stocks move? It is the arrival of *new* news--rain on the Kansas wheat fields, loss of an antitrust court case by IBM. These chance events make speculative prices vibrate randomly--wobble up and down." See Paul A. Samuelson, *Economics* 11th ed. (New York: McGraw-Hill, 1980), pp. 69-70.

62. With respect to explaining recent developments in the foreign exchange market, the news hypothesis was first suggested by Jacob A. Frenkel and Michael L. Mussa, "The Efficiency of Foreign Exchange Markets and Measures of Turbulence," *American Economic Review: Papers and Proceedings* 70 (May 1980), pp. 374-381. For the monetarist version of the news hypothesis, see Jacob A Frenkel, "Flexible Exchange Rates, Prices, and the Role of 'News'," in Jagdeep S. Bhandari and Bluford H. Putnam, eds., *Economic Interdependence and Flexible Exchange Rates* (Cambridge: MIT Press, pp. 3-41. A more eclectic version can be found in Rudiger Dornbusch, "Exchange Rate Economics: Where do We Stand?" in Jagdeep S. Bhandari and Bluford H. Putnam, eds., *Economic Interdependence and Flexible Exchange Rates* (Cambridge: MIT Press, 1983), pp. 45-83. For a critical evaluation of both versions of the news hypothesis, see Chapter 4. It should be noted that evidence against the random walk hypothesis may indicate that there is a lack of stabilizing speculation in the foreign exchange market. This position is advocated by Goodhart, "The Foreign Exchange Market," pp. 448-450 and by Thomas D. Willett and Clas Wihlborg, "International Capital Flows, the Dollar, and U.S. Financial Policies," in William Haraf and Thomas D. Willett, eds., *Monetary Policy in an Era of Change: The International Dilemma* (Washington D.C.: American Enterprise Institute, 1990), p. 78.

63. See William Poole, "Speculative Prices as Random Walks: An Analysis of Ten Time Series of Flexible Exchange Rates," *Southern Economic Journal* 33 (April 1967), pp. 468-478 and William Poole, "The Stability of the Canadian Flexible Exchange Rate," *Canadian Journal of Economics* 33 (1967) pp. 205-217.

64. Laurence A. Krause, *A Theoretical and Empirical Examination of Speculation in the Foreign Exchange Market: A Search for Speculative Bubbles* (Ann Arbor, Michigan: University Microfilms International, 1989), pp. 79-83. Goodhart states that hourly data show negative

correlation, especially following large jumps in exchange rates. Goodhart, "The Foreign Exchange Market," p. 442.

65. See Blanchard and Watson, "Bubbles, Rational Expectations, and Financial Markets," pp. 310-312.

66. Kunio Okina, "Speculative Bubbles and Official Intervention," Unpublished, University of Chicago, (May 1983), pp. 35-36.

67. For reviews of this literature, see Susan Schadler, "Sources of Exchange Rate Variability: Theory and Empirical Evidence," IMF *Staff Papers* (July 1977), pp. 265 and Isard, "Exchange Rate Determination," pp. 16. For some recent empirical work see Richard J. Sweeney, "Stabilizing or Destabilizing Speculation? Evidence from the Foreign Exchange Markets," in Sven W. Arndt, Richard J. Sweeney, and Thomas D. Willett, eds., *Exchange Rates, Trade, and the U.S. Economy* (Cambridge: American Enterprise Institute/Ballinger, 1985), p. 117.

68. See Blanchard and Watson, "Bubbles, Rational Expectations, and Financial Markets," pp. 312-314 and Okina, "Speculative Bubbles and Official Intervention."

69. Blanchard and Watson, "Bubbles, Rational Expectations, and Financial Markets," p. 313.

70. The test results are reported below from 3/1/73 to 12/31/84:

	Mean	Standard Deviation	Skewness	Kurtosis	Minimum	Maximum
German mark (N = 3061)						
	.000	.007	-.25	9.00	-.057	.038
French franc (N = 3059)						
	.000	.007	-.45	10.6	-.057	.040
Swiss franc (N = 3049)						
	.000	.009	.00	14.6	-.098	.052
Japanese yen (N = 3049)						
	.000	.007	.23	13.8	-.068	.040
British pound (N = 3033)						
	.000	.006	-.22	6.1	-.046	.031

Source:
Exchange rate data are from the Federal Reserve's interest rate and exchange rate tape.

4

Market Fundamentals

In this chapter, I will review several approaches to exchange rate formation in order to examine the interconnection between market fundamentals and speculative bubbles. Conventional theorists have long argued that large swings and trends in currency rates, if not day-to-day fluctuations, can be explained by changes in market fundamentals. While there is no agreement about just what constitutes the foreign exchange market's fundamentals, they generally are thought to include the monetary and fiscal policies of nation-states as well as the "preferences" of the international investment community which underlie portfolio selection.

In my survey of the reigning theories, I will focus upon those empirical models that have captured the imagination of the economics profession by attempting to explain the major exchange rate developments of the floating rate era. A number of models will be considered and the empirical relevance of each of these models will be examined.[1] I will then argue that the bubble hypothesis offers a reasonable and interesting explanation for the empirical conundrums found in the literature.

THE FLEXIBLE-PRICE MONETARY MODEL

Until quite recently, the most fashionable view of the underlying market fundamentals governing the behavior of currency rates was the flexible-price monetary approach to the exchange rate.[2] The flexible-price monetary approach is a theoretical extension of monetarism to an open economy with flexible exchange rates. In the monetarist tradition, the exchange rate is viewed as the relative price of national monies. This monetarist premise gives rise to two important claims about exchange rate economics. The first is that the exchange rate is an asset price since it represents the relative price of monies. This first claim has generated an entire literature devoted to proving that the foreign exchange market (like other asset markets) is an efficient market.[3] (I have already taken exception to this claim in Chapter 3.) The second major monetarist claim states that the exchange rate is a monetary phenomenon, i.e., exchange rate movements result from disturbances that are transmitted to the exchange rate via the money market.[4] It is this second claim that has played a fundamental role in transforming the theoretical and empirical building blocks of exchange rate economics in the 1970s.

In the monetarist approach to flexible exchange rates, the link that connects national money markets to the foreign exchange market is the international arbitrage of commodity prices or, as it is known in the literature, absolute purchasing power parity.[5] The complete process of exchange rate formation is envisioned in the following way. In the event of a monetary disturbance in the domestic economy, *ceteris paribus*, the excess supply in the domestic money market would cause the domestic price level to rise relative to the foreign price level. The "law of one price" would then ensure that the domestic currency depreciates, thus eliminating any profitable commodity arbitrage opportunities that might occur between domestic and world markets. In short, according to the monetarists, exchange rate movements are the by-products of disturbances in money markets which are then transmitted to the foreign exchange markets by changes in price levels. From this approach, one can then conclude that *exchange rate movements mirror the relative inflationary intentions of governments*.[6]

For purposes of econometric testing, the flexible-price model is usually specified as follows:[7]

$$m - p = ky - bi \text{ (domestic money market equilibrium)} \quad (4.1)$$

$$m^* - p^* = k^*y^* - b^*i^* \text{ (foreign money market equilibrium)} \quad (4.2)$$

$$e = p - p^* \text{ (purchasing power parity)} \quad (4.3)$$

where:

m = the log of the domestic money supply
p = the log of the domestic price level
y = the log of domestic real activity
i = the domestic short-term interest rate
e = the log of the home currency (dollar) price of foreign exchange
k = the activity elasticity of money demand
b = the semi-log interest elasticity of money demand
$*$ = foreign variable

Combining and solving for the exchange rate (the dollar price of foreign exchange), and assuming that $k = k^*$ and $b = b^*$, we get:

$$e = p - p^* = m - m^* + k(y^* - y) + b(i - i^*) \quad (4.4)$$

The model specified in equation 4.4 states that the exchange rate is determined by the relative supply and demand for money across nations. If, for example, the domestic money supply begins to increase more rapidly

than the foreign money supply, then the domestic price
level and the exchange rate would immediately begin to
follow the same upward trend as domestic money, as
illustrated in Diagram 4.1.

Diagram 4.1

**Money, the Price Level, and the Exchange Rate in the
Flexible-Price Monetary Model**

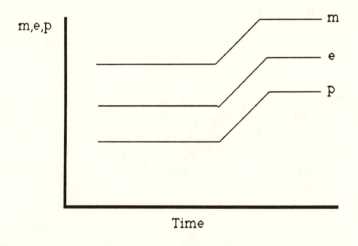

Moreover, an increase in domestic activity relative to
foreign activity would cause the home currency to
appreciate as domestic prices fall. And finally, the
interest differential is said by monetarists to represent
the difference in expected inflation between the home
country and the rest of the world. This conclusion is the
result of two highly restrictive assumptions. In the first
assumption, the nominal interest rate is assumed to equal
the real rate plus the expected inflation trend (the Fisher
hypothesis), as shown in equations 4.5 and 4.6.

$$i = r + z \qquad (4.5)$$

$$i^* = r^* + z^* \qquad (4.6)$$

where:

r = the real interest rate
z = the anticipated inflation trend

Assuming further that the real component is equal from country to country, the interest differential is then equal to the expected inflation differential, as shown in equation 4.7.[8] Moreover, in a world where exchange rates

$$i - i^* = z - z^* \qquad (4.7)$$

follow relative price levels and foreign exchange speculators hold model consistent expectations, the difference in the expected inflation trends is equivalent to the expected depreciation of the home currency. These links suggest that an increase in expected inflation in the home country also would bring about a parallel rise in the domestic interest rate and a decline in domestic money demand, thus depreciating the home currency. Therefore, in the monetarist tradition (which is in direct opposition to the Keynesian tradition on this issue), it is argued that there is a *positive* relationship (a rise in the domestic interest rate forces the home country currency to depreciate) between the exchange rate and the interest differential.[9]

From equation 4.4, several specifications of the basic flexible-price model can be estimated. Essentially one can test either purchasing power parity or, assuming that the empirical pertinence of the model's assumptions are irrelevant, the basic monetary model itself. Employing a standard simple regression equation, the purchasing power parity doctrine predicts that the intercept should be zero, the coefficient on the relative price levels should be equal to one, and the explanatory power of the model "relatively high."[10] On the other hand, the empirical content of the flexible-price monetary model indicates that the coefficient on the relative money supplies should equal one (reflecting purchasing power parity and monetary neutrality), the signs on the activity and interest differentials should be positive and reasonably close to estimated money demand elasticities,[11] and, of course, the explanatory power of the model should be "relatively high."

Table 4.1 reports the results of testing absolute purchasing power parity for the dollar-deutsche mark rate and a trade weighted basket of currencies from March 1973 to November 1988. The dollar-mark rate was chosen for individual attention because it is considered to be the key exchange rate in the world economy and also because it is as close to a genuine free market rate as there is in the currency system. The foreign countries chosen for the weighted basket include the members of the Group of Seven (Canada, France, Germany, Italy, Japan, United Kingdom, and the United States) less the U.S. plus Switzerland.

Regressions 1 through 2 test for the existence of purchasing power parity.[12] Using the consumer price index to measure the price level in each country, the estimates in these regressions demonstrate that short-run absolute purchasing power parity has little, if any, explanatory power. Moreover, the constants are significantly different from zero, and the coefficients on the price levels significantly less than one.[13] Regressions 3 and 4 test to see if there is any relationship between price levels and the exchange rate. The results indicate that a rise in the U.S. price level indeed is associated with dollar depreciation (both against the German mark and the weighted basket of currencies) and, conversely, a rise in the foreign price level with dollar appreciation (both against the German mark and the weighted basket of currencies). In addition, the explanatory power of the models increases significantly when we split the explanatory variable into separate variables. However,

Table 4.1

Analysis of Purchasing Power Parity:
March 1973 to November 1988
And Analysis of the Flexible-Price Monetary Model:
March 1973 to September 1988
(The Dependent Variables are the Log of $/German Mark Rate and the Log of the Weighted Exchange Rate)

Regressions No.	Analysis of Purchasing Power Parity					
	(1)	(2)	(3)	(4)	(5)	(6)
cpi-cpi*	.32				-.007	
	(3.96)				(-.47)	
cpi-wtcpi		.65				-.15
		(1.55)				(-2.36)
cpi			3.72			
			(11.64)			
cpi*			-6.69			
			(-11.33)			
cpi				1.42		
				(3.64)		
wtcpi				-1.65		
				(-4.10)		
e_{t-1}					.99	
					(74.7)	
wte_{t-1}						.99
						(88.5)
Intercept	4.42	4.43	17.9	5.38	.06	.03
	(285)	(406)	(14.4)	(38.7)	(1.09)	(.52)
R-Squared	.08	.01	.43	.21	.97	.98
First-Order Rho	.98	.99	.95	.98		
Durbin-Watson	.03	.02	.07	.03		

(Continued)

Table 4.1 (Continued)

	Analysis of the Flexible-Price Monetary Model			
Regressions No.	(7)	(8)	(9)	(10)
m-m*	-.71			
	(-3.75)			
m		-.75		
		(-4.59)		
m*		.98		
		(5.35)		
m-fnm			.40	
			(3.20)	
m				-.01
				(-.09)
fnm				.21
				(1.66)
ip*-ip	-.74			
	(-3.43)			
ip*		2.66		
		(6.21)		
ip		-.98		
		(-3.02)		
wtip-ip			.85	
			(3.26)	
wtip				3.82
				(8.30)
ip				-2.36
				(-6.60)
is-is*	.003			
	(.41)			
is		-.001		
		(-.22)		
is*		-.004		
		(-.50)		

(Continued)

124

Table 4.1 (Continued)

Analysis of the Flexible-Price Monetary Model

Regressions No.	(7)	(8)	(9)	(10)
is-wtis			.03	
			(5.41)	
is				.03
				(6.42)
wtis				-.07
				(-8.03)
Intercept	4.89	-4.12	4.65	-.53
	(33.1)	(-3.70)	(48.3)	(-.59)
R-Squared	.15	.41	.27	.48
First-Order Rho	.97	.87	.96	.84
Durbin-Watson	.05	.25	.08	.33

Legend:
cpi = the log of the U.S. consumer price index.
wtcpi = the log of the weighted foreign consumer price index.
m = the log of U.S. M1, seasonally adjusted.
fnm = the log of foreign money.
ip = the log of U.S. industrial production, seasonally adjusted.
is = the U.S. short-term interest rate.
wtis = the weighted foreign short-term interest rate.
wtip = the log of the weighted foreign industrial production, seasonally adjusted.
* = a German variable.

(Continued)

Table 4.1 (Continued)

Source:
All data are from the IMF, *International Financial Statistics*.
Exchange rate data are monthly average data. The weighted
foreign CPI is the weighted sum of the price levels of Canada,
France, Germany, Italy, Japan, Switzerland, and the United
Kingdom. The weights are derived by the size of each countries
imports and exports relative to the entire group in 1980. The U.S.
money supply is the Federal Reserve's measure of M1, seasonally
adjusted. Foreign money is the dollar value of Canadian money,
French money, German money, Italian money, Japanese money,
and the United Kingdom's money, transformed into dollars
byusing 1980 exchange rates. Weighted foreign industrial
production is the weighted sum of industrial production indices
from Canada, France, Germany, Italy, Japan, and the United
Kingdom. The weights are derived as above. The short-term
interest rates are the Federal funds rate for the U.S. and call
money rates, or their equivalent, for foreign countries. The
weights for the purchasing power parity estimates are Canada
.0896, France .1614, Germany .2326, Italy .1208, Japan .1775,
Switzerland .0456, and the United Kingdom .1525. The weights for
the flexible-price monetary model are Canada .0940, France .1691,
Germany .2647, Italy .1265, Japan .1859, and the United Kingdom
.1598.

the serial correlation in the error terms demonstrates that deviations of the exchange rate from purchasing power parity are not self-correcting.

This last point can be underscored by estimating the following model. Assuming the current exchange rate adjusts over time to its equilibrium rate, we can write:

$$e_t - e_{t-1} = \emptyset(e - e_{t-1})$$

where:

$\emptyset$ = the adjustment coefficient
e = the log of the equilibrium exchange rate

Furthermore, assuming that the equilibrium rate is given by purchasing power parity, and solving for e_t, we derive:

$$e_t = (1 - \emptyset)e_{t-1} + \emptyset(p - p^*)$$

In the above lagged adjustment model, the anticipated values on the coefficients for the lagged exchange rate are expected to be less than one and the coefficient on the relative price levels to be greater than zero. In regressions 6 and 7, the above model is estimated, using both the German and the weighted foreign data. The results confirm that there is no evidence of a lagged adjustment to purchasing power parity. In fact, the results confirm that once the exchange rate deviates from its purchasing power parity value, *it tends to move even further away*. In results not shown, I restricted the sum of the coefficients to unity ($\emptyset + (1 - \emptyset) = 1$). In both cases, the lagged adjustment back to equilibrium tended to be slow (.006 and .004 per month, respectively), and the coefficients were statistically insignificant. We can conclude that there is no evidence that deviations from purchasing power parity are self-correcting, but there is much evidence to suggest that deviations are persistent.[14]

A preliminary summary of the econometric evidence about purchasing power parity suggests, first, that the exchange rate and price levels are loosely associated in the predicted fashion; second, that price level movements "explain" only a small part of exchange rate movements; and third, that deviations from parity tend to be persistent. Therefore, it is evident that short-run continuous purchasing power parity is actually a poor building block for a theory of exchange rate formation.

Table 4.2 provides further evidence of the breakdown of purchasing power parity in the postwar float. The relative purchasing power parity doctrine predicts that inflation differentials between the U.S. and its industrial and financial rivals should result in an offsetting depreciation of the dollar, thus preventing changes in the real exchange rate. Table 4.2 shows that both the *direction* and *magnitude* of currency rate changes on a year-to-year basis bear little relationship to inflation differentials. This is true for all the individual countries examined as well as for a combined weighted index of foreign countries. To give an example of the breakdown of relative purchasing power parity, during the 1977-1978 period, the inflation differential between the U.S. and the group of foreign countries examined averaged 1.1 percent while the dollar depreciated on average by 12.4 percent!

Finally, it is necessary to consider the issue of whether purchasing power parity holds over the long run. It is arguable that purchasing power parity must hold between major industrial countries lest free trade eliminate the productive capacity in any country with an overvalued currency. In Figures 4.1 and 4.2, I plotted first the U.S. CPI over the German CPI along with an index of the dollar-mark exchange rate, taking 1980 as a common reference point. Next, I did the same with the U.S. CPI, a weighted foreign CPI, and a weighted foreign exchange rate. The plots suggest that, in the early part of the float, the exchange rate gyrated around its purchasing power parity rate, but large, temporary changes in real

Table 4.2

Relative Purchasing Power Parity:
1973 - 1987

Year	U.S Price Inflation (%)	German Price Inflation (%)	$/DM Rate (%)	Japanese Price Inflation (%)	$/¥ Rate (%)	Swiss Price Inflation (%)	$/SF Rate (%)	Foreign Price Inflation (%)	$ / Foreign Rate (%)
1973	6.2	7.2	19.3	11.7	11.6	8.8	20.7	8.7	6.9
1974	10.9	6.8	3.3	23.3	-7.0	9.7	6.2	14.3	-4.0
1975	9.2	5.9	5.2	11.6	-1.6	6.8	15.4	12.6	1.7
1976	5.8	4.3	-2.3	9.5	0.1	1.7	3.3	9.6	-3.5
1977	6.4	3.8	8.4	8.1	10.4	1.2	4.0	9.3	1.0
1978	7.6	2.6	15.6	4.3	27.6	1.1	34.4	6.5	12.4
1979	11.2	4.1	9.6	3.7	-4.0	3.6	7.5	8.2	4.2
1980	13.5	5.5	0.8	7.7	-3.6	4.1	-.8	11.3	0.7
1981	10.3	6.3	-19.6	5.0	2.8	6.4	-14.7	10.2	-13.9
1982	6.2	5.2	-6.9	2.7	-11.5	5.7	-3.3	9.2	-10.8
1983	3.2	3.4	-5.0	1.8	4.9	3.0	-3.3	5.8	-5.3
1984	4.3	2.4	-10.3	2.3	-0.0	3.0	-10.7	4.8	-8.1
1985	3.5	2.1	-3.3	2.0	-0.4	3.4	-4.4	4.4	-3.4
1986	2.0	-0.2	35.6	0.6	41.6	0.8	36.6	2.3	28.5
1987	3.6	0.3	20.8	0.1	16.5	1.4	20.6	2.3	15.9

Source:
All data are from the IMF, *International Financial Statistics*. The inflation rates are measures of consumer price inflation in the respective countries. For the weights used in computing the foreign inflation rate and the $/foreign exchange rate, see the first set of weights (including Switzerland) in Table 4.1.

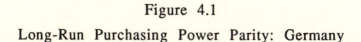

Figure 4.1

Long-Run Purchasing Power Parity: Germany

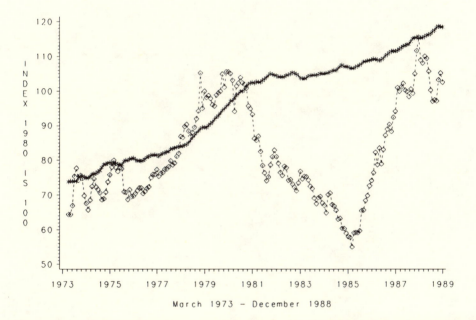

March 1973 — December 1988

Legend:
Star = U.S. consumer price index/German consumer price index.
Diamond = dollar/German mark exchange rate.
Source:
All data are from the IMF, *International Financial Statistics*.

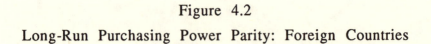

Figure 4.2

Long-Run Purchasing Power Parity: Foreign Countries

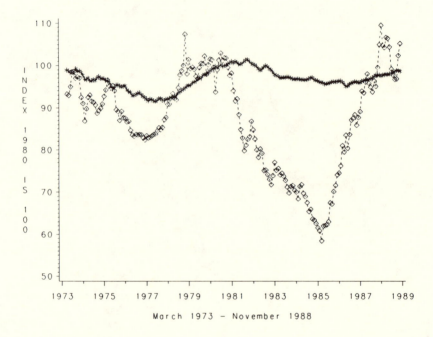

Legend:
Star = U.S. consumer price index/weighted foreign consumer price index.
Diamond = weighted exchange rate.
Source:
All data from IMF, *International Financial Statistics*. For weights see the first set of weights (including Switzerland) in Table 4.1.

exchange rates seemed to prevail. However, beginning in June 1977, the dollar depreciated significantly above its purchasing power parity rate, thus improving the price competitiveness of U.S. industry. The weak dollar era ended by 1980 and was followed by a sustained appreciation of the dollar that significantly overvalued the dollar. Thus, since the Plaza accord, the dollar depreciation has more or less restored U.S. price competitiveness to its 1980 level. Casual observation therefore suggests that, even in the long run, there is at best a loose relationship between relative price levels and the exchange rate. Moreover, it is difficult to claim, as we shall see, that market adjustments instead of government intervention have kept the international value of the dollar consistent with underlying differences in inflation rates over the long run.

In conclusion, whatever the long-term relationship between prices and exchange rates, the evidence is clear that the two have an extremely loose short- to medium-term relationship. It is fair to conclude that in the short to medium term, exchange rates have tended to detach themselves from price level movements, thus resulting in significant changes in real exchange rates.

In Table 4.1, in regressions 7 through 10, I tested two specifications of the flexible-price monetary approach to the exchange rate. Regression 7 tests the basic flexible-price monetary model using U.S. and German data. In regression 7, as with all the estimations of the monetary approach using monthly data, I used industrial production as a proxy for economic activity since gross national product figures are available only on a quarterly basis. The results demonstrate that the key variable, the money supply differential, is statistically significant with the wrong sign. This suggests that, over the float, deutsche mark appreciation has been associated with money supply growth in Germany and dollar appreciation with money supply growth in the U.S.![15] Thus the central hypothesis of the monetary approach is clearly contradicted by this finding. Besides the money supply

differential having the wrong sign, the activity
differential also has the wrong sign and is statistically
significant, while the short-term interest differential has
the "right" sign but is statistically insignificant. The
money supply sign reversal problem is confirmed by
regression 8, where I split the relative money supply
variable into separate variables to test whether the sign
reversal is spurious.[16] However, the signs on the activity
variables do become significant and correct, but the
short-term interest rate coefficients remain statistically
insignificant. Thus the results from regression 8 confirm
the apparent empirical riddle of the value of the dollar
varying directly with increases in its supply.

In results not reported, I attempt to "repair" the
model, first by including the lagged exchange rate as an
independent variable, and second by restricting the
relative money supply coefficient to unity. The inclusion
of the lagged exchange rate here can be justified on the
grounds that it would capture any lagged adjustment
process[17] and, furthermore, that it is "normal" to include
a lagged dependent variable in estimating money
demand equations.[18] Yet the money supply differential
still has the wrong sign but is statistically insignificant.
Restricting the coefficient on the money supply
differential to unity is equivalent to imposing "monetary
neutrality" (this means that a doubling of the money
stock will double prices and cause a commensurate
depreciation of the home currency). The signs on the
activity and interest differential become correct and
significant. However, the restriction causes the sum of
squared errors to explode (i.e., it reduces the explanatory
power of the model significantly), thus suggesting that
the restriction is inappropriate. Therefore, it is safe to
conclude that all of the attempts to "rescue" the flexible-
price monetary model mentioned above have been
failures.

If we cannot rescue the model, then perhaps we can
at least determine *why* it fails to predict correctly. It is
conceivable that the monetary model fails because of the

failure of purchasing power parity. In results not shown, I have reestimated the flexible-price monetary model using the errors from a purchasing power parity model as an additional explanatory variable. The results suggest that including the deviations from purchasing power parity greatly improve the fit (as expected) and that the relative money supply variable becomes correct and significant, though the coefficient remains considerably less than one (.09). Moreover, the sign on the activity differential is incorrect and highly significant. We can conclude, therefore, that the failure of the flexible-price monetary model is only partly due to the failure of purchasing power parity.[19]

Next, we turn to the estimations of the flexible-price monetary model using a broader data sample. In Table 4.1, in regressions 9 and 10, I compare money markets in the U.S. with those of Canada, France, Germany, Italy, Japan, and the United Kingdom. In regression 9, I estimate the basic monetary model. At first glance, the results appear consistent with flexible-price monetary model's central claims. The money supply differential is significant with the correct sign, although its coefficient is considerably less than one (.40). And both the activity and short-term interest differentials are correct and statistically significant. However, there are many disturbing indicators as well.

To highlight some of the problems with the model, I plotted in Figure 4.3 the actual and predicted values using the coefficients estimated in regression 9. First, the model seems to capture the trend of the weighted exchange rate well, but it underpredicts both the sharp depreciation of the dollar in 1977-1978 and the spectacular appreciation of the dollar in 1980-1985. Furthermore, the model fails to explain the subsequent depreciation of the dollar after February 1985. Second, in results not shown, I imposed monetary neutrality on the model by restricting the coefficient on the money supply to one. The restriction increases substantially the sum of squared errors (F-tests easily reject the null hypothesis

134

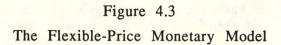

Figure 4.3

The Flexible-Price Monetary Model

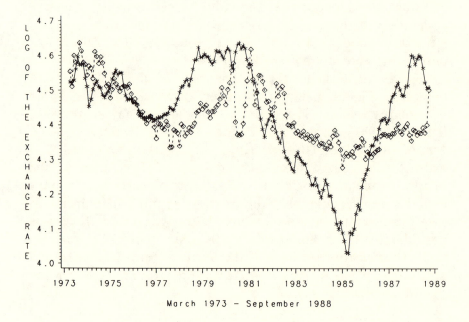

March 1973 — September 1988

Legend:
Star = actual exchange rate.
Diamond = predicted exchange rate.
Source:
See Table 4.1.

that there is no statistical difference between the sum of the squared errors of the restricted and unrestricted models), suggesting that imposing monetary neutrality on the model, the key claim of the monetarist model, substantially reduces its explanatory power.

This point is underscored by the results reported in regression 10, wherein I reestimated the model by splitting up the explanatory variables into separate variables. The results show that the sign on the U.S. money supply becomes incorrect but statistically insignificant. In short, these results suggest that we still have a problem with the monetary model's basic claim: *exchange rates do not tend to move with the relative size of the money stocks.*

Finally, it must be noted that the high degree of serial dependence in the error term (the estimate of first-order rho is .96) in regression 9 suggests that deviations from the hypothesized "fundamentals" are self-feeding. In other words, the estimates suggest that, once the exchange rate deviates from its "fundamentals," our results suggest that it is more than likely to continue to do so for some time into the future. Therefore, much like the deviations from purchasing power parity, exchange rate deviations from underlying money market conditions are not self-correcting.

To summarize briefly, I have shown that the empirical evidence seems to contradict one of the central claims of the monetary approach--that the exchange rate is a monetary phenomenon. Unfortunately, there seems to be no clear-cut explanation for the failure of the value of the dollar to vary inversely with its supply. Furthermore, the evidence suggests that the weakness of the flexible-price monetary model cannot be attributed entirely to the failure of purchasing power parity.[20]

The Flexible-Price Monetary Model and the Current Account

One possible reason for the above-mentioned failure of the monetary approach is that the money demand function is incorrectly specified. A popular alternative specification of the flexible-price monetary model incorporates the current account balance as an additional explanatory variable.[21] In order to incorporate the current account into the basic model, the money demand function must be altered to include real wealth. In an open economy, real wealth would have to include a domestic as well as a foreign component. The channel for accumulating (or deaccumulating) foreign wealth is the current account balance. A current account deficit in the home country implies that domestic wealth holders are in the process of deaccumulating wealth by redistributing their wealth to the rest of the world. So in order to achieve full asset market equilibrium in an expanded flexible-price monetary model, it is necessary that the current account be in balance.

In a period of international asset market disequilibrium, domestic and foreign wealth holders would experience net losses (or gains) in their wealth, thereby altering their demand for money and, ultimately of course, affecting the exchange rate. One can see that, in the monetary tradition, a current account shock would transmit its effects to the exchange rate by altering the composition of world wealth, which in turn alters the relative demand for money. Furthermore, in a perfectly flexible-price world, the disturbance to the money demand function would cause an immediate alteration in the domestic price level and thus the exchange rate.[22]

The introduction of the current account balance into the monetary model was motivated by the apparent tendency of current account shocks to coincide with exchange rate movements in the 1970s.[23] Table 4.3 shows that, except for 1973 and 1982-1985, there has

Table 4.3

The Current Account and Exchange Rate Adjustment:
1973 - 1987

(Billions of Dollars)

Year	United States Current Account	Trade Weighted Dollar (MERM)	Foreign Current Account
1973	+7.1	+9.0%	+2.3
1974	+1.9	-2.2%	-14.4
1975	+18.3	+1.0%	+0.7
1976	+4.2	-4.8%	-1.5
1977	-14.5	+0.5%	+16.0
1978	-15.5	+9.4%	+40.3
1979	-1.0	+2.2%	-7.5
1980	+1.8	-0.3%	-33.8
1981	+6.9	-11.2%	-2.2
1982	-8.6	-10.5%	+7.6
1983	-46.3	-5.5%	+31.8
1984	-107.1	-7.4%	+52.1
1985	-115.2	-3.9%	+71.9
1986	-138.8	+22.0%	+123.3
1987	-154.0	+13.5%	+120.6

Source:
All data are from the IMF, *International Financial Statistics*. The U.S. current account balance is the dollar value of the U.S. current account balance, billions. The trade weighted dollar is the IMF's MERM, appreciation (-). The Foreign current account balance is the sum of the dollar values of the Canadian, French, German, Italian, Japanese, Swiss, and the United Kingdom's current account balances.

been a consistent relationship between current account imbalances and exchange rate adjustment. As the augmented monetarist model suggests, large current imbalances have been associated with sizeable currency rate adjustments.

Thus the empirical prediction is that a current account surplus in the home country, by increasing domestic wealth and money demand, induces home currency appreciation. On the other hand, a current account deficit in the home country would reduce domestic wealth and money demand, thereby causing home currency depreciation. In order to respecify the basic empirical monetarist model, equation 4.4 (page 118) now would have to include the relative current account balances, as in equation 4.4'.

$$e = m - m^* + k(y^* - y) + b(i - i^*) + d(cab^* - cab) \qquad (4.4')$$

where:

    cab = the log of the dollar value of the home country's (U.S.) current account balance

The predicted sign on the added current account variable is anticipated to be positive.

The introduction of current account "shocks" into the model may provide a solution to the empirical failure of the flexible-price model. This would be the case if the incorrect sign on the money supply differential were the result of the "missing demand" for money generated by current account shocks. Therefore, it is conceivable that ignoring current account disturbances could account for the failure of the monetarist model. Table 4.4 summarizes the results of testing the flexible-price monetary model (respecified) to include current account shocks. Quarterly data were used since current account data for the U.S. are only available on a quarterly basis. Furthermore, I substituted real GNP (or GDP) data for industrial production as the proxy for economic activity.

Table 4.4

Analysis of the Flexible-Price Monetary Model with a
Current Account Balance Variable:
1973:2 to 1988:2
(The Dependent Variables are the Log of $/German Mark
Rate and the Log of the Weighted Exchange Rate)

Regression No.	(1)	(2)	(3)	(4)
m-m*	-1.47 (-4.70)	1.00		
m-fnm			-.06 (-.42)	1.00
gnp*-gnp	.24 (.17)	-3.42 (-1.80)		
fngnp-gnp			-2.90 (-2.45)	-8.75 (-7.20)
is-is*	.02 (4.71)	.01 (2.30)		
is-wtis			.004 (.40)	-.05 (-3.92)
cab*-cab	1.46 (2.66)	-1.20 (-1.94)		
fncab-cab			-.51 (-2.09)	-2.00 (-10.34)
Intercept	5.51 (2.85)	-.81 (-.32)	8.26 (5.30)	17.81 (14.82)

(Continued)

Table 4.4 (Continued)

Regression No.	(1)	(2)	(3)	(4)
R-Squared	.46	-.12	.36	-.24
First-Order Rho	.79	.88	.84	.67
Durbin-Watson	.39	.19	.25	.64

Legend:
m = the log of U.S. M1, seasonally adjusted.
fnm = log of dollar value of the foreign money supply.
gnp = the log of the real U.S. gross national product.
fngnp = the log of the real foreign gross national (or domestic) product.
is = the U.S. short-term interest rate.
wtis = the weighted foreign short-term interest rate.
cab = the log of the U.S. current account balance in billions of dollars.
fncab = the log of the foreign current account balance in billions of dollars.
* = a German variable.

Source:
All data are from the IMF, *International Financial Statistics*. For the weights used, see the second set of weights (excluding Switzerland) in Table 4.1.

In regressions 1 and 2, I tested the augmented flexible-price monetary model using the German data. In regression 1, the sign on the money supply differential remains incorrect and significant. However, all other signs are correct and significant. In regression 2, I restricted the relative money supply coefficient to one. The restriction, though, reverses the signs on the activity and current account variables. Furthermore, imposing monetary neutrality on the model forces the sum of the squared errors to explode. The estimates using the Group of Seven countries are reported in regressions 3 and 4. The results confirm that the addition of the current account variable does not rescue the flexible-price model. Furthermore, imposing monetary neutrality on the model, as I did in regression 4, once again appears only to underscore the empirical failure of the model.

In conclusion, it is clear from the evidence that the inclusion of the current account into the monetarist model does little, if anything, to improve the empirical performance of the model. Therefore, the failure of the simple monetary model cannot be explained by the inclusion of current account shocks.[24]

THE STICKY-PRICE MONETARY MODEL

A more interesting formulation of the monetary approach to the exchange rate was developed by Rudiger Dornbusch.[25] The Dornbusch model is known in the literature as the sticky-price monetary model or the nominal overshooting model.[26] Dornbusch claims that the primary problem with the flexible-price monetary model is that it assumes that asset and goods prices adjust at the same speed. In the monetarist flexible-price model, a monetary disturbance causes both an instantaneous adjustment in the exchange rate and the price level. However, if the exchange rate adjusts immediately while the price level adjusts slowly to a monetary disturbance (as in a "Keynesian" world), the model would yield a different set of predictions. The differential adjustment speeds between asset and goods markets can cause the exchange rate to overshoot its purchasing power parity equilibrium for as long as the goods market remains in disequilibrium.

In the sticky-price model, an increase in the supply of money has the impact effect of lowering the domestic interest rate while the price level remains constant. Moreover, in a world with perfect foresight (clairvoyant speculators) and uncovered interest rate parity (perfectly arbitraged money and foreign exchange markets), the exchange rate has to depreciate below its long-run equilibrium for clairvoyant speculators to expect an appreciation of the home currency large enough to equalize the expected nominal returns across countries. This is the basic principle of all overshooting models--if a variable is expected to fall tomorrow, it must rise above its equilibrium today.

Once the process of price adjustment begins due to an excess demand for goods, the real money supply begins to contract, thus forcing the domestic interest rate to rise. In order to maintain continuous arbitrage across financial centers, the exchange rate has to appreciate toward its long-run equilibrium value. At full equilibrium in the sticky-price model, the domestic interest rate is again equal to the world rate, and the exchange rate is back in line with purchasing power parity. Furthermore, as the exchange rate approaches its long-run equilibrium value, speculators anticipate zero gains from altering the currency denomination of their wealth.

A simple version of the overshooting model can be described as follows:

$$m - p = ky - bi \quad \text{(money market equilibrium)} \qquad (4.8)$$

$$E[e_{t+1}] - e_t = i - i^* \quad \text{(uncovered interest rate} \qquad (4.9)$$
parity)

$$E[e_{t+1}] - e_t = \emptyset(e - e_t) \quad \text{(expected exchange rate} \qquad (4.10)$$
depreciation with rational expectations)

$$z = w[u + d(e - p) + (a - 1)y - ci] \quad \text{(price} \quad (4.11)$$
$$\text{adjustment)}$$

where:

$E[e_{t+1}]$ = the log of the expected exchange rate in
    period $t+1$
e_t = the log of the exchange rate in period t
e = the log of the equilibrium exchange rate
p = the log of the domestic price level
z = the rate of change in the domestic price level
u = exogenous aggregate demand factors
a = the marginal propensity to spend
y = the log of domestic income
i = the domestic interest rate
$\emptyset$ = an adjustment coefficient

In the model, price adjustment depends upon the difference between expenditure and output, which is assumed fixed.[27] Further, the anticipated depreciation of the home currency $(E[e_{t+1}] - e_t)$ is the difference between the equilibrium exchange rate and the current exchange rate. And finally, the more slowly the current rate adjusts to the equilibrium rate (i.e. the smaller $\emptyset$), the more overvalued the exchange rate must be to produce a given expected depreciation of the home currency. One can see that the Dornbusch model assumes well-behaved Friedman-like speculators.

The model is solved graphically in Diagram 4.2. Here we assume that the foreign price level is equal to unity so the long-run purchasing power parity equilibrium is represented by a forty-five degree line coming out of the origin. Short-run equilibrium is maintained when there is simultaneous equilibrium in the money market and no excess profit opportunities between financial centers, as represented by the following:

$$m - p = ky - b(i^* + \emptyset(e - e_t))$$

Graphically, the above equation is the QQ locus in Diagram 4.2. Let us assume that the economy is initially in both long-run and short-run equilibrium, as in point A. If the equilibrium is disturbed by a monetary expansion, the impact effect is to reduce the domestic interest rate to maintain equilibrium in the domestic money market. The reduction of the domestic interest rate below the world rate stimulates a capital outflow, which forces the exchange rate to depreciate well beyond its new equilibrium value.[28] It is necessary for the exchange rate to overshoot in order to convince the clairvoyant speculators that the home currency will rebound. (Thus the model assumes away bubble problems, too.) The magnitude of the initial rate depreciation below its long-run equilibrium depends upon the initial size of the interest differential and how fast prices adjust to the increase in money. In Diagram 4.2, the impact effect of the increase in money moves the economy from point A to point B. At point B, the exchange rate is above its new long-run equilibrium value, e_1. As prices adjust to the excess demand created by both the fall in the interest rate and the depreciation of the home currency, the economy moves along the Q'Q' locus until a new long-run equilibrium is established at point C.

The main claim of the sticky-price monetary model is that the short-run behavior of exchange rates is determined by asset markets, i.e., exchange rates must be consistent with money market equilibrium and uncovered interest parity. In terms of the simple model, this means that the exchange rate must always lie on the QQ locus. In the model, purchasing power parity will hold only over the longer term after goods prices fully respond to monetary disturbances. Therefore, we can see that international commodity arbitrage plays no role in this model. Changes in the price level only affect the exchange rate through contracting or expanding the real money supply.

Diagram 4.2

The Dornbusch Overshooting Model

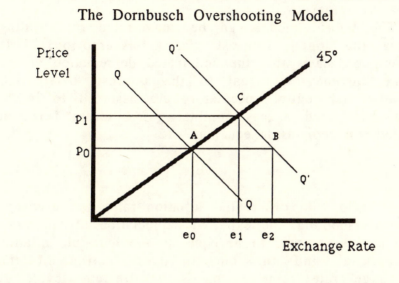

The sticky-price monetary model makes the following empirical predictions: (1) Purchasing power parity will not hold continuously, but only over the longer run; (2) Monetary shocks will produce an adjustment period where prices and exchange rates will move in the opposite direction predicted by the flexible-price model; (3) Short-run changes in the real exchange rate will arise from monetary shocks which induce nominal exchange rate overshooting; (4) The exchange rate will be more volatile than either relative money supplies or prices; and (5) In the adjustment period there will be short-run nominal and real interest rate differentials between financial centers.

An interesting and empirically relevant specification of the nominal overshooting model has been developed by Jeffrey Frankel.[29] Frankel attempted to wed the insight of the Dornbusch model (that the exchange rate tends to overshoot in a world with sticky prices and highly flexible exchange rates) with the monetarist flexible-price model's main contribution (that in an inflationary world, exchange rates tend to follow relative inflation rates).

The hybrid model can be constructed by building upon the open interest parity assumption. This assumption states that the anticipated depreciation of the home currency is equal to the interest differential, because risk-neutral speculators are assumed to insure that anticipated excess nominal gains across financial centers are zero, as in equation 4.12.

$$E[e_{t+1}] - e_t = i - i^* \qquad (4.12)$$

In a world with differential inflation rates and exchange rate overshooting, the expected depreciation of the home currency is assumed to be equal to the long-run inflation differential and the current overvaluation of the exchange rate relative to its equilibrium level, as specified in equation 4.13.

$$i - i^* = \emptyset(e - e_t) + z - z^* \qquad (4.13)$$

where:

z = the inflation trend in the home country

Rearranging equation 4.13 we get:

$$e_t = e - (1/\emptyset)[(i - z) - (i^* - z^*)] \qquad (4.13')$$

Equation 4.13' shows us that the exchange rate is determined by the equilibrium exchange rate and the real interest differential across financial centers. In the hybrid model, a real interest differential in favor of the home country brought on by tight money in the home country forces the home currency to appreciate well beyond its equilibrium level. As in the tradition of the monetary approach, it is also assumed that the equilibrium exchange rate is determined by long-run purchasing power parity or long-run equilibrium in the money markets, as shown in equation 4.14.

$$e = p - p^* = m - m^* + k(y^* - y) + b(i - i^*) \qquad (4.14)$$

where:

x = the long-run equilibrium value of variable x

Assuming that the equilibrium values of the explanatory variables are equal to their actual values, and substituting into equation 4.13' we get:

$$e_t = m - m^* + k(y^* - y) - (1/\emptyset)(i - i^*) + ((1/\emptyset) + \qquad (4.15)$$
$$b)(z - z^*)$$

Equation 4.15 states that the exchange rate is determined by (1) the relative supply and demand for money; (2) the short-term interest differential, which now reflects the temporary disequilibriums in the system; and (3) the differences between anticipated inflation trends across economies.

For econometric purposes, a proxy is needed for the long-run anticipated inflation differential. Frankel suggests using the long-term interest differential. The reason for this is that the long-term rate is assumed to embody the market's best forecasts of future interest rates, which in turn are assumed to be a function of anticipated future inflation rates. As a proxy, the long-term interest differential has the advantage of immediately reflecting changes in the market's inflationary expectations and, therefore, should be considered a superior proxy. Alternatively, the long-term inflation trend can be proxied by an average of the previous year's inflation rate.

The empirical model to be tested is specified in equation 4.16.

$$e_t = B_O + B_1(m - m^*) + B_2(y^* - y) + B_3(is - is^*) + \qquad (4.16)$$
$$B_4(z - z^*)$$

where:

    is = the short-term interest rate

In the Dornbusch-Frankel model, the anticipated signs are $B_1 = 1$, reflecting monetary neutrality,[30] $B_2 > 0$, $B_3 < 0$, since the short-term interest differential captures the temporary liquidity effect of monetary policy during disequilibrium states, and $B_4 > 0$ and, in absolute terms, larger than B_3.

The logic behind the anticipated signs of the interest differentials in equation 4.16 is that, in the short run, when the money supply is expanded and before prices can adjust, short-term interest rates will fall and the domestic currency will depreciate sharply to create the anticipation of the currency rebounding in the near future. The short-term interest rate differential is, therefore, predicted to move in the opposite direction of the exchange rate, as in most Keynesian models. On the other hand, over the long run, as changes in money growth alter the long-term inflation differential, the home currency will depreciate and thus the anticipated sign on the long-term inflation trend will be positive, as in the monetarist tradition.

The results from testing the sticky-price monetary model are reported in Table 4.5.[31] In regressions 1 and 2, I tested with the German data the model specified in equation 4.16 using, respectively, the long-term interest differential and the previous year's inflation differential as proxies for the anticipated inflation differential. As in the flexible-price monetary model, the sign on the money supply differential is incorrect, but in regression 2 it is insignificant. Furthermore, the signs on the short-term

Table 4.5

Analysis of the Sticky-Price Monetary Model
(The Dependent Variables are the Log of $/German Mark Rate and the Log of the Weighted Exchange Rate)

March 1973 to November 1988 / 1973:2 - 1988:2					
Regression No. (1)	(2)	(3)	(4)	(5)	(6)
m - m* -1.04	-.09				
(-5.28)	(-.62)				
m-fnm		-.05	.71	-1.99	-.64
		(-.39)	(8.81)	(-6.44)	(-5.05)
ip*-ip -1.55	.69				
(-5.48)	(-4.14)				
wtip-ip		-.29	.96		
		(-1.01)	(5.78)		
fngnp-gnp				-.21	1.07
				(-.17)	(1.09)
is-is* .01	-.01				
(2.49)	(-2.73)				
is-wtis		.04	-.002	.02	-.01
		(8.12)	(-.68)	(6.40)	(-1.04)
il-il* -.04					
(-4.20)					
il-wtil		-.08		-.03	
		(-6.86)		(-3.94)	
z-z*	.06				
	(11.38)				
z-wtz			.07		.07
			(16.5)		(7.60)
fncab-cab				2.00	.01
				(3.93)	(.51)
Intercept 5.22	4.39	4.39	4.87	5.24	3.89
(32.2)	(36.0)	(46.4)	(77.9)	(3.04)	(3.13)

(Continued)

Table 4.5 (Continued)

| | March 1973 to November 1988 | | | | / 1973:2 -1988:2 | |
Regression No.	(1)	(2)	(3)	(4)	(5)	(6)
R-Squared	.22	.50	.42	.71	.58	.69
First-Order Rho	.94	.94	.91	.87	.64	.72
Durbin-Watson	.11	.11	.17	.26	.69	.46

Legend:
m = the log of U.S. M1, seasonally adjusted.
fnm = the log of the dollar value of foreign money.
ip = the log of U.S. industrial production, seasonally adjusted.
wtip = the log of weighted foreign industrial production, seasonally adjusted.
gnp = the log of real U.S. gross national product.
fngnp = the log of real foreign gross national (or domestic) product.
is = the U.S. short-term interest rate.
wtis = the weighted foreign short-term interest rate.
il = the U.S. long-term interest rate.
wtil = the weighted foreign long-term interest rate.
z = the U.S inflation rate for the previous year.
wtz = the weighted foreign inflation rate for the previous year.
cab = the log of the U.S. current account balance in billions of dollars.
fncab = the log of the foreign current account balance in billions of dollars.
* = a German variable.

Source:
For money supply, industrial production, short-term interest rates, and consumer price index data, see Table 4.1. For gross national product and current account balance data, see Table 4.4. For weights used, see the second set of weights (excluding Switzerland) in Table 4.1. And for long-term interest rate data, see IMF, *International Financial Statistics*.

and the long-term interest differentials in regression 1 do not support the overshooting hypothesis. However, in regression 2, the long-term inflation trend and the short-term interest differential both have the correct signs and are significant.

In regressions 3 through 6, I employed the foreign data (Group of Seven nations) to estimate the model's parameters. In regressions 3 and 4, I used the long-term interest differential and and the inflation differentials, respectively. In regression 3, the relative money supply coefficient has the wrong sign but is insignificant. And both the long-term and short-term interest rate differentials are statistically significant with the wrong signs! However, in regression 4, the coefficient on the relative money supply coefficient is correct and significant, as are all the remaining coefficients with the notable exception of the short-term interest differential, which has the correct sign but is statistically insignificant. In regressions 5 and 6, I report the results of moving to quarterly foreign data (the results from using German data, not reported, were poor) in order to add a current account variable. The results confirm, once again, that current account shocks are not responsible for the empirical failure of the monetary approach. The empirical evidence establishes that even in the sticky-price version, the monetary approach is, as an empirical model, still significantly flawed.

PORTFOLIO BALANCE MODELS

A popular alternative to the money market approaches to exchange rate formation are the portfolio balance models.[32] Unlike the monetary approach, portfolio models assume that domestic and foreign assets are imperfect substitutes for each other. Money market models assume the "law of one bond," or that all nonmonetary assets are perfect substitutes for one another. This assumption is embodied in the uncovered interest rate parity relationship that is essential to many versions of the flexible-price and sticky-price monetary models. On the other hand, in the portfolio balance tradition, portfolio selection by wealth holders is said to depend upon interest rates, the size and distribution of their wealth, investor preferences, and exchange rate expectations.[33] Unfortunately, empirical work on the portfolio balance approach is underdeveloped, and we cannot really assess its value in exchange rate formation.[34] However, the portfolio balance perspective is relevant in that it reminds us that changing assessments of risk on the part of the international financial community is likely to be a possible source of shocks to asset and exchange rate markets. In short, portfolio balance models have focused on some interesting aspects of exchange rate determination, although in their present form they offer limited insights.

The one exception to the rule is the ongoing search for a risk premium based on an open economy, capital asset pricing model.[35] Rudiger Dornbusch has demonstrated that, if investors are assumed to maximize a function consisting of the end-of-period expected return and variance of their wealth, a simple exogenous risk premium model can be developed.[36] The basic relationship that this model establishes is that the share of foreign assets in a well-managed portfolio would be determined by the degree of risk aversion, the expected real return differential on foreign assets, and the variance of the return differential. The formal result is:

$$x_t^* = a + [cv]^{-1}(r_t^* - r_t) \qquad (4.17)$$

where:

x_t^* = the share of foreign wealth in the portfolio
c = the degree of risk aversion
v = the variance of the return differential

r_t^* (r_t) = the real return on the foreign (domestic) bond

a = a constant

The model demonstrates that an increase in the supply of outside foreign assets, given the degree of risk aversion and the variance of the return differential, increases the return on foreign assets relative to the return on domestic assets. The increase in the return differential is necessary to induce wealth holders to accept the increased risk associated with placing a larger share of their wealth in the foreign asset.

The existence of risk premia invalidates one of the central premises of the monetary approach--namely, the law of one bond. The risk premium factor also raises some new questions: (1) What is the qualitative impact of changes in risk premiums on exchange rates? (2) What is the likely quantitative impact of changes in risk premiums on exchange rates?

The qualitative impact of changing assessments of risk on exchange rates can be easily shown within the confines of the sticky-price model. If we let the risk premium on domestic assets equal rp, then to maintain uncovered interest parity the following relationship must hold (cf. page 142):

$$E[e_{t+1}] - e_t = i - rp - i^* \qquad (4.9')$$

Equation 4.9' states that the nominal risk adjusted return differential must equal the anticipated depreciation of the home currency. Combining equation 4.9' with equation 4.10, we can derive the following relationship between the current exchange rate and the risk premium on domestic assets:

$$e_t = e - (1/\emptyset)(i - rp - i^*) \qquad (4.18)$$

Equation 4.18 shows that for a given equilibrium exchange rate *and* nominal interest differential, there is a

positive relationship between the current exchange rate
and the risk premium on domestic assets. In other words,
if the risk premium on domestic assets were to increase,
then the domestic currency would have to depreciate
below its long-run equilibrium value to create an
anticipated future appreciation of the home currency to
compensate investors for the perceived risk on home
currency denominated assets. The depreciation of the
home currency serves to create an additional expected
exchange gain from holding domestic assets because it is
assumed that investors know that the currency is
undervalued and thus believe that the home currency
will appreciate as it adjusts back toward its long-run
equilibrium value.

The analysis above assumed that domestic interest
rates do not rise to absorb the increased risk. However, if
we assume the exchange rate is fixed and the interest
rate is flexible, then the interest rate would have to rise
to compensate investors for the increased risk. One could
also imagine cases where both the interest rate and
exchange rate changed due to alterations in risk. The
issue of whether exchange rates or interest rates are the
ultimate shock absorbers depends upon the current
policy regime. Assuming relatively free international
capital markets, the policy authority has to decide
whether it is better to permit the exchange rate or the
interest rate to adjust to wealth holders' changing
assessments of risk.

Ronald McKinnon argues that the typical policy regime
in industrial countries is one where domestic monetary
policies are geared toward the stabilization of domestic
interest rates, and thus exchange rates, not interest rates,
become the shock absorbers.[37] In his view, interest rates
behave as if they were caught in a "liquidity trap." In a
policy regime of this type, a shift in portfolio preferences
does not affect interest rates because the domestic
monetary authority is willing to change monetary policy
to keep interest rates pegged at existing levels. Since the
Plaza accords, however, policymakers have put increasing

emphasis on exchange rate management, though governments are still reluctant to make large adjustments in interest rates to meet their exchange rate targets, preferring instead to rely on sterilized currency market interventions as the primary instrument in achieving their exchange rate goals.

While the qualitative dimension of risk premiums is fairly well understood, the same cannot be said for the quantitative dimension. The empirical literature has failed to show us any significant relationship between the supply of outside assets and risk premiums.[38] Therefore, risk premiums of the Dornbusch variety have been fairly difficult to measure. Jeffrey Frankel has argued that this is not surprising since these risk premiums should be extremely small.[39] For example, the unconditional return variance on outside assets issued by governments with major financial centers is roughly .001 on a monthly basis. Estimates on the degree of risk aversion put the coefficient no higher than two. This implies that a one percent increase in the supply of outside foreign assets only increases the return differential by .002 on a monthly basis and by .024 on an annual basis. Since return differentials can be as high as three hundred basis points, a one percent increase in the supply of outside assets only increases the return differential by 2.4 basis points! Therefore, the empirical literature has demonstrated that, as an empirical matter, risk premiums of the Dornbusch variety can be safely ignored.

However, in general, the literature has not demonstrated that risk premiums can be safely ignored as quantitatively unimportant. It is better, perhaps, to consider changes in risk premiums as exogenously determined by major economic and political events in the world economy which force investors to alter their assessments of risk on competing stores of value. International investors must be concerned with two types of risk--political risk and exchange risk.[40] From the viewpoint of an investor, there are two important differences between foreign and domestic assets that give rise to risk premiums. The first is the political jurisdiction where assets are located, and the second the currency in which they are denominated. Political risk arises because the probability of the imposition of exchange controls on foreign-held assets differs from country to country. On the other hand, exchange risk results from differing probabilities that the exchange rate will change.

Without a firm measuring rod to gauge the size of risk premiums, only informed judgments can be made about whether or not major exchange rate movements can be attributed to changes in risk premiums. In this vein, I will consider in later sections whether or not changing assessments of risk could be responsible for some empirical anomalies found in the exchange rate literature.

ALTERNATIVE APPROACHES

The empirical failure of the standard monetary models has created fertile ground for the growth and emergence of numerous alternatives which attempt to reconcile exchange rate theory to the empirical evidence. In the following sections, I will examine those attempts at reconciliation which have had, for one reason or another, a significant impact on exchange rate economics. The purpose of these sections is twofold: first, to critique further the existing literature on exchange rate economics in order to highlight its inability to explain floating rates; and second, to mine the literature for the components of a hybrid model capable of serving as a basis for exploring the relationship between the fundamentals and speculative bubbles.

Early Views of Exchange Market Turbulence

One popular argument claims that the early turbulence from March 1973 through July 1974 can be attributed to currency traders undergoing a "learning process."[41] The proponents of this argument claim correctly that traders in the foreign exchange marketswere making the transition to a more competitive environment and, in doing so, made some large mistakes. They argue incorrectly, however, that the management practices that were responsible for the initial period of destabilizing speculation were rectified quickly. From this perspective, the calm that followed was claimed to be the normal state of affairs in the market. Unfortunately, the markets became disorderly once again in June 1977. Therefore, arguments predicated on the assumption that this early turbulence was merely an aberration fail to be persuasive.

A more interesting argument has been suggested by the monetarists.[42] They have argued that since the exchange rate is an asset price, sudden and dramatic changes in exchange rates must be due exclusively to "news." In "newsy" periods, rapid changes in exchange rates are to be expected as new information is quickly incorporated into market prices. In this view, the early turbulence and the turbulent dollar market of the late 1970s are both attributable to news-related disturbances.

From a strict monetary perspective, if news is to affect exchange rates, it must be able to alter the traders' view of the future path of the relative supply or demand for money. According to this perspective, during a news-related disturbance the exchange rate may appear to move in ways that appear to be inconsistent with current monetary policy. But that is because today's monetary policy may alter the market's expectation of future monetary policy.

To take a classic example of this kind of thinking, monetary policy under the Carter administration may have generated expectations that future monetary policy was going to be highly expansionary. So even though actual monetary growth was slower in the U.S. than in Germany, Japan, and other industrial nations, the anticipated future growth in U.S. money may have exceeded the anticipated future money growth of other nations!

For the monetarists, then, anticipated money growth is as important as actual money growth. However, their argument becomes difficult to accept when it requires us to believe that anticipated money growth has no relationship to actual money growth, as would have to be the case in the late 1970s. Table 4.6 compares money growth in the U.S. to money growth in Germany and to a group of foreign nations (Canada, France, Germany, Italy, Japan, Switzerland, and the United Kingdom). The data show that, although foreign money growth exceeded U.S. money growth by several percentage points in 1977-1978, the dollar nonetheless depreciated dramatically.

Rudiger Dornbusch has argued for a nonmonetarist version of the news hypothesis.[43] He claims that (1) exchange rate movements of the 1970s were mostly unanticipated developments; (2) unanticipated current account, cyclical, and interest rate shocks can explain most of the unanticipated component of the trade weighted dollar in the 1970s; and (3) currency rate movements were exaggerated by interest rate policies which had been geared toward internal objectives, thereby forcing large, private sector portfolio shifts to bear the burden of short-term adjustment.

While Dornbusch has presented some evidence for his claims, subsequent research has shown us that "news" announcements, even broadly considered, cannot explain currency rate movements. For example, econometric evidence attempting to link economic news announcements of all sorts to daily changes in exchange rates typically explains less than ten percent of such changes. Moreover, there seems to be no consistent relationship between economic "news" and exchange rate movements. For instance, one thorough study found that exchange rates react somewhat to unanticipated changes in the money supply but do not respond at all to unanticipated inflation or unanticipated changes in real activity.[44] Therefore, it is safe to conclude that surprise

Table 4.6

Money Growth and Exchange Rates
1973 - 1987

Year	United States Money Growth (%)	German Money Growth (%)	$/DM Rate (%)	Foreign Money Growth (%)	$/Foreign Rate (%)
1973	5.5	1.7	18.4	9.4	2.6
1974	4.3	10.7	12.2	10.0	2.8
1975	4.9	14.3	-8.1	14.0	-4.8
1976	6.6	3.3	11.0	8.9	-1.9
1977	8.0	12.0	12.2	15.8	9.6
1978	8.3	14.6	15.2	15.0	3.0
1979	7.7	2.9	5.6	7.2	7.2
1980	6.5	4.0	-11.6	4.6	-7.5
1981	6.4	-1.6	-13.1	7.8	-13.6
1982	8.6	7.1	-5.1	9.2	-7.5
1983	9.5	8.4	-12.8	8.6	-11.1
1984	5.8	6.0	-13.5	9.8	-4.6
1985	12.5	6.7	27.9	9.6	21.7
1986	16.5	8.2	26.8	11.3	20.8
1987	3.0	7.5	22.7	8.9	13.0

Source:
All data are from the IMF, *International Financial Statistics*.
Appreciation of the $/German mark and the $/Foreign rates is
denoted by (-). For the weights used, see the first set of weights
(including Switzerland) in Table 4.1.

news announcements concerning economic fundamentals have not been responsible for fueling exchange rate movements in the 1970s and 1980s.

The Safe Haven Effect and U.S. Capital Flows in the 1980s

A popular explanation for the spectacular rise of the dollar from 1980-1985 is that the portfolio shift into dollar denominated assets was the by-product of investors seeking a safe haven for their wealth.[45] According to this view, the election of a free market conservative to the presidency of the U.S., combined with political and economic disruptions abroad, produced an enormous flight of short- and long-term capital from countries and currencies perceived to be "unsafe" to the world's safe haven, the U.S. dollar.

In the late 1970s and early 1980s, chaos in the Middle East, the second oil price shock, growing economic and political uncertainty in Europe, and the Soviet invasion of Afghanistan[46] supposedly turned Western Europe's formerly strong currencies into "unsafe" stores of value, thus unleashing the first of two waves of capital flight to the U.S. dollar. The second wave of flight to the dollar began in late 1982 when the international debt crisis deepened with the de facto default by Mexico on its foreign debt.[47] The Mexican crisis was soon followed by similar debt problems throughout Latin America and thus set the stage for the second upward spiral in the dollar. According to this view, therefore, the economic disintegration of Latin America triggered an outflow of capital in search of a safe haven while simultaneously halting the outflow of bank loans from the U.S. to large Latin America debtors.[48] Both of these factors created a large, net capital flow into dollar denominated assets, thus raising the exchange value of the dollar.

While the safe haven argument contains several grains of truth, it also has some glaring logical flaws. To begin with, there is no clear and logical relationship between the events of the early 1980s and the transformation of the U.S. dollar into a safe haven. For example, it is difficult to posit a link between political turmoil in the Middle East or, for that matter, the Soviet invasion of Afghanistan and the emergence of the dollar as a safe store of value and the German mark into an unsafe one. Nor is it obvious that the election of a conservative president in the U.S. would necessarily transform the dollar into a desired store of value. This is especially true in the 1980s because conservative governments were becoming the norm throughout the industrial capitalist world. In short, the safe haven argument is certainly correct in pointing to the significance of the Third World debt crisis in generating a significant outflow of capital from Latin America. However, no convincing argument is offered for why the dollar was the preferred store of value for this international pool of "hot money" rather than either the mark, the yen, or the Swiss franc.

Empirically speaking, there is little if any evidence that confirms the safe haven argument.[49] Unfortunately, the U.S. balance of payments accounts have too many data problems to confirm or refute the safe haven argument. However, if the United States were considered a safe haven by investors in the 1980s, then we would expect real interest rates to be reduced in the U.S. relative to real interest rates in the "unsafe" nation-states such as West Germany.[50] In fact, however, real interest differentials over the period moved sharply in favor of the U.S. thus contradicting the safe haven argument. Moreover, the safe haven argument provides no real explanation as to why the dollar followed a continuous appreciation path. Assuming that asset markets adjust rapidly, then the safe haven effect should have produced a one-time change in exchange rates, not a prolonged appreciation of the dollar. Furthermore, the safe haven argument does not explain why the dollar subsequently depreciated after February 1985.

Therefore, there is little or no support for the safe haven explanation for the spectacular appreciation of the dollar in the first half of the 1980s. While most observers would agree that the early 1980s was a period of shifting economic and political currents, it is doubtful, however, that these economic and political shifts by themselves brought about the unprecedented appreciation of the dollar from 1980-1985. Furthermore, the observed movement in both interest rates and exchange rates in the 1980s does not fit well with the safe haven argument.

The Mundell-Fleming Model

One result of the failure of the monetary approach as well as widespread dissatisfaction with the news hypothesis and the safe haven argument has been to push exchange rate economics down the path of searching for applicable general equilibrium models. The objective of these models is to incorporate the interaction of many markets (goods markets, money markets, other asset markets, and labor markets) in order to explain exchange rate developments. At the theoretical level, the principal result of this development has been to view the exchange rate as a macroeconomic variable which adjusts to disturbances originating from a variety of sources, both monetary and nonmonetary.

At the core of most macroeconomic approaches to exchange rate modelling is the so-called Mundell-Fleming model.[51] The Mundell-Fleming model builds on the textbook closed-economy, Keynesian macroeconomic model in which markets for goods, money, and bonds interact to determine key macroeconomic variables such as output, employment, and interest rates. To explore the determinants of exchange rates, the international flows of goods and capital between domestic and foreign markets are needed.

Capital flows are assumed to depend upon the difference between domestic and foreign interest rates, while trade flows are a function of the real exchange rate (the exchange rate adjusted for differences in price levels) and domestic and foreign income. External equilibrium in the model rests on the assumption that net capital inflows from abroad must equal the deficit on trade. In a floating exchange rate system, this implies that any macroeconomic disturbance must not only force the interest rate and output to adjust to maintain equilibrium in goods and money markets, but also that capital flows, trade flows, and the exchange rate need to adjust to maintain the external conditions of equilibrium.

The macroeconomic disturbances that are usually considered are changes in government fiscal and monetary policy. In the Mundell-Fleming model, a fiscal expansion in the home country raises the domestic nominal and real interest rate above the world rate, thus inducing a capital inflow into the home country. In turn, this incipient capital inflow causes the domestic currency to appreciate, and with prices assumed fixed (or at least sticky), the real exchange rate appreciates, too. Moreover, if it is assumed that the home country is "small" relative to world capital markets and capital is perfectly mobile, the home currency has to appreciate sharply enough to result in the fiscal expansion causing a dollar-for-dollar reduction in net exports, thus the decline in net exports completely crowds out the fiscal expansion.

On the other hand, if the country is "large" in relation to world capital markets (like the U.S.), then the benefits of a fiscal expansion are shared throughout the world economy. Once again, the fiscal expansion raises the domestic nominal and real interest rate, which in turn attracts a large capital inflow. But now the capital inflow results in higher world nominal and real interest rates. This suggests that, if capital is highly mobile, a fiscal expansion in a large country can result in both an increase in world interest rates along with a real appreciation of the home currency.

In the Mundell-Fleming model, contractionary monetary policy also can cause nominal and real currency appreciation. In the "small" country case, a monetary contraction in the home country raises the domestic nominal and real interest rate above the world rate, attracting a capital inflow which again causes a real appreciation of the home currency. The real currency appreciation then leads to a reduction in net exports and thus domestic income. Equilibrium is restored once the fall in income reduces the demand for money sufficiently to bring the domestic interest in line with the foreign rate.

In the "large" country case, the monetary contraction appreciates the home currency and raises the domestic and world nominal and real rates of interest. Therefore, the Mundell-Fleming model suggests that both monetary and fiscal policy can move the nominal and real exchange rate by raising the domestic nominal and real interest rate temporarily above (or below) the world rate.[52]

Fiscal Policy, Real Interest Rates, and the Dollar in the 1980s

The Mundell-Fleming model has been seen by some observers as an inadequate basis for examining the impact of fiscal policy because it assumes that output is demand-determined and also because it gives no role to exchange rate expectations.[53] While it is possible to incorporate exchange rate expectations into the Mundell-Fleming model, it is difficult to get away from its "Keynesian" roots. For these reasons, a host of recent models attempting to understand the relationship between fiscal policy and exchange rates build on the Mundell-Fleming insights, although they do so within a full-employment, classical model that allows for an active role for exchange rate expectations.

This change in theoretical perspectives has come as many conventional theorists in the 1980s have all but abandoned monetary explanations of the exchange rate in favor of "fiscal policy" explanations. From the perspective of the monetary approach, fiscal policy can affect the exchange rate only by altering the relative supply or demand for money. In other words, the monetary approach assumes that fiscal policy has *no independent role* in determining the exchange rate. However, in recent years a "fiscal policy approach" to the exchange rate has been developed in an attempt to explain the startling rise in the *real* value of the dollar in the 1980s.[54] It is now widely accepted that the unprecedented peacetime budget deficits in the U.S., along with the rise of full-employment fiscal surpluses in Europe and Japan, are directly responsible for the huge overvaluation of the dollar from 1980-1985.

In this vein, an interesting and influential model has been developed by William Branson.[55] In Branson's model, the real exchange rate and interest rate in the home country are determined, simultaneously, by the overall savings balance and the requirements for international financial equilibrium.

Consistency in the savings balance in an open economy requires that the domestic budget deficit (the negative of government savings) equals the gap between savings and investment (domestic savings minus domestic investment) plus net foreign borrowing (the negative of net exports). The savings balance can be derived from the standard national income identities shown in equations 4.19 and 4.20.

$$Y = C + I + G + NX \qquad (4.19)$$

$$Y = C + S + T \qquad (4.20)$$

where:

   Y = real domestic gross national product
   C = real domestic consumption spending
   I = real domestic investment spending
   G = real government purchases
   NX = real net exports of goods and services

S = real domestic savings
T = real domestic taxes net of transfers

Setting equations 4.19 and 4.20 equal (spending equal to income) and rearranging, we derive the savings balance specified in equation 4.21:

$$G - T = S - I - NX \qquad (4.21)$$

Equation 4.21 states that the domestic budget deficit must be financed by a surplus of domestic savings over domestic investment and/or by borrowed foreign savings.

Equation 4.21 can be thought of in either Keynesian or classical terms. From a Keynesian perspective, savings must adjust to alterations in expenditure changes, whether the change in expenditure originates from either the private or public sector. However, recent literature adopts the classical approach, which assumes that the proper mode of interpreting equation 4.21 is to "standardize" the equation at "full-employment" income, thus weeding out cyclical influences which are assumed to be short-run in nature in order to achieve a long-run, full-employment (usually interpreted to mean when the economy is close to its "natural" rate of unemployment) perspective. In the long run, when the economy is at "full employment," it is assumed that expenditure must adjust to savings.

Branson develops his model further by assuming that the gap between savings and investment $(S - I)$ is an increasing function of the real interest rate (r) as investment demand is inversely related to the real interest rate, while net exports (NX) is an increasing function of the real exchange rate $(q,$ where q measures international price competitiveness as a ratio of foreign to domestic prices denominated in the home currency). From this we derive a simple relationship between the savings balance, the real interest rate, and the real exchange rate. For a given budget deficit, there is a locus of points in r-q space that satisfies the savings balance equation, as shown by the S-B locus in Diagram 4.3.

Diagram 4.3

The Real Interest Rate and the Real Exchange Rate

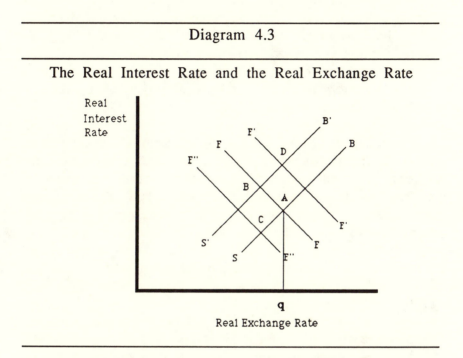

q

Real Exchange Rate

Moreover, in a world with integrated financial markets, the equilibrium between financial centers must be maintained in order to prevent disequilibriating capital flows. Usually this implies the absence of risk-adjusted profit opportunities between financial centers. In Branson's model, speculators are assumed to arbitrage *real* returns across financial centers by forcing the real expected return differential to equal the risk premium on domestic assets. Furthermore, the risk premium on domestic assets is assumed (following Dornbusch) to be an increasing function of the supply of government debt, as shown in equation 4.22.[56]

$$r - r^* - (E[q_{t+1}] - q_t) = rp(B) \qquad (4.22)$$

where:

r = the real domestic interest rate
$E[q_{t+1}] - q_t$ = the expected real depreciation of the
    home currency (the dollar)
rp = the risk premium on domestic (dollar
    denominated) assets
B = the domestic (U.S.) supply of government debt
* = a foreign variable

If traders in the market have rational expectations, then the anticipated real depreciation of the home currency depends upon the degree of undervaluation of the real exchange rate and the speed at which the actual rate adjusts to its equilibrium value, as shown in equation 4.23.

$$E[q_{t+1}] - q_t = \phi(q - q_t) \qquad (4.23)$$

where:

ϕ = the adjustment coefficient
q = the equilibrium real exchange rate (assumed
    constant)
q_t = the current real exchange rate.

Combining equations 4.22 and 4.23 we get:

$r - r^* - \phi(q - q_t) = rp(B)$

And solving for q_t:

$$q_t = q - (1/\phi)(r - r^*) + rp(B) \qquad (4.24)$$

Equation 4.24 states that, for a given equilibrium exchange rate and risk premium, there is an inverse relationship between the current real exchange rate and the real interest rate. The inverse relationship is required in order to maintain equilibrium in international financial markets. Equilibrium requires that a rise in the domestic real interest rate must be offset by the expectation of a future real currency depreciation made possible by real domestic currency appreciation today. By overvaluing the exchange rate in the current period, real currency appreciation creates an expectation of a compensating real depreciation of the exchange rate in the future. The relationship between the real exchange rate and the real domestic interest rate is shown by the F-M locus in Diagram 4.3.

Combining the saving and financial market balance conditions, we get a unique determination of the real interest rate and exchange rate, as shown in Diagram 4.3. Initially, let us assume that $q = q$, i.e., that the actual real exchange rate is equal to its long-run equilibrium value. The long-run equilibrium real exchange rate is assumed by Branson to be that level of international competitiveness which yields a balanced current account at full employment. Branson argues the dollar was approximately in long-run equilibrium in 1980, judging from the U.S. current account balance and unemployment rate.

According to Branson, the subsequent changes in fiscal policy in the U.S. increased the full-employment budget deficit, shifting the S-B locus up and to the left (S'B'). This produced a rise in both the real interest rate and the real value of the dollar (a fall in the real exchange rate), as depicted by the movement from point A to point B in Diagram 4.3. His argument (consistent with its classical roots) holds that the rise in the real value of the dollar and the real interest rate were necessary to crowd out domestic investment and net exports, thereby providing the financing for the U.S. budget deficits while at the same time maintaining the zero excess profits condition between dollar and foreign denominated assets.

The "dynamics" of this process are that the forced reduction in savings drove up the real domestic interest rate which in turn attracted an inflow of foreign savings, thus bidding up the value of the dollar. According to proponents of this argument, the rise in both real interest rates and the real value of the dollar in the 1980s are attributable directly to the large budget deficits in the U.S. as well as to budget tightening abroad.

Unfortunately, an examination of the U.S. macroeconomic accounts shows that the above analysis cannot explain the *timing* of the rise in real interest rates and exchange rates--since they preceded the rise in the U.S. budget deficits by about two years! The rise in the real interest rate and the exchange rate began before 1981, while the U.S. fiscal expansion did not begin until 1982-83. Branson attempts to reconcile the timing problem by arguing that the markets anticipated the increase in the deficit and therefore began to bid up real interest rates and the dollar long before the actual increase in the deficit. As Branson explains:

> The Economic Recovery Tax Act of 1981 had one particular aspect that is unusually useful for macroeconomic analysis. It provided an example of a clear-cut and credible announcement of future policy actions at specified dates. A three-stage tax cut was announced in the Tax Act in March 1981. Simultaneously, a multi-stage buildup in defense spending was announced. This implied a program of *future* high-employment--now "structural"--deficits, beginning late 1982. The fundamentals framework tells us that this would begin a process which starts with the . . . [S-B] curve shifting up . . . causing a rise in real interest rates and appreciation of the dollar.[57]

Moreover, Branson argues that the announcement of tax cuts and a military buildup forced traders in financial markets to consider the following questions and to arrive at answers that were consistent with the anticipated changes in fiscal policy:

> (1) What will have to be crowded out to make room for the deficit? Answer: investment and net exports.

(2) How will net exports be crowded out? Answer: dollar appreciation. Or one could reason that the rise in interest rates would attract financing from abroad, leading to appreciation of the dollar. . . . [T]hese are two views of the same adjustment mechanism. Either says the dollar would appreciate. Once that expectation takes hold, the dollar should be expected to jump immediately.[58]

Branson recognizes that the "premature" rise in real interest rates and the value of the dollar cannot be explained in his framework by a safe haven effect, as many observers at the time believed. An exogenous reduction in the risk premium on dollar denominated assets which was caused by, let us say, the 1980 Reagan victory would shift the F-M locus in and to the left, as depicted by the movement from point A to point C in Diagram 4.3. This shift reflects the enhanced preference for dollar denominated assets on the part of the international investment community. In efficient capital markets, the anticipated return on dollar denominated assets must be reduced to prevent disequilibrating capital flows. In the model, this is achieved by a *fall* in the domestic real interest rate and a real appreciation of the dollar. Branson dismisses this possibility since both the real interest rate and the value of dollar climbed together.

And finally, according to Branson, the rise in the value of the dollar cannot be sustained. Sooner or later the large current account deficits would increase the risk premium on dollar denominated assets, thus shifting the F-M locus up and to the right and moving the economy's equilibrium from point B to point D, as illustrated in Diagram 4.3. This anticipated shift would result from the eventual refusal of wealth holders to allocate an increasing share of their portfolios to dollar denominated assets. As a result of these portfolio shifts, real U.S. interest rates would skyrocket and the value of the dollar could tumble. In other words, Branson's fundamentals framework predicts that the full burden of the budget deficit would be shifted onto domestic investment when the market began to balk at holding increasing amounts of U.S. Treasury debt.

Table 4.7 shows the estimates and summary statistics for a reduced form version of Branson's model, using both U.S.-German and U.S.-foreign data (Group of Seven countries plus Switzerland).[59] Regressions 1 and 3, are different specifications of Branson's model using U.S.-German data, and regressions 2 and 4 employ U.S.-foreign data. Regressions 1 and 2 test the relationship between the real interest rate differential and the real exchange rate. In both cases there is a highly significant inverse relationship between the real interest rate differential and the real exchange rate, as predicted by Branson's model. Moreover, the model explains most of the variation in the real exchange rate (62 and 64 percent, respectively), though there is a high degree of first-order serial correlation in each case (.94 and .89, respectively).

Figure 4.4 shows the actual and predicted values for the model, using regression 2 for the entire sample period. The most interesting thing that stands out is that the model performs rather poorly for the 1980s.[60] It predicts the appreciation of the dollar from the third quarter of 1980 to the second quarter of 1984, but it fails to predict the subsequent appreciation which lasted until February 1985. In addition, the fit of the model is even worse when explaining the rapid depreciation of the dollar that followed after February 1985.

In Branson's framework two explanations are possible for the depreciation of the dollar after February 1985. First, Branson himself argued that the appreciation could not last forever due to the increasing supply of U.S. debt which would increase the risk premium on U.S. assets. Let us suppose that the risk premium on U.S. assets began to increase significantly after February 1985, forcing the dollar to depreciate. This would imply that the real interest differential would have to move sharply in favor

Table 4.7

Analysis of the Fiscal Policy Model:
March 1973 - December 1988
(The Dependent Variables are the Log of the Real
$/German Mark Rate and the Log of the Real Weighted
Exchange Rate)

Regression No.	(1)	(2)	(3)	(4)
r-r*	-.05 (-17.6)		-.05 (-17.0)	
r-wtr		-.06 (-18.2)		-.06 (-18.9)
q			-.02 (-1.00)	
wtq				.05 (3.18)
Intercept	4.46 (716)	4.45 (716)	4.46 (425)	4.44 (635)
R-Squared	.62	.64	.62	.66
First-Order Rho	.94	.89	.94	.89
Durbin-Watson	.12	.17	.12	.18

(Continued)

Table 4.7 (Continued)

Legend:

r = the real interest rate on long-term U.S. bonds.
r* = the real interest rate on long-term German bonds.
wtr = the real weighted interest rate on long-term foreign bonds.
q = a dummy variable intended to capture any change in the real, long-term equilibrium $/German Mark exchange rate after February 1985.
wtq = a dummy variable intended to capture any change in the real, long-term equilibrium weighted exchange rate after February 1985.

Source:

All data are from the IMF, *International Financial Statistics*. The logs of the real exchange rates are derived by multiplying the respective exchange rates by the corresponding ratio of foreign to U.S. consumer prices and then taking the log of the variable. Real interest rates are simply the long-term government bond rate less an average of the previous year's consumer price inflation. For the weights used, see the first set of weights (including Switzerland) in Table 4.1.

Figure 4.4

The Branson Model: Actual and Predicted Values

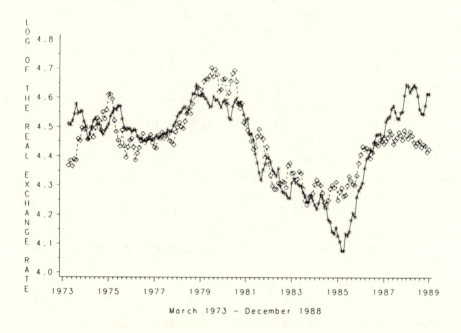

Label:
Star = actual trade weighted exchange rate.
Diamond = predicted trade weighted exchange rate.
Source:
See Table 4.7.

of U.S. assets to crowd out domestic investment spending as net exports are crowded in by the depreciating dollar. In Figure 4.5, I plotted measures of the real interest differential and the real exchange from 1973 through 1988. The data clearly show that the real interest differential *fell* after February 1985, and thus Branson's own scenario is not supported by the data.

A second possibility is that the large current account deficits generated by the spectacular appreciation of the dollar altered the market's view of the long-run equilibrium exchange rate. Persistent current account deficits will alter a nation's net foreign asset position and transform a creditor nation into it a debtor nation. This change in status requires future current account surpluses to pay the interest and principal on the accumulated net foreign debt. If the market understands the long-run implications of debt accumulation, they would realize that, in order to create future surpluses, real exchange rate depreciation would be needed. Therefore, persistent current account deficits as occurred in the U.S. would require the long-run equilibrium exchange rate to depreciate.

In our estimates of Branson's model, the long-run equilibrium rate is given by the constant term. To test whether or not a shift in the long-run equilibrium rate is responsible for the depreciation of the dollar, I allowed the constant to change after February 1985. The results indicate that in the case of the German data, no statistically significant shift occurred. In the foreign data, however, there was evidence of a small depreciation of the dollar. The size of the shift, though, is too small to explain the actual depreciation of the dollar after 1985.

In conclusion, the proposed "reconciliation" suggested by Branson and others is appealing on the surface, although a closer examination of the argument reveals significant flaws that vitiate the analysis. Besides the econometric problems noted above, two additional problems stand out. First, Branson's solution to the timing problem is extremely suspect. It must be remembered

Figure 4.5

The Real Exchange Rate and Interest Differential

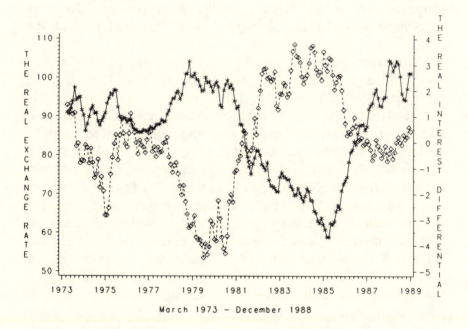

March 1973 − December 1988

Legend:
Star = trade weighted exchange rate.
Diamond = real interest rate differential.
Source:
See Table 4.7.

that the spectacular rise in the value of the dollar and real interest rates was wholly unprecedented, as were the budget deficits. And, therefore, it is obviously unlikely that the markets could have known what was coming several years in advance! Given the statistical and historical information available to the markets in the early 1980s, it would have been highly improbable for them to have forecasted, with any certainty, the future course of foreign exchange and bond markets from the proposed shifts in fiscal policy. Furthermore, there is absolutely no evidence to suggest that this was in fact the case.

Some economists recognize this weak link in the argument and attribute the early rise in real U.S. interest rates and the value of the dollar to tight monetary policy in the United States.[61] In their view, only the continued rise in real interest rates and the appreciation of the dollar after 1982 is due to divergent fiscal policies. However, the data on relative money growth do not support this hypothesis. For example, Table 4.6 shows that from 1980 to 1982, German money growth was slower than U.S. money growth, and a weighted index of foreign money growth was not significantly different from U.S. money growth. This should not be surprising in light of the fact that monetary policy was tightening up throughout the industrial world in this period. While it was true that monetary policy was becoming more restrictive in the U.S. in the early 1980s, this by itself cannot explain the "premature" appreciation of the dollar since there is no evidence that U.S. monetary policy was *more* restrictive than monetary policy abroad.

Second, there is little evidence connecting budget deficits to interest rates and currency rates. For years, scholars have been attempting to establish an empirical relationship between budget deficits and interest rates, with little success. Ironically, prior to the 1980s, many economists were convinced that budget deficits caused currencies to depreciate! This was because "the historical record concerning budget deficits and real exchange rates," as Jacob Frenkel notes, "is not unambiguous. As a matter of fact the experiences of other countries as well as that of the United States during other periods do not suggest a clear cut, strong, and universal relation."[62]

TOWARDS A SYNTHESIS

My survey of the empirical and theoretical literature has revealed that there are good empirical and theoretical reasons for abandoning both the monetary and fiscal policy approaches to exchange rate formation. However, there are important insights contained in each tradition which can be incorporated into a more general model of exchange rates. Thus, the road to a richer but eclectic theoretical and empirical model is already visible.

A more general model would at the very least need to incorporate certain components: from the flexible-price monetary tradition, (1) that purchasing power parity is a poor building block for a model of short-run exchange rate dynamics but may serve as a good indicator of the long-run equilibrium rate, and (2) that in an inflationary world differences in relative inflation rates should generate expectations of offsetting currency rate changes; from the sticky-price tradition, (3) that expectations are forward looking and that it is therefore reasonable to assume that traders anticipate that exchange rates adjust in the long run to their underlying equilibrium values; and from the Mundell-Fleming and asset market traditions, (4) that the exchange rate is an asset price, which in the short-to-medium run is determined by the expected relative return between domestic and foreign assets, and finally (5) that a complete specification of our model must consider that speculative bubbles (as well as exchange market intervention) may create large expected return differentials which lead to significant movements in exchange rates.

The basic building blocks of such a model have already been outlined. In equation 4.13 (page 146),

Jeffrey Frankel claimed that to combine the insights of the flexible and sticky-price traditions we can write:

$$i - i^* = \emptyset(e - e) + z - z^* \qquad (4.13)$$

Equation 4.13 states that the expected depreciation of the home currency (assumed to be equivalent to the interest differential) is determined by the current overvaluation of the exchange rate (e - e) multiplied by how fast the market anticipates the current exchange rate to adjust this period ($\emptyset$) to its long-run equilibrium rate. It also states that the inflation differential between the home country and the rest of the world (z - z*) creates as well an expectation of home currency depreciation.

Rearranging equation 4.13, we get:

$$e = e - (1/\emptyset)[(i - z) - (i^* - z^*)] \qquad (4.13')$$

Equation 4.13' states that the current exchange rate is a function of the long-run equilibrium rate and the long-term real interest rate differential, as in the Mundell-Fleming tradition. Further, if we assume that investors believe that purchasing power parity holds over the long run (e = p - p*), we can write:

$$e = p - p^* - (1/\emptyset)(r - r^*) \qquad (4.13'')$$

Equation 4.13" states that the current exchange rate is dependent on its long-run equilibrium rate given by purchasing power parity (p - p*) and the real interest rate differential between domestic and foreign assets (r - r*).

For econometric purposes, the following model can be estimated:

$$e = B_0 + B_1(p - p^*) + B_2(r - r^*)$$

The expected signs on the coefficients are $B_1 = 1$ (reflecting purchasing power parity) and $B_2 < 0$ (reflecting the Mundell-Fleming assumption that with highly mobile capital a real long-term interest differential in favor of dollar denominated assets generates capital inflows and an appreciating dollar, i.e., a fall in e.

The parameter estimates for the above model using U.S.-German and U.S.-foreign data are given in Table 4.8. Regressions 1 and 2 show that all the underlying hypotheses of the hybrid model are supported. For both the U.S.-German and U.S.-foreign data, the coefficient on the purchasing power parity variable is close to unity as hypothesized. Furthermore, in results not reported, restricting the coefficient to unity does not reduce the explanatory power of the models appreciably, nor does it alter the coefficients on the remaining variables. In addition, the real long-term interest rate differential has the anticipated sign. And the explanatory power of the model is similar to that of Branson's model.

The one significant problem is that the estimation of first-order rho is extremely high (as in all the models we tested), perhaps suggesting model misspecification. In results not reported, AR(1) estimates that eliminate first-order serial correlation in the error term of the model drastically alter the parameter estimates. For the U.S.-German data, the coefficient on the purchasing power parity variable remains correct and significant, but the coefficient on the real interest rate differential is correct but statistically insignificant. For the U.S.-foreign data, the results are nearly the opposite. The coefficient on the real interest rate differential remains correct and significant, but the purchasing power parity coefficient becomes incorrect and statistically insignificant. In addition, the explanatory power of the models are reduced dramatically (to 5 and 6 percent, respectively).

The hybrid model of the fundamentals can be used to perform a simple test of the "no bubble hypothesis." If bubbles did not exist, then the coefficients of the model would remain stable during highly speculative periods. More specifically, we can employ dummy variables to

Table 4.8

Analysis of the Hybrid Model:
March 1973 - December 1988
(The Dependent Variables are the Log of \$/German Mark
and the Log of the Weighted Exchange Rate)

Regressions No.	(1)	(2)	(3)	(4)
cpi-cpi*	.90 (13.3)		.85 (14.4)	
cpi-wtcpi		.87 (3.55)		.85 (4.35)
r-r*	-.05 (-14.0)		-.03 (-7.79)	
r-wtr		-.06 (-18.1)		-.02 (-5.87)
Period 1			.01 (1.28)	.02 (1.42)
Period 2			-.05 (-4.73)	-.02 (-1.96)
Period 3			-.03 (-4.14)	-.05 (-8.51)
Period 4			-.10 (-7.76)	-.10 (-10.73)
Intercept	4.45 (405)	4.45 (694)	4.47 (432)	4.49 (515)

(Continued)

Table 4.8 (Continued)

Regressions No.	(1)	(2)	(3)	(4)
R-Squared	.56	.64	.71	.80
First-Order Rho	.94	.90	.86	.81
Durbin-Watson	.12	.17	.27	.36

Legend:

cpi = the log of the U.S. consumer price index.
cpi* = the log of the German consumer price index.
wtcpi = the log of the weighted foreign consumer price index.
r = the real interest rate on long-term U.S. bonds.
r* = the real interest rate on long-term German bonds.
wtr = the real weighted interest rate on long-term foreign bonds.
Period 1 from January 1973 - June 1974.
Period 2 from June 1977 - January 1979.
Period 3 from July 1980 - February 1985.
Period 4 from March 1985 - February 1987.

Source:

All data are from the IMF, *International Financial Statistics*. For weights used, see the first set of weights (including Switzerland) in Table 4.1.

monitor changes in the effect the real interest rate differential is predicted to have on the exchange rate. Speculative bubbles would produce such shifts by creating prospective speculative capital gains, which make for either an appreciation-prone or depreciation-prone dollar market. In an appreciation-prone market, real interest rate differentials in favor of the U.S. become more effective in attracting capital inflows, thus making the impact of a positive real interest rate differential on the exchange rate that much stronger. A depreciation-prone market, on the other hand, exaggerates the effect of a real interest rate differential in favor of foreign countries on dollar depreciation. The prediction, therefore, is that in periods where real interest rate "shocks" predominate, the prospective capital gains created by currency bubbles magnify the effect that the real interest rate differential has on the exchange rate.[63]

In Chapter 3, I suggested that there are four periods during which it was likely that currency bubbles had a significant impact on currency rate movements. The first period began in January 1973 and lasted until May 1974. The currency market was characterized during this time by extreme market volatility and speculative pressures which alternated from favoring to not favoring the dollar's rivals. The second period was the Carter-era bubble. It began in June 1977 and lasted through January 1979. The market in this time period was characterized by extreme volatility and a prolonged and continuous bout of speculative flight from the dollar.

The third period started in July 1980 and continued through to February 1985. This was the Reagan-era bubble that was responsible for the dazzling appreciation of the dollar. And finally, the fourth period lasted from March 1985 through February 1987. The extraordinary depreciation of the dollar that followed after February 1985 was sparked by central bank intervention aimed at realigning the overvalued dollar. This successful central bank effort to depreciate the dollar induced potentially dangerous speculative flight from dollar denominated assets. The growing fear of this speculative flight and its consequences forced the central banks to agree to move away from the policy of dollar realignment to stabilizing the dollar around its 1987 level.

The results from testing the "no bubble hypothesis" are reported in regressions 3 and 4. The results demonstrate conclusively that in three of the four periods examined there were large and significant shifts in the real interest rate differential's effect on the exchange rate. As expected, however, during period one the reported shift in the coefficient was positive and insignificant. For period one the results seem to suggest that the real interest rate differential had no empirically verifiable impact on the exchange rate. This is not surprising, as the principal shocks provoking movements in currency rates--the breakup of Bretton Woods and first energy price shock--did not create the needed bouts of unidirectional speculative trading that seem to be required if real interest rate differentials are to have a powerful effect on exchange rates.

For period two, the estimates suggest that there was a dramatic coefficient shift. This period witnessed a dramatic fall in the real interest rate differential, which was accompanied by speculative flight from the dollar. The combination produced a dramatic and rapid depreciation of the dollar that was halted only by central bank intervention starting in January 1979. During period three, the interest rate differential coefficient shifted dramatically once again as both the real interest rate differential and speculative pressure began to turn in favor of the dollar. In period four, the most dramatic shift in the coefficient occurred due to the combination of central bank intervention to realign the dollar, a falling real interest rate differential, and speculative flight from the dollar.

SUMMARY AND CONCLUSIONS

In this chapter, we have examined the principal exchange rate models and arguments deemed by many in the economics profession as relevant to understanding the floating rate exchange rate system. The principal conclusion that the empirical evidence forces upon us is that for the most part, these models are empirically irrelevant to understanding the large swings in currency rates that have characterized the system since 1973. The exception to this general finding is the hybrid model based on long-run purchasing power parity and real interest rate differentials. This model, though flawed, tended to perform well relative to its competitors. Moreover, extreme parameter instability in the hybrid model's principal explanatory variable (the real interest rate differential) during the major speculative episodes suggests that researchers cannot exclude the possibility that currency bubbles and official intervention played an important, if not the major, role in rate swings in the floating rate era.

By and large, therefore, the empirical evidence overwhelmingly suggests first that the characteristic self-reversing, large changes in nominal and real exchange rates are not explicable in terms of the standard models of currency market fundamentals, as many in the economics profession claim. Second, it suggests that the state of our current knowledge is such that all we can claim with any certainty is that macroeconomic "shocks," usually of the variety capable of producing large changes in real interest rate differentials, initiate speculative anticipations of capital gains which generate extremely large movements in nominal and real exchange rates. Finally, the evidence also seems to support the added conclusion that coordinated central bank intervention plays an important role in the process as well, as I shall argue more forcefully in Chapter 5. In summary, the large nominal and real exchange rate movements of the 1970s and 1980s were shaped by real interest rate "shocks," speculative anticipations of capital gains, and the posture of central bank currency market intervention. It is to this last point that I now turn.

NOTES

1. There are a number of alternative surveys of the literature. See, for example, Ronald MacDonald, *Floating Exchange Rates: Theory and Evidence* (London: Unwin Hyman, 1988), Sven W. Arndt, Richard J. Sweeney, and Thomas D. Willett, eds., *Exchange Rates, Trade, and the U.S. Economy* (Cambridge: American Enterprise Institute/Ballinger, 1985), Rudiger Dornbusch, "Exchange Rate Economics: Where do We Stand?" in Jagdeep S. Bhandari and Bluford H. Putnam, eds., *Economic Interdependence and Flexible Exchange Rates* (Cambridge: MIT Press, 1983), pp. 45-83; Jeffrey R. Shafer and Bonnie E. Loopesko, "Floating Exchange Rates After Ten Years," *Brookings Papers on Economic Activity* 1 (1983), pp. 170; Ronald I. McKinnon, "The Exchange Rate and Macroeconomic Policy: Changing Postwar Perceptions," *Journal of Economic Literature* vol. 19 (June 1981), pp. 531-557; and Peter Isard, "Exchange Rate Determination: A Survey of Popular Views and Recent Models," Princeton University *Studies in International Finance* no. 42 (May 1978).

2. The monetary approach to the exchange rate was an outgrowth of the so-called monetary approach to the balance of payments. The foundational papers of the monetary approach to the balance of payments and the exchange rate can be found respectively in Jacob A. Frenkel and Harry M. Johnson, eds., *The Monetary Approach to the Balance of Payments* (Toronto: University of Toronto Press, 1976) and Jacob A. Frenkel and Harry M. Johnson, eds., *The Economics of Exchange Rates* (Reading, MA: Addison-Wesley, 1978).

3. For surveys of this literature see Richard M. Levich, "On the Efficiency of Markets for Foreign

Exchange," in Jeffrey A. Frankel and Rudiger Dornbusch, eds., *International Economic Policy: Theory and Evidence* (Baltimore: Johns Hopkins University Press, 1979), pp. 246-269; Richard M. Levich, "Further Results in the Efficiency of Markets for Foreign Exchange," in Federal Reserve Bank of Boston *Managed Exchange Rate Flexibility: The Recent Experience* conference series no. 20 (Oct. 1978), pp. 58-90; and Michael L. Mussa, "Empirical Regularities in the Behavior of Exchange Rates and Theories of the Foreign Exchange Market," in Karl Brunner and Allan Meltzer, eds., *Policies for Employment. Prices, and Exchange Rates*, Carnegie-Rochester conference series in public policy, a supplement to the *Journal of Monetary Economics* (1979), pp. 9-57.

4. To quote Mussa: "This approach emphasizes that both the balance of payments (meaning the official settlements balance) and the exchange rate are essentially monetary phenomena. The proximate determinants of exchange rates and the balance of payments are the demands and supplies of various national monies. When the demand for a particular money rises relative to the supply of that money, either the domestic credit component of the money supply must be expanded, or the exchange rate must appreciate, or the official settlements must go into surplus, or some combination of the three." Michael L. Mussa, "The Balance of Payments, and Monetary and Fiscal Policy Under a Regime of Controlled Floating," in *The Economics of Exchange Rates,* pp. 47-48.

5. There are various versions of purchasing power parity. The distinction commonly made is between absolute and relative purchasing power parity. Absolute purchasing power parity implies that all goods have the same price when transformed into a common currency unit. However, the existence of trade barriers and transportation costs would mean that strict absolute purchasing power parity would cease to hold. In this case, assuming the factors causing the deviations from purchasing power parity are held constant, all goods

prices would experience the same rate of price inflation when translated into world prices. This is known as relative purchasing power parity.

The mechanism that is said to assure continued adherence to parity is international commodity arbitrage. It is also possible to argue for continuous parity from an efficient markets perspective. On this point see John Pippinger, "Arbitrage and Efficient Markets Interpretations of Purchasing Power Parity," Federal Reserve Bank of San Francisco *Economic Review* (Winter 1986), p. 47.

6. In fact, Frenkel argued that the German hyperinflation was the ideal test case for the theory. To quote Frenkel: "That episode [the German hyperinflation] is of special interest since it provides an opportunity to examine the assets approach to a situation in which it is clear that the source of the disturbances is monetary." Jacob A. Frenkel, "A Monetary Approach to the Exchange Rate: Doctrinal Aspects and Empirical Evidence," in *Economics of Exchange Rates*, p. 6. A convincing argument can be made that the flexible-price monetary approach is only a hyperinflation model.

7. The money demand functions can be derived by taking the natural logs of $M/P = y^k \exp.^{-bi}$.

8. Empirical tests of these assumptions have proven them to be universally false. See, for instance, Herbert Gintis, "International Capital Markets and the Validity of National Macroeconomic Models," Unpublished, University of Massachusets, Amherst (June 1982), pp. 1-53.

9. In a crude Keynesian model, a rise in the domestic interest rate would trigger a capital inflow causing the home currency to appreciate. For a discussion of this issue see Frenkel, "A Monetary Approach to the Exchange Rate," pp. 9-11.

10. The standard comparison in the literature is to test the out of sample fit of the structural models against a random walk. See, for instance, Richard A. Meese and Kenneth Rogoff, "Empirical Exchange Rate Models of the

Seventies: Do they Fit Out of Sample?" *Journal of International Economics* 14 (1983), pp. 2-24.

11. The income elasticity of money demand is said to be about .19 in the short-run and .68 in the long-run. On the other hand, the interest elasticity of money demand is thought to be about -.045 in the short-run and -.16 in the long-run. Unfortunately, these estimates are suspect because the money demand function has been unstable. See Rudiger Dornbusch and Stanley Fischer, *Macroeconomics* 4th ed. (New York: McGraw Hill, 1987), pp. 355-359.

12. There are a number of statistical objections to the test proposed. First, it is argued that it is inappropriate to use national price indices since they generally have different weights. The different weights would bias the results--for example, suppose country A produces only wine and country B only cloth. If the price of wine rises 10% while the price of cloth falls by 10%, then the equilibrium exchange rate should not change. However, by using GNP deflators in both countries to test for purchasing power parity, the ratio of the deflators would be altered, predicting a change in the equilibrium rate. However, tests of purchasing power parity using indices with identical weights have yielded similar results to tests using national price indices. Second, it is argued that there is simultaneous bias in the simple test of purchasing power parity. However, two-stage least squares estimates produce estimates similar to OLS. Finally, it is argued that tariffs and transactions costs undermine the simple test of purchasing power parity. Once again, though, there is little or no evidence to show that this is the case. For a review of the issues see Pippinger, "Arbitrage and Efficient Market Interpretations," pp. 31-38.

13. These results are consistent with the existing literature. For example: "One of the striking facts concerning the relationship between prices and exchange rates during the 1970s has been the poor performance of the predictions of the simple versions of purchasing

power doctrine . . ." [Moreover,] "divergences from purchasing power parity, measured in terms of the relation between exchange rates and the ratio of consumer price indices, seem to persist." Jacob A. Frenkel, "Flexible Exchange Rates, Prices, and Role of 'News': Lessons from the 1970s," in *Economic Interdependence and Flexible Exchange Rates*, p. 25.

14. I also tested to see if relative purchasing power parity fares any better. The results (not shown) confirm the failure of purchasing power parity to hold over the sample period.

15. This is a well-known problem in the literature. See, for example, Dornbusch, "Exchange Rate Economics: Where do We Stand?" pp. 48-51 and the results of Thomas D. Willett, Waseem Khan, and Aida Der Hovanessian, "Interest Rate Changes, Inflationary Expectations and Exchange Rate Overshooting: The Dollar-DM Rate," in Sven W. Arndt, Richard J. Sweeney, and Thomas D. Willett, eds., *Exchange Rates, Trade, and the U.S. Economy* (Cambridge: American Enterprise Institute/Ballinger, 1985), pp. 49-71.

16. Haynes and Stone first brought attention to this possibility when the sign reversal problem originally became apparent in the literature. "[E]xchange rate models," wrote Haynes and Stone, "are inappropriate and misleading because the explanatory variables are specified in difference form (for example, the logarithmic difference between U.S. and German money supplies). Such subtractive linear constraints are especially dangerous because the specification bias which in general results from the restriction often leads to a sign reversal in the constrained coefficient. This follows because a reversal can be more likely, *ceteris paribus*, the stronger the direct correlation between the relevant domestic and foreign variables." They suggested that the relevant variables be split to avoid the problem. Stephen E. Haynes and Joe A. Stone, "On the Mark: Comment," *American Economic Review* 71 (Dec. 1981), p. 1060.

17. Dornbusch, "Exchange Rate Economics: Where do We Stand?" p. 49.

18. Stephen M. Goldfeld, "The Demand for Money Revisited," *Brookings Papers on Economic Activity* 3 (1973), pp. 577-637 and Stephen M. Goldfeld, "The Case of the Missing Money," *Brookings Papers on Economic Activity* 3 (1976), pp. 683-730.

19. A similar procedure was used and result found for the U.S.-Canadian exchange rate. See David Backus, "Empirical Models of the Exchange Rate: Separating the Wheat from the Chaff," *Canadian Journal of Economics* vol. 17, no. 4 (Nov. 1984), p. 835.

20. One way to "rescue" the theory is to assume that the monetarist model is applicable only to the hyperinflation case. In periods of moderate inflation rates, as in the case under consideration, the monetarist model is inappropriate.

21. See Pentti J. K. Kouri, "The Exchange Rate and the Balance of Payments in the Short Run and in the Long Run: A Monetary Approach," *Scandinavian Journal of Economics* 78, no. 2 (May, 1976), pp. 280-304. Alternatively, the inclusion of the current account variables can be justified in terms of portfolio balance models. See my review of portfolio balance models later in this chapter.

22. The money demand function would become: $m - p = ky - bi + cf$, where f is the natural log of the foreign wealth held by domestic residents and c is the elasticity of money demand with respect to wealth. In an open economy, the change in net foreign wealth is equal to the current account balance (cab). Furthermore, the so-called absorption approach shows that the current account balance is equal to the difference between total income (y) and spending by domestic residents-- absorption (a), where absorption is assumed to be a function of wealth. So the change in net foreign assets is: $cab = y - a$. In the model, the relationship between the domestic price level (or the exchange rate), the stock of net foreign assets, and the current account balance in a

small country model is as follows. An initial current account surplus (y > a) would increase the stock of net foreign wealth of the home country, increase domestic absorption (spending) relative to domestic income, and thus reduce the current account balance and lower the domestic price level (appreciating the domestic currency). See Kouri, "The Exchange Rate and the Balance of Payments," pp. 283-290.

23. See Richard N. Cooper, "Flexible Exchange Rates, 1973-1980: How Bad Have They Really Been?" in Richard N. Cooper, Peter Kenen, Jorge Braga De Macedo, and Jacques Van Ypersele, eds., *The International Monetary System Under Flexible Exchange Rates* (Cambridge: Ballinger Publishing Co., 1982), pp. 6-10. Cooper claims that the real exchange rate tends to move with the current account balance. Others argue that the nominal exchange rate reacts to current account shocks. See, for example, Steven W. Kohlhagen, "The Experience of Floating: The 1973-1979 Dollar," in Jacob S. Dreyer, Gottfried Haberler, and Thomas D. Willett, eds., *The International Monetary System: A Time of Turbulence* (Washington DC: American Enterprise Institute, 1982), pp. 144-149.

24. I attempted also to run the model over the subperiod 1974-1981, the period over which the evidence suggests that the predicted relationship between the relative current account balances and the exchange rate tends to hold, but with no success.

25. Rudiger Dornbusch, "Expectations and Exchange Rate Dynamics," *Journal of Political Economy* (Dec. 1976), pp. 1161-1176.

26. The literature distinguishes between nominal and real exchange rate overshooting. For examples of models of real exchange rate overshooting see Kent P. Kimbrough, "Price, Output, and Exchange Rate Movements in the Open Economy," *Journal of Monetary Economics* no. 11 (1983), pp. 25-44; Willem H. Buiter and Marcus Miller, "Real Exchange Rate Overshooting and the Output Costs of Bringing Down Inflation: Some Further Results," in Jacob

A. Frenkel, ed., *Exchange Rates and International Macroeconomics* (Chicago: University of Chicago Press, 1983), pp. 317-358; and Willem H. Buiter and Marcus Miller, "Monetary Policy and International Competitiveness: The Problems of Adjustment," *Oxford Economic Papers* no. 33 (July 1983), pp. 143-175.

27. The price adjustment equation can be derived from a simple aggregate demand and aggregate supply analysis. Price adjustment is assumed to be $z = w(y^d - y^s)$, where y^d is the natural log of aggregate demand and y^s the natural log of aggregate supply. The aggregate demand function is assumed to be $y^d = u + d(e - p) + ay - ci$, and aggregate supply is assumed to be a constant, equal to y. Therefore, $z = w[u + d(e - p) + (a - 1)y - ci]$.

28. It must be noted that there is no necessity for the exchange rate to overshoot in the Dornbusch model. For example, if the exchange rate is initially out of long-run equilibrium, and the supply of money is increased, then the exchange rate will depreciate but not overshoot. This point is made by Brian Hillier, *Macroeconomics: Models, Debates and Developments* (Oxford: Basil Blackwell, 1986), pp. 199-211.

29. Jeffrey A. Frankel, "On the Mark: A Theory of Floating Rates Based on Real Interest Rate Differentials," *American Economic Review* vol. 69, no. 4 (Sept. 1979), pp. 610-622.

30. Backus believes that to satisfy the overshooting hypothesis the coefficient on the relative money supply variable should be expected to exceed unity. See Backus, "Empirical Models of the Exchange Rate," p. 830.

31. For previous results, see Willett, Khan, and Der Hovanessian, "Interest Rate Changes, Inflationary Expectations and Exchange Rate Overshooting," Jeffrey A. Frankel, "Monetary and Portfolio-Balance Models of Exchange Rate Determination," in Jagdeep S. Bhandari and Bluford H. Putnam, eds., *Economic Interdependence and Flexible Exchange Rates* (Cambridge: MIT Press, 1983), pp. 84-115; Frankel, "On the Mark," passim; Haynes and Stone, "On the Mark: Comment," pp. 1060-1067; Robert A.

Driskill and Steven M. Sheffrin, "On the Mark: Comment," *American Economic Review* vol. 71, no. 5 (Dec. 1981), pp. 1068-1074; and Jeffrey A. Frankel, "On the Mark: Reply," *American Economic Review* vol. 71, no. 5 (Dec. 1981), pp. 1075-1082.

32. There is a vast literature on portfolio models. See, for instance, Peter Isard, "Exchange Rate Determination," and Rudiger Dornbusch, "Monetary Policy Under Exchange Rate Flexibility," in Federal Reserve Bank of Boston *Managed Exchange-Rate Flexibility: The Recent Experience* (proceedings of a conference held at Melvin Village, New Hampshire; Oct. 1978), pp. 98-101, and William H. Branson, "Asset Markets and Relative Prices in Exchange Rate Determination," *Sozialwissenschaftliche Annalen* 1 (1977), pp. 69-89.

33. See, for example, Peter Isard, "Exchange Rate Determination," passim.

34. See, for some results, David Backus, "Empirical Models of the Exchange Rate," pp. 839-840.

35. See Rudiger Dornbusch, "Exchange Rate Risk and the Macroeconomics of Exchange Rate Determination," National Bureau of Economic Research *Working Paper* series no. 493 (June 1980), pp. 1-36.

36. See Jeffrey A. Frankel, "The Dazzling Dollar," *Brookings Papers on Economic Activity* 1 (1985), pp. 207-211.

37. Ronald I. McKinnon, "Why Floating Rates Fail," Hoover Institution *Working Paper* series no. E-83-12 (July 1983), pp. 1-3.

38. See, for example, Jeffrey A. Frankel, "In Search of the Exchange Risk Premium: A Six-Currency Test Assuming Mean-Variance Optimization," *Journal of International Money and Finance* 1 (1982), pp. 255-274. For an attempt to combine the portfolio balance and monetary approach, see Jeffrey A. Frankel, "Monetary and Portfolio-Balance Models of Exchange Rate Determination," in Jagdeep S. Bhandari and Bluford H. Putnam, eds., *Economic Interdependence and Flexible*

Exchange Rates (Cambridge: MIT Press, 1983), pp. 101-105.

39. Jeffrey A. Frankel, "The Dazzling Dollar," pp. 211-213.

40. See Robert Z. Aliber, "The Interest Rate Parity Theorem: A Reinterpretation," *Journal of Political Economy* 81 (Nov.-Dec. 1973), pp. 1451-1459.

41. See, for instance, Ian H. Giddy, "Measuring the World Foreign Exchange Market," *Columbia Journal of World Business* (Winter 1978), pp. 37-38.

42. See Frenkel, "Flexible Exchange Rates, Prices, and the Role of 'News'," pp. 3-41 and Jacob A. Frenkel and Michael L. Mussa, "The Efficiency of Foreign Exchange Markets and Measures of Turbulence," *American Economic Review* 70 (1980), pp. 374-381. For an empirical critique of this position see Roger D. Huang, "The Monetary Approach to Exchange Rate in an Efficient Exchange Market: Tests Based on Volatility," *Journal of Finance*, vol. 36, no. 1 (March 1981), pp. 31-41.

43. See Dornbusch, "Exchange Rate Economics: Where do We Stand?" pp. 55-60.

44. See Craig S. Hakkio and Douglas K. Pearce, "The Reaction of Exchange Rates to Economic News," Federal Reserve Bank of Kansas City *Research Working Paper* no. 85-01 (June 1985) and Maurice Obstfeld, "Floating Exchange Rates: Experience and Prospects," *Brookings Papers on Economic Activity* 2 (1985), pp. 433-434. Goodhart argues that there is evidence that exchange rates tend to underreact to economic news. Charles Goodhart, "The Foreign Exchange Market: A Random Walk with a Dragging Anchor," *Economica* 55 (Nov. 1988), pp. 439-444.

45. See Bank for International Settlements, *Annual Report* (June 1980), pp. 134-135; *Annual Report* (June 1983), p. 149; Rudiger Dornbusch, "Flexible Exchange Rates and Excess Capital Mobility," *Brookings Papers on Economic Activity* 1 (1986), p. 216; Edward M. Bernstein, "The United States as an International Debtor Country," *The Brookings Review* (Fall 1985), pp. 31-32; and Peter

Isard and Lois Stekler, "U.S. International Capital Flows and the Dollar," *Brookings Papers on Economic Activity* 1 (1985), pp. 219-229.

46. Unfortunately, differing versions of the safe haven argument attribute the flight of investors to the safety of the dollar to different reasons. Dornbusch, for instance, summarizes the argument as follows: "Increased political uncertainty in Europe, a strengthening of the relative economic position of the United States under the Reagan Administration, and the economic disintegration in Latin America are the motivating forces in this international asset shift toward the United States." In "Flexible Exchange Rates and Excess Capital Mobility," p. 216.

47. For a brief summary of the Mexican crisis, see Martin H. Wolfson, *Financial Crises* (New York: M. E. Sharpe, 1986), pp. 102-105.

48. For estimates of the size of the capital outflow from Latin America and elsewhere see "LDC Capital Flight," Morgan Guaranty Trust *World Financial Markets* (March 1986), pp. 13-15, and Donald R. Lessard and John Williamson, eds., *Capital Flight and Third World Debt* (Washington DC: Institute for International Economics, 1987).

49. For an empirical evaluation of the safe haven argument see Isard and Stekler, "U.S. International Capital Flows." After a careful examination of the U.S. balance of payments accounts, Isard and Stekler conclude that "the composition of U.S. capital flows offers little evidence on the relative importance of various forces that might explain the recent appreciation of the dollar. Nor does the overall size of the net private capital inflow necessarily measure the upward pressures on the value of the currency." Ibid., p. 229. An interesting exception is the work Ayanian. He interprets political risk to a function of U.S. military security against the "Soviet threat." His econometric work shows a significant relationship between U.S. defense spending as a share of GNP and the real exchange rate of the dollar. Robert

Ayanian, "Political Risk, National Defense and the Dollar," *Economic Inquiry* 26 (April 1988), pp. 345-351.

50. For example, when there is a so-called "flight to quality" in the U.S., the spread between "unsafe" and "safe" assets widens considerably. Aliber claims this argument can be generalized to currency rates. "Currency brands," Aliber claims, "can be ranked like songs on a hit parade, with the standings based on the interest rates on assets which are similar except for currency of denomination." See Robert Z. Aliber, *The International Money Game* (New York: Basic Books, 1983), pp. 143.

51. See Rudiger Dornbusch, *Open Economy Macroeconomics* (New York: Basic Books, 1980), MacDonald, *Floating Exchange Rates,* Jeffrey A. Frankel, "Ambiguous Policy Multipliers in Theory and in Empirical Models," in Ralph C. Bryant, Dale W. Henderson, Gerald Holtham, Peter Hooper, and Steven A Symansky, eds., *Empirical Macroeconomics for Interdependent Economies* (Washington D.C.: The Brookings Institution, 1988), pp. 17-26, and Jacob A. Frenkel and Assaf Razin, "The Mundell-Fleming Model: A Quarter Century Later," *IMF Staff Papers* 34 (Dec. 1987), pp. 567-620.

52. There are two controversial issues surrounding the results of the Mundell-Fleming model. The first is theoretical and concerns the impact of a fiscal expansion in the home country on the home currency. In the Mundell-Fleming model, if the degree of capital mobility is limited, then a fiscal expansion could depreciate the home currency. This is due to the fact that the pressure on the home currency originating from a worsening of the trade account could overwhelm the impact of rising capital inflows. The second issue centers on the prediction that in the large country case a tightening of monetary policy in the U.S. is expansionary abroad. This is contrary to the experience of the early 1980s when tight money in the U.S. was universally seen as the catalyst for a global slump. See Frankel, "Ambiguous Policy Multipliers," for an analysis of both these points, and Jean-Paul Fitoussi and Edmund S. Phelps, *The Slump in Europe* (Oxford: Basil

Blackwell, 1988) for an extensive treatment of the second controversy.

53. See Dornbusch, "Exchange Rate Economics: Where do We Stand?"

54. See, for example, Dornbusch, "Flexible Exchange Rates and Excess Capital Mobility," pp. 212-216; William Branson, "Causes of Appreciation and Volatility of the Dollar," in Federal Reserve Bank of Kansas City *The U.S. Dollar: Recent Developments, Outlook, and Policy Options*, a symposium sponsored by the Federal Reserve Bank of Kansas City (Jackson Hole, Wyoming, August 21-23, 1985), pp. 33-53; and W. Max Corden, "Fiscal Policies, Current Accounts, and Real Exchange Rates," *Weltwirtschaftliches Archiv* 3 (1986), pp. 423-438.

55. See Branson, "Causes of Appreciation and Volatility of the Dollar," and also William Branson, "The Limits of Monetary Coordination as Exchange Rate Policy," *Brookings Papers on Economic Activity* 1 (1986).

56. This can be derived by rearranging a simple parity condition: $E[qt+1] - qt = r - rp - r^*$. The assumption that markets eliminate excess profits implies that if the real return on domestic assets is 5%, the real return on foreign assets 3%, the risk premium on domestic assets is 1%, that the configuration of real exchange rates must be such that the real exchange rate is anticipated to depreciate during the period by 1%.

57. Branson, "Causes of Appreciation and Volatility of the Dollar," pp. 45-46. Besides the increase in the U.S. budget deficit, the increases in the full-employment budget surpluses abroad are also blamed. Estimates put the increase in the U.S. full-employment budget deficit, between 1980-1985 at roughly 3.5 percent of the GNP and the increase in foreign full-employment surpluses at roughly 2.5 percent of the GNP. See William L. Helkie and Peter Hooper, "An Empirical Analysis of the External Deficit, 1980-1986," in Ralph C. Bryant, Gerald Holtham, and Peter Hooper, eds., *External Deficits and the Dollar: The Pit and the Pendulum* (Washington DC: The Brookings Institution, 1988), p. 45. For sophisticated single equation

tests of Branson's claims, see Martin Feldstein, "The Budget Deficit and the Dollar," in *National Bureau of Economic Research Macroeconomics Annual 1986* (Cambridge: MIT Press, 1986), pp. 355-392.

58. Ibid., p. 46.

59. For a survey of similar models, see MacDonald, *Floating Exchange Rates*, pp. 283-287. For a test of the Branson hypothesis using proxy measures for monetary and fiscal policy in place of the real interest rate differential, see Feldstein, "The Budget Deficit and the Dollar." For an multi-equation econometric study, see Helkie and Hooper, "An Empirical Analysis of the External Deficit, 1980-1986," pp. 44-51.

60. Empirical results from sophisticated multi-equation, macroeconometric simulations have produced similar conclusions. After surveying the simulated effect of fiscal policy on real interest differentials and the dollar Helkie and Hooper conclude: "[T]he rise in the dollar must be largely attributable to other factors." Ibid., p. 49.

61. See, for example, Jacob A. Frenkel, "Commentary on 'Causes of Appreciation and Volatility of the Dollar'," in *The U.S. Dollar: Recent Developments, Outlook, and Policy Options*, p. 57; Rudiger Dornbusch, "Exchange Rate Theory and the Overvalued Dollar," in *Dollars, Debts, and Deficits* (Cambridge: MIT Press, 1986), pp. 5-7; and MacDonald, *Floating Exchange Rates*, pp. 281-283.

62. Ibid., p. 58.

63. Some theorists have posed an alternative way of using exchange rate models to detect bubbles. They argue that when exchange rates move in ways that are clearly contrary to observed fundamentals that this indicates the presence of bubbles. Using this methodology, the remarkable appreciation of the dollar in 1985 and, on a smaller scale, the appreciation of the dollar in 1988-1989 are deemed to be bubble periods. Unfortunately, this approach by assumption rules out the possibility of bubbles playing any role during episodes in which exchange rates are moving in the "right" direction. See Frankel and Froot, "Chartists, Fundamentalists, and

Trading in the Foreign Exchange Market," *American Economic Review: Papers and Proceedings* 80 (May 1990), pp. 181-185, Paul R. Krugman, *Exchange-Rate Instability* (Cambridge: MIT Press, 1989), and Helkie and Hooper, "An Empirical Analysis of the External Deficit, 1980-1986."

5

The Political Exchange Rate Cycle

In this chapter, I will investigate the relationship between central bank intervention and speculative bubbles. The first two sections will examine the general mode of management of the exchange rate system that emerged with the demise of the Bretton Woods fixed exchange rate regime. In particular, I will focus on clarifying the basic determinants of central bank currency market interventions. Then I will consider the role played by central bank exchange rate management during the major speculative episodes of the post-Bretton Woods float. The final section will conclude with a summary statement describing what I believe to be the relationship that has developed since March 1973 between market fundamentals, bubbles, and central bank intervention, which I term the "political exchange rate cycle."

EXCHANGE RATE MANAGEMENT

Since the breakdown of the Bretton Woods adjustable peg currency system and the advent of the float, central banks have attempted to regulate currency rates using a variety of policy instruments, most frequently by varying official foreign exchange holdings. This process has become so ingrained in the post-Bretton Woods float that it is often referred to in textbooks or by economists as either a "managed" or "dirty" float. In theory, the manipulation of international reserve holdings can be used as a policy instrument to affect domestic employment, the price level, and/or the balance of payments. However, in practice, the overriding policy objective behind official intervention has been to bring a semblance of stability to the currency system. I will argue that harsh experience has taught central bank managers that the exchange rate system does not manage itself, particularly during key junctures which require that the central banks act as the providers of "stability of last resort."

The Channels of Influence

Before examining the the post-Bretton Woods policy regime which began to take shape after 1973, it is necessary to consider first the channels through which the buying and selling of reserves by central banks can operate to influence currency rates.[1] There are at least four such channels of influence. First, the regulatory authorities can influence the short-run behavior of exchange rates by buying or selling dollars, and thereby alter the market period forces of supply and demand that determine the day-to-day rates of exchange. Second, large-scale concerted and nonsterilized interventions can influence the exchange rate by changing the relative supply of money--one of the fundamentals which underlies the exchange rate. In periods of extreme distress, the monetary authorities usually signal their willingness to alter monetary policy to accommodate exchange rate objectives by backing up their currency interventions with substantial changes in interest rates.

In the third channel of influence, pronounced sterilized interventions can alter market fundamentals by changing the relative supplies of outside assets, which are assumed to influence exchange rates by altering risk premia. However, it is generally recognized that changes in official reserves usually are not large enough to have any significant impact on the relative supplies of outside debt. In the fourth instance central bank intervention can affect currency rates by altering the market's expectations about future rate movements.[2] This channel is particularly important during periods of intense speculative trading because, during such highly speculative periods, expectations concerning future rate movements dominate current developments. The effectiveness of this channel depends upon how strongly expectations are held and also on the perceived willingness and ability of the central banks to act.

From this perspective, the central bankers' ultimate basis for control of the market lies in their ability to buy or sell unlimited quantities of currencies in order to impose losses on private traders who bet against the monetary authorities. When central banks successfully use the threat of their market power to force a change in the market's psychology, they are able then to alter the trajectory of the exchange rate. At the very least, concerted intervention can force speculators to hedge their open positions to avoid potential short-term trading losses, and thus bring at least a temporary calm to the market.

Central Bank Management

The conventional view of the political economy of central bank intervention is that the regulators attempt to "lean against the wind"--in effect, to smooth out the volatility of currency rates when the markets become disorderly.[3] "Leaning against the wind" occurs when central banks support their own currency by selling their international reserves in order to moderate currency depreciations or by purchasing international reserves to partially offset currency appreciations. The supposed intent of the intervention is not to prevent exchange rate adjustments or to "correct" misaligned rates, but to smooth out short-run disorderly swings in rates. While "leaning against the wind" appears to be the normal policy stance of the major central banks, I will argue that the major central banks periodically have gone significantly beyond the usual boundaries consistent with smoothing operations.

During the Bretton Woods era, the U.S. central bank was more or less passive about the management of currency rates. Generally speaking, foreign central banks were to keep their currencies aligned to the dollar while U.S. authorities were responsible for keeping the dollar pegged to gold.[4] Under this arrangement, the major European powers and Japan needed large foreign exchange holdings (mainly dollars) in order to fix their currency rates to the dollar. For its own part, the U.S. required large gold reserves in order to stabilize the dollar price of gold.

In the early 1960s, an informal mechanism for central bank cooperation in managing currency rates was added to the system.[5] The need for central bank cooperation became evident when the U.S. began to experience growing balance of payments problems in the mid-1960s. In response to perceived threats to the fixed rate regime, a swap network was arranged, allowing the U.S. central bank to have a reciprocal credit line with its counterparts in Europe and Japan. In effect, each central bank could get limited and temporary access to the other's printing press when necessary to manage currency rates. The precedent for using this swap network to fend off market speculation came in the late 1960s when the Bank of England needed foreign exchange reserves to defend the pound from speculative attack.

At the start of the floating era, the primary responsibility for managing the key exchange rates in the world system continued to be left (by default) to the major European and Japanese central banks, since U.S. authorities were still content to remain relatively passive. The U.S. maintained this posture of relative nonintervention until a speculative attack on the dollar occurred in 1977-1978. Figure 5.1 shows both U.S. foreign exchange reserves as well as U.S. total reserves minus gold holdings over the period of the float. What immediately stands out here is just how insignificant and nonvarying U.S. official reserve holdings were until the late 1970s. In contrast, Figure 5.2 demonstrates that right from the start of the float the major foreign central banks (from Canada, France, Germany, Italy, Japan, the U.K., and Switzerland) played a much more active role in managing the currency system.

A more precise picture of the official reserve policy of the major central banks with respect to the dollar is provided by Table 5.1. Table 5.1 presents the summary results of a simple model of official reserve policy in managing the dollar. In the model, central banks are assumed to adjust their reserves when confronted with changes in the exchange value of the dollar. Thus, the desired reserves of dollars held by central banks are said to increase when the dollar tends toward depreciation and to decrease when the dollar strengthens.

The empirical evidence suggests several broad generalizations about the reserve policy of the central banks examined. The first is that the use of official intervention to further domestic policy goals (the inflation rate and industrial production) seems to be, judging from the Japanese and German experiences, either nonexistent or at best insignificant. The inclusion of domestic inflation and domestic industrial production in the German and Japanese intervention functions reveals that, in the Japanese case, a rise in industrial production produces a small *increase* in reserves.

Using slightly different specifications of the intervention function, Rudiger Dornbusch has found that the German unemployment rate has a statistically significant but small positive effect on German intervention; and I have shown elsewhere that a rise in Japan's trade balance induces the Bank of Japan to buy small amounts of dollars.[6] From all this we can conclude

Figure 5.1

U.S. Official Intervention: March 1973 - December 1988

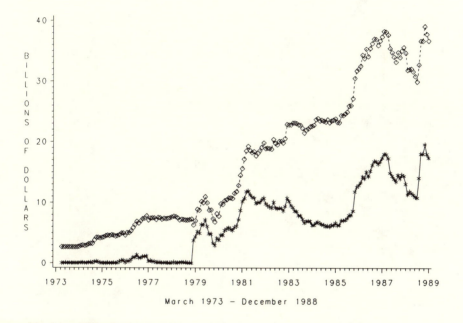

Legend
Star = U.S. foreign exchange reserves.
Diamond = total U.S. reserves less gold.
Source:
All data are from the IMF, *International Financial Statistics.**
*The data used here and in subsequent analyses are *reported* reserves. Actual intervention may differ from that reported.

Figure 5.2

Official Intervention on the Part of Major Central Banks:
March 1973 - December 1988

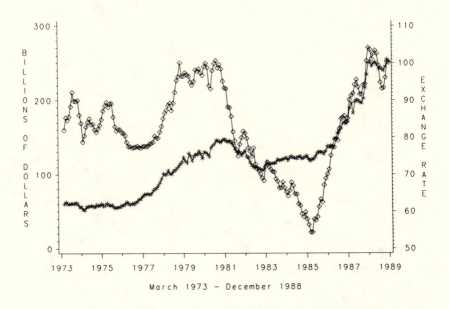

March 1973 – December 1988

Legend:
Star = adjusted foreign exchange reserves of Canada, France, Germany, Italy, Japan, the U.K., and Switzerland.
Diamond = A reserve weighted exchange rate.
Source:
All data are from the IMF, *International Financial Statistics*. Central bank foreign exchange reserves are adjusted by subtracting the previous period's reserves times the U.S. treasury bill rate from the contemporaneous value of reserves. The weights used are the share of each central bank's reserve holdings relative to the group in 1980.

Table 5.1

Analysis of Reserve Use by Central Banks:
March 1973 - December 1988
(The Dependent Variables are the Change in Reserves
Billions of Dollars)

Variable	Germany	Japan	Five Central Banks
Change in Dollar/Mark Rate			
Estimated Beta	.52		
T Value	(9.19)		
Change in Dollar/Yen Rate			
Estimated Beta		.25	
T Value		(7.86)	
Change in Weighted Dollar			
Estimated Beta			1.10
T Value			(10.60)
Domestic Activity			
Estimated Beta	-.01	.02	
T Value	(-.68)	(3.08)	
Domestic Inflation			
Estimated Beta	-.02	-.008	
T Value	(-.70)	(-.84)	
Reagan Dummy			
Estimated Beta	-.27	-.17	-.67
T Value	(-2.29)	(-2.20)	(-2.96)
Intercept	1.40	-1.46	.28
T Value	(2.00)	(-2.48)	(1.37)

(Continued)

Table 5.1 (Continued)

	Germany	Japan	Five Central Banks
R-Squared	.34	.33	.39
First-Order Rho	-.01	.20	.16
Durbin-Watson	2.00	1.59	1.67

Source:

All data are from the IMF, *International Financial Statistics*. Central bank reserves are corrected foreign exchange reserves. The reserves are corrected by subtracting the previous period's reserves times the U.S. treasury bill rate from the contemporaneous value of reserves. The five central banks are those countries from the Group of Seven plus Switzerland whose reserves consistently vary with the exchange value of the dollar. These include the central banks of Canada, Germany, Japan, the U.K., and the U.S. The weights for the reserve weighted dollar are determined by the relative size of a country's reserves in 1980. Domestic activity variables are indices of industrial production. Domestic inflation variables are indices of consumer price inflation. The Reagan Dummy is an interactive dummy variable that allows for a change in the degree of intervention from 1981 through February 1985.

from the size of the estimated coefficients that these domestic policy variables are economically insignificant in setting intervention policy. In other words, there has been no systematic effort by either the Germans or the Japanese to rig the exchange rate system to their competitive advantage or, for that matter, to promote their domestic policy objectives.

Second, the major policy objective behind foreign central bank intervention appears to have been managing the currency system and, in particular, "leaning against the wind," or buying and selling dollars to counter market pressures--although, as Table 5.1 illustrates and I will argue later, there have been times (January 1981 to February 1985, during the "Reagan dummy") when central banks have forsaken their responsibilities. On average, though, the interventions have been modest. The central banks that manage the dollar have purchased collectively 1.1 billion dollars in foreign exchange reserves for every one point change in the weighted dollar.

Third, the major central banks intentionally have increased their average reserve holdings over time. This accumulation of reserves is necessary in order to enhance their capacity to intervene effectively in regulating currency rates. As reported in Table 5.1, the estimated accumulation of reserves, independent of changes in the value of the dollar, amounts to a little less than three and one half billion dollars per year (.28 billion per month).

Perhaps a more accurate perspective on this issue of reserve accumulation through the years can be gleaned from Table 5.2. In Table 5.2, I show the foreign exchange reserves of Germany, Japan, the U.S., and industrial countries as a whole from 1970 through 1988. Generalizing from the pattern of reserve accumulation in industrial countries, the data indicate that after some initial increases in foreign exchange reserves in the early 1970s, coinciding with the breakup of Bretton Woods, reserve accumulation became very modest until the speculative attack on the dollar began in the second

Table 5.2

Central Bank Foreign Exchange Reserves:
1970 - 1988
(Billions of U.S. Dollars)

Year	Germany	Japan	United States	Industrial Countries
1970	8.5	3.2	.6	29.7
1971	12.6	13.8	.3	55.5
1972	18.7	18.0	.3	73.4
1973	25.1	10.2	.0	78.3
1974	24.0	11.3	.0	77.9
1975	24.7	10.6	.1	83.0
1976	25.5	13.9	.3	84.6
1977	30.6	20.1	.0	117.0
1978	42.4	28.9	4.4	159.0
1979	47.3	16.4	3.8	175.6
1980	44.5	21.6	10.1	214.1
1981	39.6	24.7	9.8	188.3
1982	39.6	19.1	10.2	168.5
1983	37.3	20.4	6.3	179.7
1984	35.0	22.3	6.7	189.4
1985	39.0	22.3	12.9	191.0
1986	45.9	37.7	17.3	245.5
1987	72.9	75.7	13.1	365.5
1988	53.3	90.5	17.4	414.7

Source:
The data are from the IMF, *International Financial Statistics: Yearbook* (1989). The foreign exchange reserves of the industrial countries (by IMF classification) were transformed from billions of SDRs to billions of dollars using dollar/SDR conversion rate.

half of 1977. This was followed by moderate dollar sales in the strong dollar era from 1980 - February 1985. However, after 1985, reserve accumulation accelerated, perhaps suggesting that the Plaza and Louvre accords had an impact on central bank reserve policy.

Overall it is safe to conclude that the accumulation of reserves has been modest, especially when one contrasts official reserve accumulation with the spectacular growth of the foreign exchange market. One possible consequence of the failure of central banks to augment their reserves significantly before the late 1970s was the growing perception in the late 1970s that the central banks were losing the war to control the foreign exchange markets.

Finally, it appears that the accumulation of reserves by the leading foreign central banks has not been sterilized, resulting in significant changes in the supply of money. In Table 5.3, I show the relationship between reserve accumulation by foreign central banks and their money supplies since 1973. If foreign central banks routinely sterilized their interventions, then we would expect there to be no relationship between the level of their foreign exchange reserves and the supply of money. However, the data in Table 5.3 indicate that, for Germany considered individually and for the foreign members of the Group of Seven nations (Canada, France, Germany, Italy, Japan, and the U.K.), there is a strong positive relationship between foreign exchange reserves and the money supply. Thus, large increases in reserves seem to be associated with substantial increases in foreign money supplies, both in absolute terms as well as relative to the U.S. money stock.

This combination of policies by the foreign central banks of "leaning against the wind" while not sterilizing their interventions perhaps accounts for the apparent perverse relationship between relative money growth and the exchange rate found in analyzing the monetary approach to the exchange rate. For example, while the dollar was depreciating from 1977-1978, the purchases of foreign exchange by foreign central banks may have

Table 5.3

Foreign Central Bank Reserves and Money Supplies: 1973 - 1988
(Billions of Dollars)

Year	Germany			Group of Seven		
	Reserves	Money	% of U.S. M1	Reserves	Money	% of U.S. M1
1973	25	75	28	50	441	166
1974	24	83	30	51	490	179
1975	25	94	32	49	554	190
1976	26	97	31	53	613	197
1977	31	109	33	85	707	210
1978	42	125	34	108	812	224
1979	47	129	33	117	880	225
1980	44	134	32	134	919	220
1981	40	132	30	119	1004	226
1982	40	141	29	98	1106	230
1983	37	153	29	106	1191	226
1984	35	162	29	104	1307	234
1985	39	173	28	111	1409	225
1986	46	187	26	142	1561	214
1987	73	201	27	251	1684	224
1988	53	207	26	241	1692	216

Source:
All data are from the IMF, *International Financial Statistics*. Reserves are foreign exchange reserves, billions of U.S. dollars. Money supplies are in billions of U.S. dollars, 1980 exchange rates. The relative money supplies are foreign money supplies divided by the Federal Reserve's measure of M1. The foreign country members of the Group of Seven include Canada, France, Germany, Italy, Japan, and the United Kingdom. December's observation was used in each case, except for 1988 when September's data was used.

been responsible for bloating their money supplies, thus raising foreign money stocks relative to the U.S. money stock. Therefore, the apparent paradox of the value of the dollar decreasing while its relative supply was diminishing can be explained by the policy response of the foreign central banks to speculative currency bubbles.[7]

OFFICIAL INTERVENTION AND CURRENCY BUBBLES

While enabling us to make some important generalizations concerning the nature of exchange rate management, the broad picture presented still does not provide the detailed information necessary to understand the relationship between exchange rate bubbles and central bank management of the market. In order to explore this side of the picture, it is necessary to rely on the limited but suggestive historical evidence available.

The Early Turbulence: March 1973 - July 1974

The early turbulence in the floating exchange rate system, which occurred from the beginning of the float in March 1973 through the virtual collapse of the market in July 1974, can be divided into three phases.[8] During the first phase, which was roughly from mid-March to early July 1973, the dollar was under intense selling pressure. By February 1973, the markets sensed that further devaluations of the dollar were imminent, and investors began to sell dollars and buy German marks. The collapse of the fixed exchange rate regime in March came as the result of this enormous speculative pressure against the dollar.[9] After purchasing billions of surplus dollars during "the most concerted flight there had ever been out of the dollar,"[10] the major central banks still were forced to close the foreign exchange market and devalue the dollar. However, the markets were persistent, and the selling pressure against the dollar resumed, forcing the reclosing of the market two weeks later and the advent of generalized floating. Thus, currency speculators forced a rapid transition from the more tightly managed Bretton Woods system to the current market-dominated exchange rate regime.

The market continued to sell dollars even after the collapse of the Bretton Woods exchange rate system. The selling pressure continued until the beginning of July 1973, at which point "conditions in the market had become so disorderly that the usual trading was difficult."[11] At their regular monthly meeting at the Bank for International Settlements, the central bank governors decided that an announcement was needed to "notify [traders] that arrangements were in place for official intervention to restore a more orderly market situation."[12] Shortly afterward, a combination of coordinated intervention in the market with shifts in U.S. and German monetary policy halted the slide of the dollar.

The second phase of speculative activity began at the end of July 1973 and lasted through January 1974. This period was dominated by the market's nervousness about the impact of the first energy crisis on the international monetary system.[13] At first, the rise in energy prices increased the value of the dollar. This was the result of the then universal belief that the U.S. economy would be less affected by the energy crisis because it was relatively more self-sufficient in energy than any of its industrial competitors. The trade weighted dollar soared back to its post-Smithsonian level, effectively undoing two official devaluations and several months of depreciation. At the time, the appreciation of the dollar was welcomed in Europe and Japan since those governments were primarily concerned about their deteriorating competitiveness in trade vis-a-vis their American rivals. This concern and the belief that the previous depreciation of the dollar had gone too far underlay the anaemic reaction by the major central banks to the rise of the dollar. Ironically, the central banks began to sell dollars just when the market began to reverse its bullish outlook on the dollar.

In the third phase of the turbulence which began at the end of January 1974 and lasted through May 1974, the dollar once again came under intense selling pressure. The reversal in the dollar's fortunes was the result of a shift in market psychology fueled by mounting evidence which suggested that the U.S. economy was not better suited to a world of high energy prices. This shift in outlook also brought into question the basis for the dollar's recent meteoric appreciation. As a result, speculators again began to shun the dollar and purchase German marks, Swiss francs, and increasing amounts of gold in search of a safe haven from the dollar. The renewed speculative flight from the dollar was interrupted only when creeping international financial distress brought the international banking network and the floating rate currency system to the brink of collapse.

The cause of this near collapse, as noted in Chapter 3, can be traced to the fact that several major banks overextended themselves and were caught with positions that proved to be highly unprofitable.[14] Trading in the foreign exchange market was disrupted when the Herstatt bank in Germany was closed by the Bundesbank after it had collected on its debts in the spot market but before it had paid out on its liabilities in spot transactions. This started a panic in the interbank foreign exchange market as well as in the interrelated interbank Eurocurrency market.

The initial losses that triggered this near disaster were attributable, in part, to the inexperience of currency dealers with speculation in the new floating rate currency system. Dealers naively discounted the increased risk involved in speculating in the new floating rate system and engaged in what can only be described as reckless currency speculation, which literally put major financial institutions at risk of default over short-term bets on the dollar.

It must be remembered that currency traders were schooled in the art of currency speculation in the relatively safe Bretton Woods environment.[15] In order to speculate successfully in the fixed rate era, traders had to guess which country was likely to devalue and when. Normally it was relatively easy to surmise the answer to the first question, though more difficult to answer the second. Experience had taught the currency markets that countries with chronic balance of payments difficulties and eroding competitive positions had to devalue their currencies sooner or later, unless they were willing to either see their international reserves be substantially reduced or to undergo severe internal policy adjustments. However, the exact timing of a devaluation depended on a host of economic and political variables which made it difficult to forecast in practice. If speculators anticipated a devaluation and were proved wrong, they could always close their positions without fear of large losses. In effect, there was little downside risk to speculation. To be right would yield huge rewards, but to be wrong would generally entail no large losses.

The asymmetric system of rewards for speculation in the fixed rate era was replaced in the floating era by a more symmetric system, with the potential for vastly enlarged rewards and losses. Unfortunately, many trading rooms in the large multinational banks did not adjust their trading guidelines and supervision to suit the more competitive trading environment. The failure to adjust adequately produced the large losses of mid-1974.

A panic and a complete breakdown of the international currency and banking system were averted by (1) quick support operations to protect the creditors of the failing institutions, (2) sweeping changes in regulations, and (3) the introduction of official supervision of trading practices.[16] The banks themselves also introduced tighter self-supervision of their trading practices and control over open positions. As a result of timely intervention, the market was quickly revived but without the speculative excesses that characterized it since the demise of Bretton Woods, and with an enhanced role for central bank management.

In summary, speculative bubbles in the early part of the float from March 1973 through July 1974 revolved around the aftermath of the breakup of the Bretton Woods system and the first oil price shock. The "turning points" of the three speculative phases were influenced, respectively, by official intervention, changes in market psychology, and creeping financial fragility.

From the perspective of regulation, this period can be classified as a time when the major central banks were in a learning process about their new role as the providers of "stability of last resort" in a foreign exchange market now dominated by private traders. The central banks were pushed into this new role in the deregulated market by the continuous bouts of instability that threatened to undermine what had become an increasingly fragile international monetary order.

Over the course of the period, several precedents concerning the role of central banks were established. The first and foremost rule established was that central bank intervention was going to be an integral component of the currency system since it was needed to maintain a semblance of stability in the face of destabilizing speculative activity. The second rule was that positions taken by currency dealers had to be supervised and regulated to prevent reckless speculative activity from producing periodic panics that would put the integrity of the emerging "free market" international monetary order at risk. And third, in case of financial distress induced by large speculative losses, the regulatory authorities had to engage in extensive support operations if they wished to prevent a collapse on the scale of the 1930s. Thus, the early turbulence provoked the establishment of a mode of currency regulation that went significantly beyond the confines of merely "leaning against the wind."

The Free Fall of the Dollar:
June 1977 - January 1979

A major test of the ability of regulatory authorities to manage the floating exchange rate system came with the speculative flight from the dollar in the late 1970s. The dollar flight had its origins in major policy shifts made in Washington in 1976.[17] At the time, the newly-elected Carter administration was faced with a difficult policy dilemma. On the one hand, the administration wanted to reflate in order to stimulate domestic production and employment, both of which were still considered unsatisfactory after the worldwide slump of 1974-1975. The problem was that the administration simultaneously wanted to improve, or at least not worsen, its current account position, which was already in deficit. To improve both its internal and external position, the Carter administration decided to coax the governments of Germany and Japan into a coordinated expansion so that the "three locomotives" would drag the world out of recession without creating major payments imbalances. After being rebuked by Germany and Japan, the Carter administration decided, as a second-best strategy, to force a depreciation of the dollar, which was intended to improve its external position while at the same time reflating domestic aggregate demand.

To force a depreciation of the dollar, the Carter administration attempted to undermine the market's confidence in official support for the dollar. To do so, the administration issued a communique from an OECD meeting of finance ministers stating that member countries with current account surpluses were "ready to see a worsening in their current-account positions and an appreciation of their currencies in response to underlying market forces."[18] This was followed by periodic announcements by the Carter administration stating that it believed that the dollar was overvalued and, therefore, no official support for the dollar would be forthcoming if the dollar were to depreciate. The Carter administration's "open mouth" policy, as it was labeled, had the desired effect--the dollar began to weaken almost immediately.

Once the dollar began its decline, the market's confidence in its future prospects waned, thus feeding further flight from the dollar. In fact, speculative flight from the dollar became so intense that by the end of December, not more than six months after the start of the "open mouth" policy, the Carter administration was forced to reverse its stance from encouraging flight from the dollar to "checking speculation and restoring order in the exchange markets."[19] This was the start of what was to become a series of interventions aimed at stabilizing the dollar, each one being larger in scope and more serious in intent than the one preceding it.

The first such intervention in December 1977 was perceived by the foreign exchange market as nothing more than a cosmetic alteration in U.S. exchange rate policy.[20] Its main components were (1) a series of high level announcements expressing concern over the plight of the dollar, (2) an announcement stating that the Treasury had arranged a swap agreement with the Bundesbank for an undisclosed amount in order to participate with other central banks in supporting the dollar, and (3) a rise in the discount rate of one-half of a percentage point to make dollar denominated assets more attractive to foreign investors. Ironically, rather than reversing the market's decline, the stabilization program instead had the effect of convincing the market that the U.S. government was unwilling to provide the kind of official support necessary to stabilize the dollar-based currency system.

This set the stage for the next major stabilization program in mid-March 1978.[21] The March program included (1) a doubling of the amount of the swap line between the U.S. and Germany, (2) the sale of SDR (Special Drawing Rights at the IMF) 600 million in Treasury bonds in Germany to procure German marks for intervention, and (3) an indication to the foreign exchange market that the U.S. government was willing to draw on its reserve account at the IMF to defend the dollar. However, once again the market perceived that the program was inadequate. Thus after only two months of relative stability, the slide in the dollar resumed by the end of May.

Finally, along with the other major central banks, the U.S. government decided that it would intervene on whatever scale was deemed necessary to stem the decline of the dollar since the situation was perceived to be getting out of hand.[22] A new package in November 1978 included (1) a three billion dollar IMF drawing, (2) SDR sales totaling two billion dollars, (3) another increase in the swap line between the U.S. and the Bundesbank as well as with the the Bank of Japan and the Swiss National Bank, totaling over seven and one-half billion dollars, (4) the intention to issue up to ten billion dollars worth of government securities denominated in foreign currencies (so-called Carter bonds), and (5) a one percentage point increase in the discount rate (the largest such rise in forty-five years). After two months of concerted intervention, the slide in the dollar was finally arrested, and by January 1979 the dollar even began to climb on its own.

Throughout 1979 there were intermittent bouts of currency rate instability. However, in each case coordinated central bank intervention seemed to prevent the large, chaotic portfolio shifts between competing currencies that characterized the period from June 1977 through January 1979. Perhaps part of the reason for the relative success in controlling inter-currency speculation was the shift in speculative pressure. As the predominating fears haunting global financial markets became rising worldwide inflation, political instability, and monetary collapse, investors began to flee all paper assets for real assets in 1979.

The specter of runaway inflation and the collapse of the international monetary order ushered in global policies of deflation. Undoubtedly, the cornerstone of the new program was the deregulation of interest rates in the

U.S. with the adoption of "monetarist-like" operating procedures by Paul Volcker on October 6, 1979.[23] Interest rate deregulation, combined with monetary policies designed to raise interest rates, served to stem the flight out of paper assets. This feat was accomplished by raising interest rates throughout the world economy to unprecedented levels in order to make paper assets more attractive to investors, and also by creating a global recession that transformed workers separated from their jobs into a reserve army of inflation fighters. The net result of these policies was to start an era of high real interest rates and slow growth that became the norm of the early 1980s.

The change in monetary policy in the U.S. was a direct response to the growing fears of the consequences of the speculative/inflationary bubble. The newly appointed Chairman of the Federal Reserve Board, Paul Volcker, was searching for a policy that would be credible to the major players in the financial markets in restraining speculative activity and inflationary pressures. The hope was that a credible policy would force an immediate change in inflationary and speculative anticipations and thereby assuage the speculative/inflationary psychology that was dominating the financial and goods markets.[24] The new policy involved manipulating the Federal Funds rate as a means of achieving stringent targets for money growth. The shift towards monetary targeting meant that the Fed was going to move away from its traditional emphasis upon interest rate targeting. Therefore, the change in operating procedures is best seen as an attempt by the Fed to assert control over speculative/inflationary expectations by policies it believed best suited for imposing discipline and restraint on financial markets.

To summarize briefly, the period from mid-1977 through January 1979 was an era when the limitations of central bank control over currency speculation in the post-Bretton Woods era became apparent. The lesson from this period is clear: Once market expectations become homogeneous and one-way currency trading develops into a flight from the dollar, it can be extremely difficult and costly in the current politically fragmented world to stabilize the dollar-based currency system. This point is underscored by the dramatic policy shifts needed to halt the dollar's decline in 1978-1979. The first step in stopping the free fall of the dollar was for Washington to change its outlook on the dollar, as well as to share the European perspective that further dollar depreciation threatened the global monetary system. This became necessary because it was demonstrated clearly at the time that the Europeans and Japanese alone could not prevent the dollar from first weakening and then plummeting in world currency markets.

Once the depreciation of the dollar gathered momentum and investor confidence in the dollar waned, concerted intervention could no longer prevent a free fall of the dollar even with U.S. support and leadership. Subsequent currency market developments forced the Carter administration to reverse gears abruptly and adopt a tight money policy to complement its official support operations on behalf of the dollar. The shift in monetary policy became a necessary complement to currency market interventions in order to halt growing international monetary disorder. As the cautious observers at the Bank for International Settlements explained:

> Broadly speaking, if official intervention is to have a stabilizing influence on the exchange market, the most important requirement is that it should be convincing. This means firstly, that it should be consistent with, or backed up by, other policy measures.[25]

Furthermore, once monetary policy shifted in the U.S. to appease speculators, the tight money and high interest rate policies in the U.S. were exported throughout the world economy. Country after country found it necessary to join the policy bandwagon of tight money to avoid a speculative attack on its own currency as well as a loss of confidence in its domestic financial system. In this manner, tight global monetary policies brought the world's monetary and trading system to the brink of collapse before order was finally restored. The spread of tight money policies in this period makes a mockery of the early supporters of floating rates who claimed that a "free market" rate system would allow each country to pursue an independent monetary policy in our interdependent global economy.

The Strong Dollar Era: July 1980 - February 1985

The era of the strong dollar began by the third quarter of 1980. From January 1979 through the Spring of 1980, currency rates continued to fluctuate but no clear pattern emerged. By late 1980, several events produced large portfolio shifts into the dollar which, when combined with the unwillingness of the new Reagan administration to intervene to prevent the strengthening of the dollar, paved the way for a profound overvaluation of the dollar.

The triggering factors that generated the initial portfolio shifts into the dollar were a complex set of changes in a variety of economic and political variables that conspired to make dollar denominated assets extremely attractive to foreign investors. The most important factor, as we argued in Chapter 4, was the emergence of a long-term real interest rate differential in favor of dollar denominated assets that resulted from deregulation and relatively tight U.S. monetary policy. While a positive real interest differential may not necessarily produce capital inflows, particularly when the home currency is seen as depreciation-prone, it did so in the appreciation-prone environment created by the "successful" stabilization program and relative "undervaluation" of the dollar in the 1980s.

The second factor that came into play was the creation of a pool of international "hot" money created by speculative capital flight from Latin America and elsewhere. Moreover, a number of events occurring at the time may have created an international investment climate in the late 1970s and early 1980s when investors were desperately seeking a safe and profitable place to park their wealth. It is argued that during the turmoil of the period dollar denominated assets were seen as a temporary safe haven. However, as I have shown, no conclusive evidence exists to verify this hypothesis. Therefore, the emerging real interest rate differential (which the empirical evidence in Chapter 4 seems to confirm) and/or speculative capital flight from abroad may explain the initial rise of the dollar, though neither is capable of explaining the continued appreciation of the dollar.

To fully understand the reasons for the development of one-way trading in dollars, it is necessary to explore the political economy of the dollar at the time. Since the end of 1978, U.S. policymakers had committed themselves to supporting the dollar as part of a larger stabilization program. When the dollar began to strengthen on its own and clearly no longer needed official support, the Reagan administration withdrew from any management of the dollar.[26] At first, the Europeans and the Japanese continued to support the value of their currencies in an attempt to prevent the importation of financial instability and to resist inflationary pressures. However, they soon realized that they were fighting a losing battle, and thus by 1982 had virtually stopped their collective intervention.

This point is underscored by the results in Tables 5.1. Beginning in 1981, the leading central banks cut their support for the dollar by more than half. (See the Reagan dummies in Table 5.1.) Therefore, policymakers abroad were unwilling, if not unable, to further contract monetary policy by intervening in the foreign exchange market on a scale large enough to prevent the dollar from appreciating. Moreover, as the world recession deepened and the predominating policy problems became slumping growth and rising unemployment, foreign policymakers began to realize that an appreciating dollar would bring its own benefits by improving the relative competitiveness of their industries and thus help bring their respective economies out of recession by shifting world demand in their favor. If U.S. policymakers were unwilling to participate in the management of the dollar, it was reasoned, foreign central bankers were certainly not obligated to prevent its appreciation.

The withdrawal of official support operations paved the way for the meteoric rise in the dollar. The market was already bullish on the dollar, and now the market was given a free hand to bid the dollar up to new heights. Under the circumstances, speculators set the dollar on an appreciation path that lasted until February 1985.

The Plaza Accord: February 1985 - February 1987

The beginning of the end of the strong dollar era came in mid-January 1985 when finance ministers and central bank governors at a Group of Five meeting (France, Germany, Japan, Britain, and the U.S.) began to reaffirm "their commitment to undertaking coordinated intervention."[27] Unfortunately, the small scale of dollar sales that followed and the lack of any demonstrated effort in fulfilling the new commitment left the markets unconvinced. This set in motion a "euphoric" rise in the dollar lasting through to February 1985. At that point, the Deutsche Bundesbank led a large-scale coordinated intervention aimed at halting the dollar's rise. Between the January meeting and the first of March, dollar sales by the Group of Ten countries totaled about ten billion dollars. While supporting the measure, the United States only contributed seven-hundred million of the total. However, even with only nominal support from the U.S., the February-March intervention succeeded at least in restoring two-way trading in dollars.[28]

The February-March intervention set the stage for a second and more successful attempt at bringing down the value of the dollar. In a Group of Five meeting at the Plaza Hotel in New York City on September 22, the U.S. surprised the world by reversing its own policy stance and supporting coordinated intervention to force a depreciation of the dollar.[29] Once the shift in policy was announced but before the intervention began, the dollar fell nearly six percent in one trading day, the largest such decline since March 1973. The leading central banks then proceeded to intervene by selling about thirteen billion dollars in order to convince the market of the seriousness of their intentions. The intervention was eventually successful in reversing the pattern of trading and produced a depreciation-prone dollar market.

Continuing official pressure on the U.S. dollar through 1986 produced a dramatic collapse in the dollar's exchange value. The trade weighted dollar fell twenty-two percent in 1986 and continued to depreciate by another thirteen and a half percent in 1987. In fact, the Plaza policies were so successful that by early 1987 there was growing concern among foreign policymakers that the depreciating dollar might be headed for a "hard landing" in which speculative flight from the dollar would become so pronounced that it would threaten the stability of the dollar-based international monetary system.[30]

This episode demonstrates two related points that are contrary to the conventional wisdom. The first is that the dollar was not grossly overvalued due to divergent monetary and fiscal polices between the U.S. and its principal economic rivals. For while the Plaza accords did attempt to coordinate monetary and fiscal policies in the Group of Five, the adjustments that were made in this area were by all accounts very modest.[31]

And second, it was demonstrated that central bank intervention could achieve dramatic results in the right circumstances. By 1985 both the market and the central banks were not only convinced that further dollar appreciation was unlikely in the face of the bloated U.S. trade and current account deficits, but also that correcting these imbalances would require a much weaker dollar. Therefore, the international situation created by the overvalued dollar made it relatively easy for the central banks to burst the dollar bubble and initiate a bear dollar market.

The Louvre Accord: February 1987 - Present

Once the dollar's depreciation brought it close to levels that existed in 1980, foreign policymakers began to argue that further depreciation would be harmful to their trading interests. Therefore, they began to push for stabilizing the dollar at then-current levels. Washington agreed to move away from the policy of realignment toward one of stabilization in exchange for a firmer commitment on the part of Japan and Germany to expand their economies and shrink the U.S. trade deficit.[32]

The first sign of the new consensus on managing the dollar came in early February 1987 at a Group of Seven meeting (the Group of Five plus Canada and Italy) in which policymakers agreed in principle to use their intervention strategies in order to stabilize the dollar at then-current levels. This new strategy was formalized at a Group of Five meeting in Paris on February 21-22 at the Louvre. The finance ministers of the Group of Five declared that since currency rates were now consistent with economic fundamentals, it was appropriate to stabilize rates.

The Louvre accord was surprisingly successful at limiting further dollar depreciation. To stabilize the dollar, foreign central banks in 1987 bought large quantities of dollars, intervening at every sign of weakness in the dollar. The success of the Plaza and Louvre agreements raises the question of whether the increased awareness to the "exchange rate problem" and the growing willingness of policymakers to engage in concerted interventions to police the exchange rate system would prove to be a lasting solution, or merely a temporary fix.

The answer to this question depends upon whether or not the leading central banks will continue to work collectively to police the exchange rate system. As Charles Kindleberger, the dean of international economic historians, explains:

> Is a foreign-exchange crisis likely? . . . So long as the G-7 central banks are committed to something like the Plaza or the Louvre agreement, however modified, the dollar will be supported by public authorities if private investors should experience revulsion from it. This is the lender-of-last-resort function at the international level. But like any lender-of-last-resort exercise, it requires political acceptance. If the financial authorities of say, Japan and Germany become locked in disagreement with those of the United States over where the responsibility for stabilizing exchange markets lie, the markets might fall freely between two or more stools.[33]

In the world in which we live where political, economic, and ideological differences abound, it is highly unlikely that the current cooperative arrangements can be counted on to prevent future outbreaks of instability in the dollar-based international monetary system. If the history of the exchange rate system is any guide, the type of cooperation needed to police the exchange rate system tends to emerge only when problems become so pressing that they can no longer be ignored. Clearly a more permanent and lasting solution to the "exchange rate problem" is required.

THE POLITICAL ECONOMY OF THE DOLLAR

Since the fall of the Bretton Woods system, exchange rates between key currencies have been in constant turmoil except for a brief and partial respite from July 1974 to June 1977. The origins of this disarray can be located in the explosive combination of destabilizing currency speculation, unstable exchange rate fundamentals, and a fragmented political system that prevented effective management of currency rates.

The pattern that has emerged from this turmoil is one where "shocks" of a political or economic nature force large, intercurrency portfolio shifts that soon produce one-way speculative betting. As a bubble develops, conflicting views of national self-interest, conflicting ideologies, as well as differences in policy goals inhibit the emergence of effective preventive policy measures.

So far, official intervention has been effective enough in preventing a worldwide collapse by setting limits on rate movements, as we saw in 1978-1979, 1985, and in 1987, and by intervening as a lender of last resort when speculative losses threatened the stability of the international financial system, as in mid-1974. However, the inability of central banks to manage the exchange rate system cooperatively in order to prevent major policy problems from developing in the first place has meant that their role in the arena of international finance has been effectively reduced to "providers of stability of last resort" for an increasingly unstable currency system.

NOTES

1. See Owen F. Humpage, "Exchange Market Intervention: The Channels of Influence," Federal Reserve Bank of Cleveland *Economic Review* (Quarter 3 1986), pp. 2-13 and Anatol B. Balbach, "The Mechanics of Intervention in Exchange Markets," Federal Reserve Bank of St. Louis *Review* (Feb. 1978), pp. 2-7.

2. Humpage, "Exchange Market Intervention," pp. 10-11.

3. See Ronald MacDonald, *Floating Exchange Rates: Theories and Evidence* (London: Unwin Hyman, 1988), pp. 249-259. Rudiger Dornbusch, "Exchange Rate Economics: Where do We Stand?" in Jagdeep S. Bhandari and Bluford H. Putnam, eds., *Economic Interdependence and Flexible Exchange Rates* (Cambridge: MIT Press, 1983), pp. 67-73, Paul Wonnacott, "U.S. Intervention in the Exchange Market for DM, 1977-80," Princeton University *Essays in International Finance* no. 51 (December 1982), Peter J. Quirk, "Exchange Rate Policy in Japan: Leaning Against the Wind," *IMF Staff Papers* (November 1977), pp. 642-664; and George M. von Furstenberg, "New Estimates of the Demand for Non-Gold Reserves under Floating Exchange Rates," *Journal of International Money and Finance* 1 (1982), pp. 81-95.

4. Formally speaking, each currency was pegged to gold, not the dollar. See John Williamson, *The Failure of World Monetary Reform, 1971-1974* (New York: New York University Press, 1977), p. 4.

5. Andrew Shonefield, "International Economic Relations of the Western World: An Overall View," in Andrew Shonefield, ed., *International Economic Relations of the Western World: 1959-1971*, vol. 1 of *Politics and Trade* (London: Oxford University Press, 1976), pp. 20-23 and Charles Coombs, *The Arena of International Finance* (New York: John Wiley & Sons, 1976), pp. 69-91

6. There have been periodic suggestions that the exchange rate system has been rigged by large and small powers alike to further their own domestic policy goals. In this view, exchange rate turbulence is merely a by-product of interstate conflict. See, for example, Riccardo Parboni, *The Dollar and its Rivals: Recession, Inflation, and International Finance* (London: Verso, 1981), passim. Dornbusch found some evidence that Germany used its intervention strategy to export some of its unemployment problem in the 1970s. See Dornbusch, "Exchange Rate Economics: Where do We Stand?" p. 70. I

found no support for Dornbusch's finding, but some support for the Bank of Japan using its interventions to limit the size of its trade surplus. Laurence A. Krause, *A Theoretical and Empirical Examination of Speculation in the Foreign Exchange Market: A Search for Speculative Bubbles* (Ann Arbor, Michigan: University Microfilms International, 1989), pp. 201-202.

7. McKinnon makes a similar point in Ronald I. McKinnon, "Currency Substitution and Instability in the World Dollar Standard," *American Economic Review* 72 (June 1982), pp. 320-333. Maurice Obstfeld has argued that there was quite a bit of sterilization in the fixed rate era. See Maurice Obstfeld, "Can We Sterilize? Theory and Evidence," *American Economic Review: Papers and Proceedings* 72 (May 1982), pp 45-50.

8. See Bank for International Settlements, *Annual Report* (June 1974), pp. 29-32.

9. See Michael Moffitt, *The World's Money* (New York: Simon and Schuster, 1983), ch. 3.

10. Ibid., p. 74.

11. Bank for International Settlements, *Annual Report* (June 1974), p. 29.

12. Ibid., p. 29.

13. See Charles Coombs, "Treasury and Federal Reserve Foreign Exchange Operations," *Federal Reserve Bulletin* (Sept. 1974), pp. 636-650.

14. See Joan Edelman Spero, *The Failure of the Franklin National Bank* (New York: Columbia University Press, 1980), pp. 63-67 and pp. 76-89 and Hyman Minsky, *Stabilizing an Unstable Economy* (New Haven: Yale University Press, 1986), ch. 3.

15. See Aliber, *The International Money Game*, pp. 9-10 and ch. 4.

16. See Bank for International Settlements, *Annual Report* (June 1975), p. 123.

17. Moffitt, *The World's Money*, ch. 5.

18. Bank for International Settlements, *Annual Report* (June 1978), p. 112.

19. Ibid., p. 112.

20. Ibid., p. 112.

21. Ibid., pp. 112-113.

22. Bank for International Settlements, *Annual Report* (June 1979), pp. 136-137.

23. Whether or not the monetary policy experiment of 1979-1982 can be considered monetarist was the subject of much debate. See Benjamin M. Friedman, "Lessons from the 1979-82 Monetary Policy Experiment," *American Economic Review: Papers and Proceedings* 74 (May 1984), pp. 382-387 and Milton Friedman, "Lessons from the 1979-82 Monetary Policy Experiment," *American Economic Review: Papers and Proceedings* 74 (May 1984), pp. 397-400.

24. To quote one observer: "From the perspective of the Fed in October 1979, the overriding imperative for monetary policy was to assuage the inflationary psychology of the public that manifested itself in speculative activity in commodity and foreign exchange markets and threatened to spread to wage setting behavior." Robert Hetzel, "Monetary Policy in the 1980s," Federal Reserve Bank of Richmond *Economic Review* (March/April 1986), p. 22. For an interesting and detailed account of Volcker's monetary policy experiment see William Greider, *Secrets of the Temple: How the Federal Reserve Runs the Country* (New York: Simon and Schuster, 1987).

25. Bank for International Settlements, *Annual Report* (June 1986), p. 142.

26. The policy of nonintervention was announced by the Under Secretary of the Treasury for Monetary Affairs Beryl W. Sprinkel in April 1981. See I. M. Destler and C. Randall Henning, *Dollar Politics: Exchange Rate Policymaking in the United States* (Washington D.C.: Institute for International Economics, 1989), pp. 20-26.

27. For details see Bank for International Settlements, *Annual Report* (June 1986), p. 142. An interesting question is why did it take so long for the political pressure to build to change the policy of nonintervention? Destler and Henning argue that one

reason for the long delay was that exchange rate policy in the U.S. is controlled by a small group in the Treasury and Federal Reserve who are shielded from political pressures. See Destler and Henning, *Dollar Politics*, pp. 33-47.

28. Bank for International Settlements, *Annual Report* (June 1986), p. 145.

29. For the details of the initial currency market interventions, see Yoichi Funabashi, *Managing the Dollar: From the Plaza to the Louvre* (Washington DC: Institute for International Economics, 1989), pp. 22-24.

30. From the beginning Paul Volcker, the Chairman of the Federal Reserve Board, and Karl Otto Pohl, the Bundesbank President, were worried about this prospect: Volcker believed that "self-reinforcing, cascading depreciation of a nation's currency, undermining confidence and carrying values below equilibrium levels, is not in the nation's interest or that of its trading partners." Pohl argued that: "It is hard to trigger an avalanche, but once it starts, it is much harder to stop." They are cited by Funabashi, *Managing the Dollar*, p. 25. Furthermore, an interesting analysis of the likelihood of a "soft" versus a "hard" landing for the dollar and the implications for policy was presented by Stephen N. Marris, "The Decline and Fall of the Dollar: Some Policy Issues." *Brookings Papers on Economic Activity* 1 (1985), pp. 237-249.

31. The coordinated fiscal policy measures called for a reduction in the U.S. budget deficit by 1 percent of GNP for 1986 with more significant reductions to come sometime in the future. Japan agreed to stimulate domestic demand and economic growth, but at the same to *reduce* its fiscal deficits. And Germany agreed to reduce the size of its public sector by cutting taxes and *tightening* spending. With respect to monetary policy, the agreements were even more vague. See Funabashi, *Managing the Dollar*, p. 21, for the agreement on fiscal policy, and pp. 32-36 for the monetary policy side of the agreements.

32. Ibid., 178-182.

33. Charles P. Kindleberger, "Is There Going to be a Depression?" in *The International Economic Order: Essays on Financial Crisis and International Public Goods* (Cambridge: MIT Press, 1988), p. 10.

6

Consequences and Policy

The major claims presented in the preceding chapters raise important policy issues. A strong case for a regulatory offensive against currency speculation rests upon an assessment of its economic and political repercussions. On the one hand, if the spillover effect of speculative bubbles is found to be negligible, then one possible conclusion is that foreign exchange speculation should be tolerated and seen as an international safety valve for the propensity to gamble: After all, destabilizing speculation probably thrives in many asset markets without being much more than a periodic nuisance. But if, on the other hand, foreign exchange market turmoil imposes substantial costs on the world economy, then active policy intervention would be justified. In the main body of this chapter, I will address this issue in an attempt to demonstrate the importance of speculative currency bubbles for international economic policy. The final section will be devoted to outlining briefly, as well as examining critically, the available policy remedies.

Currency bubbles can transmit their effects through a number of channels, but three cases in particular will be examined. In the first instance, I will explore the case for currency bubbles affecting world trade through increasing exchange rate uncertainty.[1] Second, I will discuss the claim that large, bubble related currency misalignments can damage trade relations by increasing protectionist pressure.[2] And finally, I will consider arguments that currency bubbles affect international macroeconomic stability.[3]

TRADE AND EXCHANGE RATE UNCERTAINTY

Speculatively induced currency disturbances can affect the level of international trade by increasing the volatility of exchange rates. It is widely accepted that an increase in nominal exchange rate volatility will make the exchange rate system more unpredictable to traders by diminishing their ability to forecast rate changes. For those engaged in foreign trade, an increase in rate uncertainty multiplies the risk of currency-related loss, thus leading risk-averse agents to divert trade away from the international arena.

More precisely, the additional cost to foreign trade is the result of increased uncertainty about the domestic currency value of sales abroad: For example, an exporter who exchanges goods for foreign currency could never be certain of their domestic currency value. In general, the more uncertainty in the currency system, the greater the risk of currency loss for the exporter. Admittedly, traders could utilize the forward market or other such devices to hedge against exchange risk, but hedging itself imposes direct costs on traders. Theoretically, the additional costs associated with increased exchange rate volatility could prove to be a significant barrier to the expansion of world trade.

The controversies surrounding the link between exchange rate volatility and world trade center on an assessment of how significant a barrier exchange rate uncertainty is to the expansion of trade. If the potential marginal benefits of engaging in international trade are relatively large compared to the additional costs imposed by exchange rate uncertainty, then exchange rate bubbles would not prove to be a strong impediment to trade. In fact, the growth of world trade outstripped the growth of production throughout the 1970s, although world trade growth had diminished sharply in the early 1980s. The existing empirical work shows that the most important determinant in the growth of trade appears to be the growth of world gross domestic product (GDP) .[4]

To gauge the magnitude of the volatility effect on trade, I have estimated a model of trade growth. The model predicts the growth in OECD trade (exports plus imports) using industrial country (by IMF definition) GDP growth and the standard deviation of the trade weighted value of the dollar as a proxy for exchange rate turbulence. Examining Table 6.1, one can see that every percentage point increase in GDP growth adds 2.11 points to trade growth. Thus, over the sample period growth has had a pro-trade bias. On the other hand, for every one point increase in market turbulence, trade growth falls by .24 percentage points.

These results suggest that the volatility effect can be quite substantial. For example, in the 1980s (1980-1986) when exchange rate volatility increased on average by 4.24 points, the predicted effect on OECD trade growth was a loss on average of over one percentage point per year. Seen in this way, there are times when exchange rate-induced uncertainty can pose serious problems to the expansion of trade.[5] However, when considering the floating period as a whole, the evidence suggests that increased exchange rate volatility has hampered the growth of international trade by increasing exchange risk, but the increase in exchange risk has not proved to be an insurmountable barrier to trade growth.

The social cost of increased exchange rate uncertainty is the "efficiency" loss to the international community resulting from decreased international specialization. In other words, the social cost of the volatility effect is the reduction in productive efficiency as producers divert resources to the home market that are better suited for international trade. Yet when all is said and done, this cost is probably not substantial. It is therefore debatable whether policy intervention is warranted if the primary

Table 6.1

Analysis of OECD Trade Growth: 1971 - 1986
(The Dependent Variable is the Growth of OECD Imports Plus Exports)

Variable	OLS Estimates
Growth in Industrial Country GDP	
Estimated Beta	2.11
T Value	(8.80)
Standard Deviation of Trade Weighted Exchange Rate	
Estimated Beta	-.24
T Value	(-1.81)
Intercept	-.14
T Value	(-.99)
R-Squared	.86
Durbin-Watson	2.50
First-Order Rho	-.26

Sources:
OECD trade data (exports plus imports) are from the OECD, *National Accounts*. Industrial country GDP data are from the IMF, *International Financial Statistics*. The standard deviation of the trade weighted exchange rate was computed by taking the standard deviation of the quarterly observations of the Federal Reserve's trade weighted dollar. The Federal Reserve's trade weighted dollar data are from the *Federal Reserve Bulletin*.

social cost associated with currency bubbles is a "misuse" of resources related to increased exchange rate uncertainty.

CURRENCY MISALIGNMENTS AND PROTECTIONISM

Large currency bubbles also are capable of generating substantial competitive misalignments in exchange rates. In the era of floating rates, changes in international price competitiveness tend to occur during gyrations in nominal currency values. The system is currently structured so that nominal currency values are extremely flexible, behaving almost like asset prices. In comparison, however, goods prices tend to be relatively inflexible or even somewhat "sticky." Under this arrangement, significant movements in currency rates are not offset by price level adjustments. This results in large changes in real exchange rates which are the accepted measures of price competitiveness across economies. It is not surprising then that from 1975 through 1987, 99% of the variation in the real exchange rate of the dollar (which is a measure of the relationship of prices converted into a common currency unit between the United States and its industrial rivals) can be accounted for by variations in nominal currency values.[6]

The source of currency misalignments in the current floating exchange rate regime stands in sharp contrast to the origin of competitive misalignments under the Bretton Woods system. In the twilight of the Bretton Woods system, significant competitive disequilibriums began to emerge when policymakers kept exchange rates fixed even as inflation rates differed across economies. During this period, the example most often cited is the overvaluation of the dollar--estimated to have been 15 to 20 percent between 1971 and 1973.[7] At the time, the economics profession was convinced that such "severe"

Table 6.2

United States External Balances: 1970 - 1988
(Billions of Dollars)

Year	Current Account Balance	As a % of GNP	Merchandise Trade Balance	As a % of GNP
1970	+2.3	.2	+2.6	.3
1971	-1.5	-.1	-2.3	-.2
1972	-5.8	-.5	-6.4	-.5
1973	+7.1	.5	+.9	.1
1974	+1.9	.1	-5.5	-.4
1975	+18.1	1.1	+8.9	.6
1976	+4.2	.2	-9.5	-.5
1977	-14.5	-.7	-31.1	-1.6
1978	-15.5	-.7	-34.0	-1.5
1979	-1.0	-.0	-27.5	-1.1
1980	+1.8	.1	-25.5	-.9
1981	+6.9	.2	-28.0	-.9
1982	-8.6	-.3	-36.5	-1.2
1983	-46.3	-1.4	-67.1	-2.0
1984	-107.1	-2.8	-112.5	-3.0
1985	-115.2	-2.9	-122.2	-3.0
1986	-138.8	-3.3	-144.5	-3.4
1987	-154.0	-3.4	-160.3	-3.5
1988	-135.1	-2.8	-126.3	-2.6

Source:
All data are from IMF, *International Financial Statistics.*

competitive imbalances, which resulted in U.S. current account deficits on the order of .5 percent of GNP, could be avoided if exchange rates were permitted to float.

In contrast, the most severe currency overvaluation in the current floating era occurred during the period from 1980 to the second quarter of 1985, when a fifty-four percent swing in the trade weighted exchange rate of the dollar (as estimated by the IMF's MERM) produced over a forty percent loss in real price competitiveness for U.S. industry. Prior to the overvaluation of the dollar, the external position of the United States in 1980, as measured by the current account balance, was roughly in balance. Not surprisingly by 1984, after four years of currency overvaluation, the United States current account balance was over one hundred billion dollars in the red. And large deficits have been the rule ever since. (See Table 6.2 for a summary of the external position of the United States since 1970.) In short, the problem of currency misalignment in the 1980s has dwarfed the competitive disequilibriums created in the final years of the Bretton Woods fixed rate system. It is reasonable to conclude that the "free market" currency system seems capable of producing longer and more severe currency misalignments than policymakers themselves produced in the era of managed currencies.

Once exchange rates do become misaligned, trade imbalances follow. Those nations whose currencies become overvalued (such as the U.S. in the 1980s) experience ballooning trade deficits which result from their industries being at a competitive disadvantage. Conversely, those countries with undervalued currencies run up large trade surpluses due to their favorable competitive positions. Subsequently, currency related trade imbalances generate political pressure for unilateral protection of industry and employment against "unfair" foreign competition in the trading system.

In the deficit countries, the traded goods sector--i.e., the import and export competing industries--come under intense competitive pressure as foreign firms gain cost advantages over domestic producers. The threat of losing both market share and employment in the industries affected increases the political pressure for protectionism. Fred Bergsten and John Williamson claim that the "overvaluation of the dollar has proved to be an accurate 'leading indicator' of trade policy in the United States-- perhaps the most accurate of all such indicators--in the postwar period."[8] The immediate pressure to increase protectionism, therefore, comes from the deficit countries' desires not to suffer any of the consequences of this loss in industrial competitiveness.

Paradoxically, currency misalignments not only generate protectionist pressure in the deficit countries, but also indirectly in the surplus countries as well. During prolonged periods of currency undervaluation, productive capacity and employment in the traded goods sector of surplus countries are increased to take advantage of the competitive imbalance. Once the competitive imbalance disappears, employers and employees in the affected industries put pressure on their governments to protect their newly won but now threatened market positions.[9] The pressure to maintain the profitability and viability of a bloated trade surplus by subsidizing exports, restricting imports, and intervening to maintain the currency undervaluation can be every bit as great as the pressure to protect industries at a competitive disadvantage in deficit countries.

Perhaps the single best contemporary illustration of the effect of currency misalignment on trade relations is the intermittent bilateral trade problem between the U.S. and Japan.[10] Over the last fifteen years there have been three major incidents of trade conflict between the two countries. Before each incident Japan ran up large bilateral trade surpluses, primarily due to currency undervaluation.[11]

The first episode occurred from 1971-1972 during the twilight of the Bretton Woods system. In the late 1960s and early 1970s the yen became undervalued because U.S. inflation exceeded price increases in Japan. This currency misalignment preceded a sevenfold increase in the bilateral trade surplus between the U.S. and Japan. (The surplus went from .5 to 3.5 billion dollars.[12]) A second burst in the bilateral trade surplus occurred in the period from 1976-1978 after the central bank of Japan intervened in the currency markets to block the strengthening of the yen.[13] At this time there was a fivefold increase in the bilateral trade imbalance with Japan. (The trade imbalance rose from around 1.5 to 8 billion dollars.[14])

The dollar bubble from 1980 through February 1985 has produced the largest and perhaps the most damaging jump in the bilateral trade imbalance between the U.S. and Japan. From the first quarter of 1979 through the fourth quarter of 1984 (by the measure constructed in Table 6.3), U.S. industry experienced a thirty-eight percent decline in price competitiveness. This produced a rise in the bilateral trade surplus from around nine billion dollars to over fifty-two billion dollars. The subsequent increase in trade friction between the two countries is too well known to need reiteration.

In the current environment, once any large member in the trading system succumbs to protectionist pressure the most likely response will be retaliatory trade practices by its trading partners. Behind every unilateral decision to protect an industry or group of industries from the competitive disequilibriums produced by the exchange rate system lies the risk of trade wars. But it is clear that the advent of trade wars in an international trading system where all the key economies are heavily dependent for their own economic health on the continued growth of international trade, would be nothing short of economic and political disaster.

In the worst case scenario, the current multilateral trading system would crumble, generating worldwide depression and political disintegration much like that of the interwar period.[15] Even if complete disintegration of the trading system did not occur, trade wars would still

Table 6.3

United States-Japan Trade and Price Competitiveness:
1979:1 - 1984:4

Period	U.S. Producer Prices/Japanese Producer Prices (P/P*)	Exchange Rate (¥/$)	Real Exchange Rate (¥/$)(P/P*)	Bilateral Trade Balance
1979:1	1.01	201.5	203.5	-9.2
1979:2	1.01	217.6	219.8	-12.7
1979:3	1.01	218.9	221.1	-10.0
1979:4	1.01	238.6	241.0	-10.4
1980:1	1.01	243.6	246.0	-10.8
1980:2	.98	232.7	228.0	-13.2
1980:3	1.00	220.1	220.1	-13.2
1980:4	1.02	210.7	214.9	-14.0
1981:1	1.06	205.6	217.9	-14.0
1981:2	1.09	220.0	239.8	-19.6
1981:3	1.09	231.9	252.7	-20.0
1981:4	1.09	224.7	244.9	-18.8
1982:1	1.09	233.5	254.5	-21.2
1982:2	1.10	244.3	268.7	-20.4
1982:3	1.10	258.9	284.8	-20.4
1982:4	1.10	259.7	285.7	-16.8
1983:1	1.10	235.7	259.3	-18.4
1983:2	1.11	237.5	263.6	-20.8
1983:3	1.13	242.5	274.0	-19.3
1983:4	1.13	234.2	264.6	-30.0
1984:1	1.14	231.1	263.5	-27.6
1984:2	1.16	229.6	266.3	-35.6
1984:3	1.14	243.5	277.6	-45.6
1984:4	1.14	246.0	280.4	-52.8

Source:
Producer prices are from OECD, *Main Economic Indicators*, 1980 = 100. The exchange rate data are from IMF, *International Financial Statistics*. The trade data are from IMF, *Direction of Trade Statistics*, billions of dollars, annualized.

produce some or all these effects: a slowdown in the growth of international trade, an accompanying slowdown in economic growth, dislocations in many major industries as the reparcelization of markets takes effect, and an increase in political tension among major trading partners. In any case, a disorganized retreat from current trading relations would result in major economic and political dislocations.

THE MACRO CONSEQUENCES OF CURRENCY BUBBLES

Another spillover effect of currency bubbles is exchange rate-induced "macro shocks." Conservative economists, going back to Milton Friedman's "The Case for Flexible Exchange Rates," have claimed that chaotic exchange rate movements are merely a sign of underlying turbulence in the world economy.[16] In contrast to the conservative view, I will argue that the volatile nature of the exchange rate system is, in part, responsible for the macroeconomic disorder experienced since the advent of generalized floating in March of 1973.

It is indisputable, of course, that since the modern float began the macroeconomic performance of the major industrial economies has worsened significantly. From Table 6.4 one can see that there has been considerable decline in economic growth, a rise in inflationary pressures, and a pronounced increase in unemployment, beginning with the fall of the Bretton Woods system in 1970 and the switch to floating exchange rates in 1973. In short, by standard measures of macroeconomic performance, the floating era has been an economic disaster. However, whether this is due in any part to the performance of the exchange rate system is a matter of contention.

The preceding chapters have shown that both the nominal and real exchange rates have gyrated continuously since the floating era began. These gyrations

Table 6.4

Indicators of Macroeconomic Performance: 1960 - 1986

OECD Economies	1960-69	1970-72	1973-86
Average Growth Rate	4.95%	4.12%	2.50%
Average Inflation Rate	2.84%	5.20%	7.80%
Average Unemployment Rate	2.73%*	3.40%	5.34%+

United States	1960-69	1970-72	1973-86
Average Growth Rate	4.09%	2.73%	2.50%
Average Inflation Rate	2.34%	4.50%	6.40%
Average Unemployment Rate	3.91%	5.36%	7.14%+

West Germany	1960-69	1970-72	1973-86
Average Growth Rate	5.56%	4.13%	1.90%
Average Inflation Rate	2.51%	4.73%	4.00%
Average Unemployment Rate	.78%	.83%	4.16%+

Japan	1960-69	1970-72	1973-86
Average Growth Rate	11.01%	7.73%	3.70%
Average Inflation Rate	5.43%	6.10%	4.80%
Average Unemployment Rate	1.20%	1.23%	2.05%+

*Unemployment data from 1964.
+Unemployment data from 1973-84.

Source:
All data are from the OECD, *Economic Outlook* and *National Accounts*.

are capable of producing fluctuations in both domestic output and inflation rates. Every alteration in the real exchange rate alters the relative competitiveness of national industries on world and domestic markets for traded goods. Exchange rate bubbles can thereby force a reallocation of world output towards depreciating currency countries. Moreover, large currency appreciations and depreciations also can affect a country's cost of competitive and noncompetitive imports. Therefore, either through induced demand pressure or cost pressures, currency bubbles are capable of affecting a country's inflation rate.

Output Shocks

It is an established principle of open economy macroeconomics that currency depreciation tends over time to be expansionary. After a lag, a depreciation of the home currency lowers the price of the home country's exports on world markets and raises the price of imports to the domestic market. A currency depreciation also raises the price of traded goods relative to nontraded goods. These changes in relative prices mean that large currency bubbles will quickly alter both the relative competitiveness of a country's goods on world markets as well as create incentives for producers to move resources into export- and import-competing industries.

Sooner or later, a depreciation of the home currency will begin to raise domestic output and employment as expenditure and resource-switching behavior is induced by the new set of relative prices. In the short run, when elasticities tend to be small, the impact of a currency depreciation may be either slight or, as is often the case, actually worsen the trade balance because prices respond more quickly than quantities. For instance, if a depreciation in the short run forces import prices to rise by ten percent and import quantities to fall by only five percent, then the trade balance may worsen.

However, the longer the period considered, the more responsive quantities will be to the changes in relative prices and the larger will be the expansionary impact of a currency depreciation. The empirical evidence suggests that in general the trade balance first will worsen and then improve in the usual J-curve manner.[17] Theoretically speaking, two exceptions are possible. First, if a country is unusually inflation prone, then a currency bubble could create a sufficient inflationary impact which would offset the nominal depreciation of its currency. Under these circumstances, currency bubbles would not alter a country's competitiveness but merely produce a purely inflationary effect. Or a large currency depreciation might not prove to be expansionary if, for structural reasons, an alteration in relative prices did not promote the necessary expenditure and resource-switching required to improve the balance of trade. In general though, large currency bubbles will alter international competitiveness, the relative price of traded goods, and the distribution of world markets between economic rivals.

Multicountry model estimates of the size of the output effects that result from exchange rate movements have been done for the U.S. and Europe. A twenty percent dollar appreciation, for example, has been estimated to slow the U.S. growth rate by .5 percent the first year and .4 percent the second year.[18] On the other hand, a ten percent depreciation of the dollar has been estimated to reduce European growth by .2 percent the second year, .4 percent the third year, and .3 percent the fourth year after the depreciation.[19] These disturbances are of a fairly large magnitude. The consequences are even worse when it is considered that the burden of these output displacements are placed mainly on the traded goods sector of the respective economies involved, which usually includes a country's most efficient and dynamic industries.[20]

The normal channel through which currency related output shocks are transmitted is a country's balance of trade. To better perceive the magnitude of the damage involved I have estimated a model of the real dollar value of the merchandise trade balance of the United States from the first quarter of 1977 to the fourth quarter of 1988. The explanatory variables in the empirical model are U.S. real GNP, the real GDP of the remaining members of the OECD, and an average of the real trade weighted dollar lagged for two years.

The results are presented in Table 6.5 for both ordinary least squares (OLS) and rho transformed (AR(1)) estimations. These estimates suggest that for every one percent increase in the real trade weighted index of the dollar the trade balance improves by about 2.25 percent. In the period from 1980 to 1984, when the trade deficit increased fourfold (Figure 6.1 shows that the trade imbalance resulted from a stagnation of export earnings combined with a sharp increase in imports), over seventy percent of the deterioration in the trade balance, using the OLS estimator, can be attributed to the dazzling heights that the dollar had climbed to in the 1980s.[21]

The large trade imbalances, besides redistributing effective demand in favor of foreign industry and slowing economic growth in the U.S., have helped "deindustrialize" U.S. manufacturing. An overvalued currency traditionally affects manufacturing more than any other sector, since manufacturing is almost entirely made up of industries that are either import competing or are heavily dependent upon export markets.

It is no surprise, therefore, that the overvaluation of the dollar in the 1980s has been devastating to U.S. manufacturing. The dazzling dollar has produced an enormous loss in price competitiveness for U.S. manufacturing. From 1979 trough February 1985, unit labor costs rose thirty-five percent and export prices thirty-four percent in U.S. manufacturing relative to its industrial competitors.[22] The result has been a significant shrinkage in the manufacturing sector as is evident from employment trends since 1979. (See Figure 6.2.)

Table 6.5

Analysis of the U.S. Trade Balance: 1977:1 - 1988:4

(Billions of 1980 Dollars)

Variable	OLS	AR(1)
U.S. GNP		
Estimated Beta	-.14	-.12
Estimated Elasticity	[6.57]	[5.62]
T Value	(-4.61)	(-3.10)
Rest of OECD GDP		
Estimated Beta	.03	.02
Estimated Elasticity	[2.59]	[1.73]
T Value	(1.77)	(.94)
Real Exchange Rate: Average of Previous Two Years		
Estimated Beta	1.60	1.61
Estimated Elasticity	[2.25]	[2.27]
T Value	(9.50)	(6.93)
Intercept	38.9	37.3
T Value	(1.37)	(.99)
R-Squared	.91	.84
Durbin-Watson	1.14	
First-Order Rho	.41	

Source:
U.S. GDP, OECD GDP, and the GDP deflator data are from OECD, *Quarterly National Accounts*. The trade balance figures are from the IMF, *International Financial Statistics*. The index of the value of the dollar is the IMF's real exchange rate index, IMF, *International Financial Statistics*.

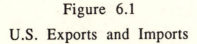

Figure 6.1

U.S. Exports and Imports

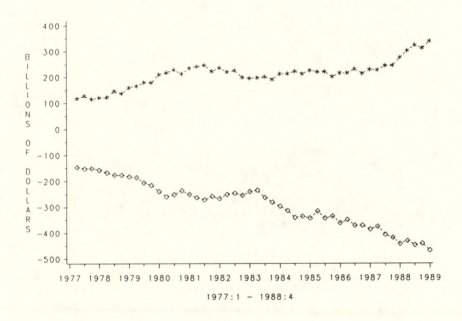

Legend:
Star = exports (+), billions of dollars, annualized.
Diamond = imports (-), billions of dollars, annualized.
Source:
All data are from the IMF, *International Financial Statistics.*

Figure 6.2

Employment Trends

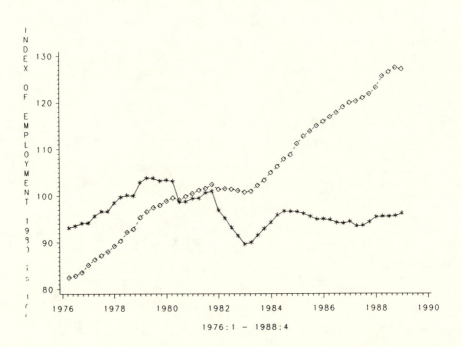

Legend:
Star = manufacturing employment, 1980 = 100.
Diamond = nonmanufacturing employment, 1980 = 100.
Source:
All data are from the *Survey of Current Business*.

This is worrisome for several reasons. If manufacturing employment suffers, not only are jobs lost but usually high-paying job opportunities for low skill workers disappear. In effect, currency overvaluation pushes industrial development in a deleterious direction by shrinking high value-added industries while freeing resources to feed low value-added service jobs. These structural shifts in industry and employment worsen income distribution and lower the effective future growth potential of high-pay blue collar jobs in the United States. In short, our current trade deficits bias current and future industrial development in the U.S. towards low value-added service jobs and away from high value-added manufacturing jobs.

Inflationary Shocks

Foreign exchange disturbances can also produce inflationary shocks. In an open international trading system, countries that experience nominal exchange rate depreciation also will feel induced inflationary pressures. A currency depreciation raises the cost of imports which, in turn, can affect the price level through a number of channels. The first is by raising the cost of imported raw materials to domestic manufacturers. Most industrial countries are import dependent for their supply of at least some basic raw materials, and so currency depreciation will thus raise prime costs, generating cost-push pressure on industrial prices.

The second channel of inflationary pressure works by altering competitive pressure on domestic import-competing industries. For example, a rise in competitive import prices slackens domestic competitive pressure, which produces higher domestic markups and prices. In this case, currency depreciation results in a profits inflation. The third channel through which currency bubbles transmit inflationary pressures is by the wage-setting process. First, a currency depreciation would raise the price of consumer goods and, where there is resistance to changes in real wages, also ignite wage inflation. Second, a currency depreciation, by reducing competitive pressure on domestic industry, would improve the bargaining position of labor, thus enhancing wage inflation.

Finally, a currency depreciation can stimulate inflationary pressures by raising aggregate demand. Sooner or later an improvement in competitiveness will result in an expansion in domestic output and hence inflation. In summary, exchange rate depreciation can transmit inflationary pressure by raising raw material prices, domestic markups, domestic money wage rates, and domestic aggregate demand.

Appreciating currencies are likely to reap the "benefit" of induced deflationary pressure. By making imports cheaper, appreciation works through the same channels but with the opposite effect. However, deflationary pressure may not work with the same force as inflationary pressure if there is a bias against downward flexibility of wages and prices. In this case, deflationary exchange rate pressure will not offset fully the inflationary pressure generated. The end result is that exchange rate gyrations will "ratchet up" world inflation by becoming a net inflationary force on a global scale.[23]

Using multicountry models, conservative estimates have been made of the overall inflationary-deflationary impact of exchange rate disturbances. The estimated effect of a twenty percent dollar appreciation is to lower the U.S. inflation rate by .4 percent the first year, .5 percent the second, and .1 percent the third year.[24] A ten percent dollar depreciation has been estimated to lower the inflation rate in Europe by .5 percent the first year, .1 percent the second year, and .6 percent the third year.[25] The magnitude of the possible inflationary shocks that can result from large currency bubbles may therefore be considerable.[26]

To better appreciate the magnitude of the effect of changes in currency values on domestic inflation rates, I will consider the predicted impact of exchange rate movements on the deceleration of U.S. inflation in the 1980s (consumer price inflation dropped from 13.5 percent in 1980 to 4.3 percent in 1984).[27] Using a conventional price-wage model of inflation, the disinflation effect of the rise in the value of the dollar reduced, on average, consumer price inflation by 1.7 percentage points from 1981 to 1984. This estimate of the disinflationary effect of the dollar's rise assumes that exchange rate appreciation influences the rate of inflation either by increasing output or lowering the cost of imports. By incorporating the effect of exchange rate movements on wage adjustments, Jeffrey Sachs has estimated that the disinflation effect over the same period averaged 2.5 percentage points.[28] In Sachs' model, changes in the value of the dollar get built into wage formation. The appreciation of the dollar is assumed first to directly decelerate consumer prices by lowering the cost of imports. In the next round, wage inflation slows and induces a second indirect round of price deceleration. The cumulative effect of the dollar's rise in Sachs' model is, therefore, larger. Regardless of which model is thought to be more appropriate, exchange rate related deflationary pressure has played a significant role in the deceleration of U.S. inflation in the 1980s.

One common argument made by defenders of the floating rate system is that, since currency depreciation in the United States raises domestic output and inflation while lowering European output and inflation, the benefits and costs to each side balance out. The problem with this claim is that it overlooks the fact that the disturbances may create a host of unwanted policy problems, both present and future, that exacerbate already difficult situations.

For example, the recent dollar appreciation, as I argued, has helped lower U.S. inflation, but only at the cost of battering the traded goods sector in the U.S. If one

takes seriously the claim that one of the goals of the
Reagan administration's supply-side program was to
"reindustrialize" U.S. industry, the strong dollar era, as
argued previously, has undermined that policy by acting
as a potent "deindustrializing" force.

In Europe, on the other hand, the dollar appreciation
came at a time when governments there were engaging
in wholesale attacks on inflation. The additional
inflationary pressure was highly unwelcome. There can
be little doubt that the appreciation of the dollar forced
harsher deflationary policies upon European
governments, which then snuffed out any output
stimulus that the strong dollar initially may have had.

Do Exchange Rates Really Matter?

Recently, economists have questioned the view that
large exchange rate movements are capable of producing
significant macro shocks. The most convincing empirical
support for this view comes from what failed to happen
as a result of the dramatic depreciation of the dollar after
February 1985. According to the existing empirical and
theoretical literature, the large depreciation of the dollar
should have greatly improved the U.S. trade deficit and
nudged U.S. inflation rates upward. Yet, neither result
seems to have materialized.

A sophisticated version of this thesis is argued by
Paul Krugman.[29] He claims that a strange dialectic has
transpired which has detached exchange rates from the
global economy as the exchange rate has been
progressively delinked itself from reality. Exchange rates
are delinked from fundamentals, Krugman argues, by
currency speculators who follow bubble paths in ignoring
the fundamentals. This has created an exchange rate
system that is both extremely volatile and subject to
large, self-reversing swings in rates. Nonfinancial firms
have reacted to these developments by detaching their
pricing and market-positioning investments from short to

medium term movements in currency rates. In turn, as an increasing number of important economic decisions are made regardless of movements in currency rates, policymakers have allowed exchange rates themselves to become further delinked from the fundamentals.

It is clear that there is some truth to Krugman's hypothesis. I believe, however, that he wrongly exaggerates the special circumstances of the post-1985 era into the misleading claim that exchange rates no longer matter. The large appreciation of the dollar from 1980-1985 allowed foreign firms to cut their prices and increase their share of the U.S. market. To increase their share of the U.S. market also required that foreign producers make large, irreversible investments in productive capacity, service outlets, and product marketing. For U.S. firms, these same circumstances forced them to do whatever it took to survive, including reducing their market positioning investments to a minimum.

After 1985, the large depreciation of the dollar forced foreign firms to choose between either (1) raising their prices to protect their markups above unit production costs and thus risk losing their newly won, but now threatened position in the U.S. market, or allowing their markups and profits to fall in order to protect their market shares. There is no doubt that foreign firms chose the latter option.

In the literature this is known as the pass through problem, because foreign firms did not pass through the the dollar's depreciation after February 1985 into import price increases.[30] To illustrate the point, I estimated a simple model of U.S. import prices in which import prices depend on the price level in the U.S. and an average of the nominal trade weighted dollar in the previous two years. I estimated the model through February 1985 so that I could observe its out-of-sample fit after February 1985.[31] As expected, given the size of the dollar's depreciation after February 1985, import prices were predicted to be substantially higher by the end of 1988 than they in fact were. (See Figure 6.3.)

The failure of import prices to rise after 1985 meant that the expected surge in inflation as well as the expected improvement in the trade balance would be severely blunted. To demonstrate this first point, in Figure 6.4 I plotted import and domestic prices. The plots suggest that after 1981 the decline in import prices slowed the rate of increase in domestic prices. However, the subsequent depreciation of the dollar after 1985 did not lead to an acceleration of import price inflation as was the case with dollar depreciation in the late 1970s. Turning to the trade balance, I reestimated the trade balance model through February 1985 to show the out-of- sample fit of the model after 1985. As expected, the model forecasts a rather substantial improvement in the trade balance that never materialized. (See Figure 6.5.)

Therefore, the evidence available points to the fact that the exchange rate pass through problem after 1985 may account for the fact that large exchange rate changes no longer seem to matter as much as they once did. However, no evidence exists to suggest that the real economy has progressively detached itself from the exchange rate system. Rather, what evidence we have suggests that the prolonged appreciation of the dollar has generated a significant long-term trade problem for the U.S. that has been difficult, if not impossible, to undo by depreciating the dollar.

Politics and Speculative Flight

The dilemmas for policy makers created by speculative foreign exchange disturbances are more complex than just those related to exchange related shocks. As Ragnar Nurkse has argued concerning the 1920s floating era, and as the current literature on the so-called peso problem suggests, speculative foreign

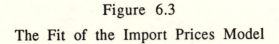

Figure 6.3

The Fit of the Import Prices Model

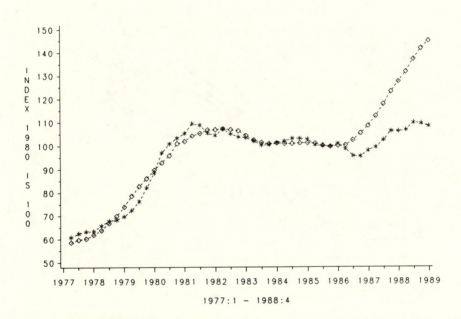

Legend:
Star = predicted import prices.
Diamond = an index of actual import prices, 1980 = 100.
Source:
All data are from the IMF, *International Financial Statistics*.

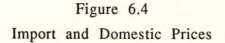

Figure 6.4

Import and Domestic Prices

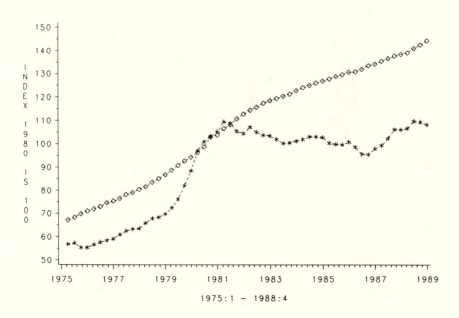

Legend:
Star = an index of import prices, 1980 = 100.
Diamond = index of domestic (U.S.) prices, 1980 =100.
Source:
Import prices are from the IMF, *International Financial Statistics*. Domestic prices (GNP deflator) are from the OECD, *National Accounts*.

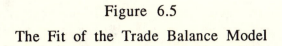

Figure 6.5

The Fit of the Trade Balance Model

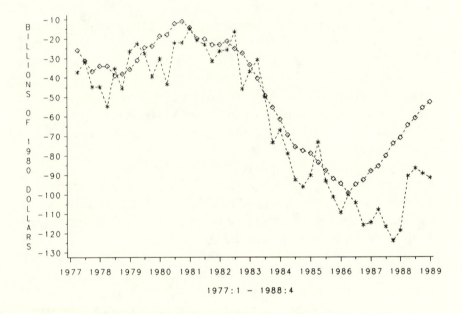

Legend:
Star = the U.S. trade balance, billions of 1980 dollars, annualized.
Diamond = predicted U.S. trade balance.
Source:
See Table 6.5.

exchange disturbances probably have undermined certain types of policies as well as aggravated political instability. For example, both the attempted economic expansion engineered by the Carter administration from 1977-1978 and more recently by the French Socialist government in the early 1980s were undermined, in part, by speculative flight from their respective currencies. We probably have already reached the point where major economic programs must be "approved" by the foreign exchange markets if they are to be effective. This will hinder, if not prevent, many liberal-left macroeconomic policy initiatives. Current arrangements leave too much power in the hands of currency speculators who decide what is "sound" policy. The current exchange rate regime in effect promotes a dictatorship of currency speculators over governments that cannot act effectively to select appropriate policies in periods where policy experimentation is needed.

In the current politically volatile environment, exchange rate movements are likely to feed instability, just as they did in the interwar period. Oil shocks, regional wars, changes in governments and even vague rumors generate an inordinate amount of currency movement. Needless to say, currency speculators do not support weak currencies or "weak" governments, but flee to strong currencies and move their wealth to "safe" political boundaries. Fragile and uncertain political situations, consequently, are exacerbated by currency speculators who jump on the bandwagon of speculative flight. The unequivocal conclusion is that present arrangements serve to complicate and magnify most political and economic problems. More and more observers of this scene are becoming convinced that change, perhaps even dramatic restructuring, is warranted before we experience a debacle of the magnitude of the 1930s.

PROPOSALS FOR REFORM

Suggested remedies for the exchange rate problem essentially break down into three categories. First, it has been suggested that floating rates be abandoned and some form of state control over exchange rates be reintroduced. The underlying theme in these proposals is that the balance between state and market control over the exchange rate must be addressed in order to begin dealing with the bubble problem. The suggested alternative currency regimes include returning to a Bretton Woods fixed parity system,[32] adopting a crawling peg that would maintain more or less constant real exchange rates[33] and, more recently, establishing broad real exchange rate zones to prevent excessive currency misalignments by central bank intervention and international policy coordination.[34] The second set of suggestions would leave in place the current floating regime, but would impose capital controls to "throw a little sand" into the well-greased machinery of the foreign capital and exchange rate markets. In this vein, recent suggestions include a foreign exchange transactions tax[35] and a real interest rate equalization tax.[36] These proposals assume that as long as financial capital is mobile and can freely and with little cost move across borders in search of higher returns, the problem of destabilizing speculation will continue to haunt the international financial system. Finally, there are a host of proposals to use existing policy instruments for policing or merely limiting the damage of foreign currency speculation. Suggestions include using interest rate policy to stabilize exchange rates[37] or offsetting exchange rate-induced disturbances with internationally coordinated monetary and fiscal policies.[38] Recently, there have also been more calls for tougher foreign exchange market intervention to prevent large currency misalignments by continuing and enlarging upon the policies initiated by the Plaza and Louvre agreements.

In the absence of the political power and will that is needed to reregulate the currency markets as well as to control capital movements, attempting to limit currency bubbles by the use of traditional policy instruments may be ineffective. Moreover, the use of traditional policy instruments to control exchange rates would, at the very least, further overburden these instruments by forcing policymakers to abandon other policy objectives altogether in order to focus their instruments on correcting currency related problems. Clearly, alternative instruments are needed to limit the damage that turmoil induced by speculation can unleash until conditions allow for the reregulation of exchange rates and capital movements.

The main channel through which exchange rate bubbles affect real activity is by significant alterations of international competitiveness. Bubbles can force large and sudden changes in nominal and real exchange rates that generate large, competitive imbalances between trading partners. The existing proposals have attempted to limit the bubble themselves rather than the competitive imbalances they create. It should be easier though to prevent the transmission of the "shock" than the bubbles themselves. For example, if an internationally agreed system of taxes on imports and subsidies on exports were put into place, then it would be possible to stabilize real competitiveness between major trading partners. Exchange rate movements then could be left to the whims of speculators while the trading system would be shielded from exchange rate related "shocks."

The initial setting of the level of real competitiveness to be defended by a multilateral tax-subsidy plan could be designed to maintain "appropriate" (i.e., mutually agreed) current account balances among trading partners. Initially such policies could be used to first reduce existing current account imbalances. Once existing imbalances are reduced and the targeted levels of competitiveness are established, they could be defended within a band of plus or minus x percent. If a sharp rise or fall in currency values forced the level of competitiveness outside the band, then a correction would be made by taxing imports and subsidizing exports to eliminate the competitive imbalance. The tax-subsidy plan would require that the rules of international trade be altered to allow for variable and temporary "barriers" to trade to protect the international trading system from the turbulence of the currency system. It may seem that the tax-subsidy plan addresses the problem but avoids dealing with the source of the problem. The rationale for this intentional evasion is that it may be easier, both technically and politically, to control goods than to control the movement of finance or currencies. The plan is clearly a "second-best" option, but perhaps in the current environment it is more feasible than the alternatives.

CONCLUSION

The "exchange rate problem" is only one of several problems that are currently haunting the global financial and trading system. Since the early 1970s the world economy has had to withstand sharp increases in oil prices, accelerating inflation, growing debt and financial problems, as well as global deceleration of economic growth with rising unemployment rates. Better management of the exchange rate problem will not in itself salvage the financial and trading system or restore pre-1973 growth and unemployment rates. However, it is becoming increasingly clear that without better management of the exchange rate system it will be difficult, if not impossible, to address the host of policy problems that now threaten to undermine global economic and political stability.

Whatever policies finally are adopted, they must suit the magnitude of the problem. The history of the interwar period has taught us that currency instability literally can destroy the pillars of the world's trading and financial system. The disequilibriums produced by the exchange rate system have not yet resulted in a collapse and may not do so, though they have certainly increased the risk of collapse. To cover our eyes to the danger signs that abound is becoming increasingly difficult. We would do better to remember the lessons of the interwar period and not continue to turn a blind eye to the problem. Given the present circumstances, it may be better to "overreact" and err on the side of caution than to be accused after the fact of having done too little too late.

NOTES

1. See M. A. Akhtar and R. Spence Hilton, "Effects of Exchange Rate Uncertainty on German and U.S. Trade," Federal Reserve Bank of New York *Quarterly Review* 9 (Spring 1984), pp. 7-16 and Thomas D. Willett, "Exchange Rate Volatility, International Trade, and Resource Allocation: A Perspective on Recent Research," *Journal of International Money and Finance* 5, supplement (March 1986), pp. 101-112.

2. See C. Fred Bergsten and John Williamson, "Exchange Rates and Trade Policy," in William R. Cline, ed., *Trade Policy in 1980s* (Cambridge: MIT Press, 1983), pp. 99-120.

3. It is interesting to note that Nurkse included two of the three arguments made here in his critique of floating exchange rates. Specifically, he argued that floating rates had three serious disadvantages: "In the first place, they create an element of risk which tends to discourage international trade. Secondly, . . . exchange fluctuations involve constant shifts of labour and other resources between production for the home market and production for export." Ragnar Nurkse, *International Currency Experience: Lessons of the Inter-War Period* (Princeton: League of Nations, 1944), pp. 210-211.

4. See Rachel McCulloch, "Unexpected Real Consequences of Floating Exchange Rates," Princeton University *Essays in International Finance* no. 153

(August 1983), p. 6 and C. Fred Bergsten and William R. Cline, "Trade Policy in the 1980s," in William R. Cline, ed., *Trade Policy*, pp. 73-75.

5. Akhtar and Hilton argue that U.S.-German trade has suffered by increased volatility in the dollar-mark market. See Akhtar and Hilton, "Effects of Exchange Rate Uncertainty on German and U.S. Trade." However, these findings of an adverse effect on trade represent the exception rather than the rule in the literature. See Willett, "Exchange Rate Volatility, International Trade, and Resource Allocation."

6. The 99% figure was derived by regressing the real value of the dollar against the nominal value of the dollar. In summary, the results of the regression analysis are:

Real Value of the Dollar = .08 + 1.00(Nominal Dollar)
$$(.10) \quad (95.6)$$

Underneath the estimated betas are the T values. Note that the constant is not significantly different from zero and the estimated slope is equal to one. These results suggest that changes in the nominal value of the dollar "explain," for all practical purposes, the movement of the real value of the dollar.

7. Bergsten and Williamson, "Exchange Rates and Trade Policy," p. 110.

8. Ibid., p. 103.

9. Ibid., pp. 102-103.

10. An alternative hypothesis put forward by Thurow is that Japan's economy is "structurally dependent" on exporting more than it imports. Historically, this "structural surplus" was hidden by: (1) the need to import to industrialize in the 1950s; (2) rapid growth in the 1960s; and (3) the rise in oil prices in the 1970s. Now that these counter tendencies have run their course, Japan is racking up record trade surpluses. See Lester C. Thurow, "Exports and the Japanese Economy," in *Japan's Economy and Trade With the United States*, Joint Economic Committee, 99th Congress (Washington DC: U.S. GPO, 1985), pp. 1-12.

11. See C. Fred Bergsten, "What to do about the U.S.-Japan Economic Conflict," *Foreign Affairs* vol. 60, no. 5 (Summer 1982), pp. 1059-1075.

12. Ibid., p. 1060.

13. Bergsten argues that "Japan had committed one of its most serious policy errors of the postwar period [by intervening in the currency markets to keep the yen undervalued]." Ibid., p. 1066. Japan more than doubled its foreign exchange holdings to keep the yen from rising in value. Official holdings increased from 16 billion dollars to 33 billion. See McClellan A. Dubois, "Japan: Foreign Exchange Policy," in *Japan's Economy and Trade With the United States,* p. 97.

14. Bergsten, "What to do about U.S.-Japan Economic Conflict, " p. 1066.

15. See Charles P. Kindleberger, *The World in Depression* (Berkeley: University of California Press, 1973).

16. To quote Friedman: "The ultimate objective is a world in which exchange rates, while free to vary, are in fact highly stable. Instability of exchange rates is a symptom of instability in the underlying economic structure. Elimination of this symptom by administrative freezing of exchange rates cures none of the underlying difficulties and only makes adjustment to them more painful." Milton Friedman, "The Case for Flexible Exchange Rates," in *Essays in Positive Economics* (Chicago: University of Chicago Press, 1953), p. 158.

17. See, for example, Rudiger Dornbusch and Paul R. Krugman, "Flexible Exchange Rates in the Short Run," *Brookings Papers on Economic Activity* 3 (1976), pp. 551-554.

18. These estimates come from the Federal Reserve's multicountry trade and payments model. The 20% appreciation is in the Federal Reserve's trade weighted effective exchange rate of the dollar. See Dornbusch, "Equilibrium and Disequilibrium Exchange Rates," National Bureau of Economic Research *Reprint* no. 388 (July 1983), pp. 590-591.

19. These estimates come from OECD's multilateral model. Ibid., p. 591.

20. One study has concluded that the dollar appreciation from 1980 to 1982 cut U.S. exports by $35 billion and increased U.S. imports by $10 billion. See Robert A. Feldman, "Dollar Appreciation, Foreign Trade, and the U.S. Economy," *Federal Reserve Bank of New York Quarterly Review* 7 (Summer 1982), pp. 1-9.

21. The model estimated in Table 6.5 does not communicate either the entire scope of the problem, or the complex relationship between the exchange rate and the trade deficit. In a previous study, I estimated a distributed lag model, which showed that it would take at least a year before any turn-around in the trade problem will begin. (This is the so-called J-curve effect, where after a real depreciation the trade balance will first worsen then improve tracing out the shape of the letter J.) Moreover, the estimates of lagged effect of the real exchange rate on the trade balance suggested it takes two and a half years before the full effect is complete. See Laurence A. Krause, *A Theoretical and Empirical Examination of Speculation in the Foreign Exchange Market: A Search for Speculative Bubbles* (Ann Arbor, MI: University Microfilms International, 1989), pp. 250-253. More sophisticated models of the U.S. trade and current account deficits also show that the overwhelming cause of the deficits was the dollar. See William L. Helkie and Peter Hooper, "An Empirical Analysis of the External Deficit, 1980-1986," in Ralph C. Bryant, Gerald Holtham, and Peter Hooper, eds., *External Deficits and the Dollar: The Pit and the Pendulum* (Washington DC: The Brookings Institution, 1988), pp. 40-42. Glick and Huctchinson argue that the appreciation of the dollar did not deindustrialize the U.S. economy. See Reuven Glick and Michael Hutchinson, "Does Exchange Rate Appreciation 'Deindustrialize' the Open Economy? A Critique of U.S. Evidence *Economic Inquiry* 28 (Jan. 1990), pp. 19-37.

22. The data are from OECD, *Economic Outlook* 38 (December 1985), p. 168.

23. This is known in the literature as the Mundell-Laffer hypothesis. For an evaluation see W. Max Corden, *Inflation, Exchange Rates, and the World Economy: Lectures on International Monetary Economics* 2nd ed. (Chicago: University of Chicago Press, 1981), pp. 77-83.

24. These estimates are from the Federal Reserve's multicountry trade and payments model. See Dornbusch, "Equilibrium and Disequilibrium Exchange Rates," pp. 589-590.

25. These estimates are from the OECD's multilateral model. Ibid., p. 591.

26. One study estimated that when the dollar fell, on a trade weighted basis by 12% from the first quarter of 1977 to the last quarter of 1978, that roughly two-thirds of the increase in the U.S. inflation, from 5 to 8%, was a result of the fall. See Joel L. Prakken, "The Exchange Rate and Domestic Inflation," Federal Reserve Bank of New York *Quarterly Review* 4 (Summer 1979), p. 49.

27. This section relies on Jeffrey D. Sachs, "The Dollar and the Policy Mix: 1985," *Brookings Papers on Economic Activity* 1 (1985), pp. 116-185.

28. Ibid., pp. 130-133.

29. Paul R. Krugman, *Exchange-Rate Instability* (Cambridge: MIT Press, 1989).

30. See, for example, Peter Hooper and Catherine L. Mann, "Exchange Rate Pass-through in the 1980s: The Case of U.S. Imports of Manufactures," *Brookings Papers on Economic Activity* 1 (1989), pp. 297-329 and Helkie and Hooper, "An Empirical Analysis of the External Deficit," pp. 51-56.

31. The estimated model is:

Import Prices = -113.5+1.07(U.S. Deflator)+1.03(Exchange
$$(-13.7)\ (32.2)(14.4)\ \ \text{Rate})$$

R-Squared   .97
Durbin Watson .47
First-Order Rho .76

Source: Import prices and exchange rate data are from the IMF, *International Financial Statistics*. The U.S. GNP deflator data are from the OECD, *National Accounts*.

32. See, for example, Michael Moffitt, "Global Monetary Mess," *New York Times* (29 July 1983), p. 23.

33. See John Williamson, "The Crawling Peg in Historical Perspective," in John Williamson, ed., *Exchange Rate Rules* (New York: St. Martin's Press, 1981).

34. John Williamson, "The Exchange Rate System," *Institute for International Economics* 5 (Sept. 1983).

35. James Tobin, "A Proposal for International Monetary Reform," *The Eastern Economic Journal* (July-Oct. 1978), pp 153-159.

36. Dornbusch, "Equilibrium and Disequilibrium Exchange Rates," pp. 593-596.

37. Ronald I. McKinnon, "Why Do Floating Exchange Rates Fail?" Hoover Institute *Working Papers in Economics* no. E-83-12 (July 1983).

38. Dornbusch and Krugman, "Floating Exchange Rates in the Short Run," pp. 573-575.

Bibliography

Ackley, Gardner (1983), "Commodities and Capital: Prices and Quantities." *American Economic Review: Papers and Proceedings* 73, Mar., pp. 1-16.

Akhtar, M. A. and Hilton, Spence R. (1984) "Effects of Exchange Rate Uncertainty on German-U.S. Trade." Federal Reserve Bank of New York *Quarterly Review* 9, Spring, pp. 7-16.

Aliber, Robert Z. (1983), *The International Money Game* New York: Basic Books.

_____ (1974), "Attributes of National Monies and the Interdependence of National Monetary Policies," in Aliber, Robert Z., ed., *International Financial System* Chicago: University of Chicago Press, pp. 111-126.

_____ (1973), "The Interest Rate Parity Theorem: A Reinterpretation." *Journal of Political Economy* 81, Nov.-Dec., pp. 1451-1459.

_____ (1970), "Speculation in the Flexible Exchange Revisited." *Kyklos* 23, pp. 303-314.

_____ (1962), "Speculation in the Foreign Exchanges: The European Experience." *Yale Economic Essays* Spring, pp. 170-245.

Artus, Jacques R. (1976), "Exchange Rate Stability and Managed Floating: The Experience of the Federal Republic of Germany." IMF *Staff Papers* July, pp. 312-333.

Ayanian, Robert (1988), "Political Risk, National Defence and the Dollar." *Economic Inquiry* 26, April, 345-351.

Backus, David (1984), "Empirical Models of the Exchange

Rate: Separating the Wheat from the Chaff." *Canadian Journal of Economics* vol. 17, no. 4, pp. 824-846.

Balbach, Anatol B. (1978), "The Mechanics of Intervention in Exchange Markets." Federal Reserve Bank of St. Louis *Review* Feb., pp. 2-7.

Bank for International Settlements (1988), *Annual Report* June, pp. 165-193.

_____ (1987), *Annual Report* June, pp. 151-178.

_____ (1986), *Annual Report* June, pp. 141-167.

_____ (1985), *Annual Report* June, pp. 140-154.

_____ (1983), *Annual Report* June, pp. 138-152.

_____ (1980), *Annual Report* June, pp. 133-145.

_____ (1979), *Annual Report* June, pp. 134-137.

_____ (1978), *Annual Report* June, pp. 111-128.

_____ (1975), *Annual Report* June, pp. 26-30 and p. 123.

_____ (1974), *Annual Report* June, pp. 28-32 and pp. 142-143.

Baumol, William J. (1957), "Speculation, Profitability, and Stability." *Review of Economics and Statistics* 39, Aug., pp. 263-271.

Begg, David K. H. (1982), *The Rational Expectations Revolution in Macroeconomics* Baltimore: John Hopkins University Press.

Bergsten, Fred C. (1982), "What to do About the U.S.-Japan Economic Conflict." *Foreign Affairs* vol. 60, no. 5, Summer, pp. 1059-1075.

_____ and Williamson, John (1983), "Exchange Rates and Trade Policy," in Cline, William, ed., *Trade Policy in the 1980s* Cambridge: MIT Press, pp. 99-120.

Bernstein, Edward M. (1985), "The United States as an International Debtor Country." *The Brookings Review* Fall, pp. 28-36.

Bilson, John F. 0. (1981), "The Speculative Efficiency Hypothesis." *Journal of Business* 54, pp. 435-451.

Blanchard, Olivier J. (1979), "Speculative Bubbles, Crashes and Rational Expectations." *Economic Letters* 3, pp. 387-389.

_____ and Watson, Mark W. (1983), "Bubbles, Rational Expectations, and Financial Markets." National Bureau of Economic Research *Reprint* no. 374, June, pp. 295-315.

Block, Fred L. (1977), *The Origins of International Economic Disorder: A Study of United States International Monetary Policy from World War II to the Present* Berkeley: University of California Press.

Branson, William H. (1986), "The Limits of Monetary Coordination as Exchange Rate Policy." *Brookings Papers on Economic Activity* 1, pp. 175-207.

―――― (1985), "Causes of Appreciation and Volatility of the Dollar," in Federal Reserve Bank of Kansas City *The U .S. Dollar: Recent Developments, Outlook, and Policy Options* Jackson Hole, Wyoming, Aug., pp. 33-52.

―――― (1977), "Asset Markets and Relative Prices in Exchange Rate Determination."*Sozialwissenschaftliche Annalen* 1, pp. 69-89.

Brown, Brendan (1987), *The Flight of International Capital* London: Croom Helm.

Bryant, Ralph C. (1987), *International Financial Intermediation* Washington DC: The Brookings Institution.

Buiter, Willem H., and Miller, Marcus (1983a), "Real Exchange Rate Overshooting and the Output Costs of Bringing Down Inflation: Some Further Results," in Frenkel, Jacob A., ed., *Exchange Rates and International Macroeconomics* Chicago: University of Chicago Press, pp. 317-358.

―――― (1983b), "Monetary Policy and International Competitiveness: The Problems of Adjustment." *Oxford Economic Papers* no. 33, July, pp. 143-175 .

Canzoneri, Matthew B. (1983), "Rational Destabilizing Speculation and Exchange Intervention Policy." *Journal of Macroeconomics* 5, Winter, pp. 75-90.

Coombs, Charles (1976), *The Arena of International Finance* New York: John Wiley & Sons.

―――― (1974), "Treasury and Federal Reserve Foreign Exchange Operations." *Federal Reserve Bulletin* Sept., pp. 636-650.

Cooper, John (1974), "How Foreign Exchange Operations

can go Wrong." *Euromoney* May, pp. 4-7.

Cooper, Richard N. (1982), "Flexible Exchange Rates, 1973-1980: How Bad Have They Really Been?" in Cooper, Richard N., Kenen, Peter, De Marcedo, Jorge Braga, and Ypersele, Jacques Van, eds., *The International Monetary System Under Flexible Exchange Rates* Cambridge: Ballinger Publishing Co., pp. 3-15.

Corden, W. Max (1986), "Fiscal Policies, Current Accounts, and Real Exchange Rates." *Weltwirtschaftliches Archiv* 3, pp. 423-438.

_____ (1981), *Inflation, Exchange Rates, and the World Economy: Lectures on International Monetary Economics* 2nd ed, Chicago: University of Chicago Press.

Cosset, Jean-Claude. (1984), "On the Presence of Risk Premiums in Foreign Exchange Markets." *Journal of International Economics* 9, pp. 139-154.

Dam, Kenneth W. (1982), *The Rules of the Game* Chicago: University of Chicago Press.

Davidson, Paul (1982), *International Money and the Real World* New York: Wiley.

Destler, I. M. and Henning, C. Randall (1989), *Dollar Politics: Exchange Rate Policymaking in the United States* Washigton D.C.: Institute for International Economics.

Diba, Behzad T. and Grossman, Herschel I. (1983), "Rational Asset Price Bubbles." National Bureau of Economic Research *Working Paper* no. 1059, Jan.

Dornbusch, Rudiger (1987), "Exchange Rate Theory and the Overvalued Dollar," in *Dollars, Debts, and Deficits* MIT Press, pp. 3-15.

_____ (1986), "Flexible Exchange Rates and Excess Capital Mobility." *Brookings Papers on Economic Activity* 1, pp. 209-226.

_____ (1983a), "Exchange Rate Economics: Where do We Stand?" in Bhandari, Jagdeep S. and Putnam, Bluford H., eds., *Economic Interdependence and Flexible Exchange Rates* Cambridge: MIT Press, pp. 45-83.

_____ (1983b), "Flexible Exchange Rates and

Interdependence." IMF *Staff Papers* 30, pp. 3-30.

_____ (1983c), "Equilibrium and Disequilibrium Exchange Rates." National Bureau of Economic Research *Reprint* no. 388, July.

_____ (1983d) "Flexible Exchange Rates and Independence." IMF *Staff Papers* 30, pp. 3-30.

_____ (1980a), *Open Economy Macroeconomics* New York: Basic Books.

_____ (1980b), "Exchange Rate Risk and the Macroeconomics of Exchange Rate Determination." National Bureau of Economic Research *Working Paper* no. 493, June.

_____ (1978), "Monetary Policy Under Exchange-Rate Flexibility," in Federal Reserve Bank of Boston *Managed Exchange Rate Flexibility: The Recent Experience* conference series no. 20, Oct., pp. 90-122.

_____ (1976a), "Exchange Rate Expectations and Monetary Policy." *Journal of International Economics* 6, pp. 231-244.

_____ (1976b), "Expectations and Exchange Rate Dynamics." *Journal of Political Economy* 84, Dec., pp. 1161-1176.

_____ and Fischer, Stanley (1987), *Macroeconomics* 4th ed, New York: McGraw-Hill.

_____ and Krugman Paul R. (1976), "Flexible Exchange Rates in the Short Run." *Brookings Papers on Economic Activity* 3, pp. 537-575.

Driskill, Robert A. and Sheffrin, Steven M. (1981), "On the Mark: Comment." *American Economic Review* 71, Dec., pp. 1068-1074.

Dubois, McClellan A. (1985), "Japan's Foreign Exchange Policy," in Joint Economic Committee, 99th Congress, *Japan's Economy and Trade With the United States* Washington DC: U.S. GPO.

Dunn, Robert M. Jr. (1983), "The Many Disappointments of Flexible Exchange Rates." Princeton University *Essays in International Finance* no. 154, Aug.

Fama, Eugene F. (1970) "Efficient Capital Markets: A

Review of Theory and Empirical Work." *Journal of Finance: Papers and Proceedings* 25, May, pp. 383-417.

Feldman, Robert A. (1982), "Dollar Appreciation, Foreign Trade, and the U.S. Economy." Federal Reserve Bank of New York *Quarterly Review* 7, Summer, pp. 1-9.

Feldstein, Martin (1986), The Budget Deficit and the Dollar," in *National Bureau of Economic Research Macroeconomics Annual 1986* Cambridge: MIT Press, pp. 355-392.

Fitoussi, Jean-Paul and Phelps, Edmund S. (1988), *The Slump in Europe* Oxford: Basil Blackwell.

Flood, Robert P. and Garber, Peter M. (1982), "Bubbles, Runs, and Gold Monetization," in Wachtel, Paul, ed., *Crises in the Economic and Financial Structure* Lexington, MA: Lexington Books, pp. 275-316.

Frankel, Jeffrey A. (1988), "Ambiguous Policy Multipliers in Theory and Evidence," in Bryant, Ralph C., Henderson, Dale W., Holtham, Gerald, Hooper, Peter, and Symansky, Steven A., eds., *Empirical Macroeconomics for Interdependent Economies* Washington D.C.: The Brookings Institution.

_____ (1985), "The Dazzling Dollar." *Brookings Papers on Economic Activity* 1, pp. 199-217.

_____ (1983), "Monetary and Portfolio Balance Models of Exchange Rate Determination," in Bhandari, Jagdeep S. and Putnam, Bluford H., eds., *Economic Interdependence and Flexible Exchange Rates* Cambridge: MIT Press, pp. 84-115.

_____ (1982), "In Search of the Exchange Risk Premium: A Six Currency Test Assuming Mean-Variance Optimization." *Journal of International Money and Finance* 1, pp. 255-274.

_____ (1981), "On the Mark: Reply." *American Economic Review* 71, Dec., pp. 1075-1082.

_____ (1979), "On the Mark: A Theory of Floating Exchange Rates Based on Real Interest Rate Differentials." *American Economic Review* 69, Sept., pp. 610-622.

_____ and Froot, Kenneth A. (1990), "Chartists, Fundamentalists, and Trading in the Foreign Exchange Market." *American Economic Review: Papers and Proceedings* 80, May, pp. 181-185.

Frenkel, Jacob A. (1985), "Commentary on Causes of Appreciation and Volatility of the Dollar," in Federal Reserve Bank of Kansas City *The U.S. Dollar: Recent Developments, Outlook, and Policy Options* Jackson Hole, Wyoming, Aug., pp. 53-63.

_____ (1983), "Flexible Exchange Rates, Prices, and the Role of 'News'," in Bhandari, Jagdeep S. and Putnam, Bluford H., eds., *Economic Interdependence and Flexible Exchange Rates* Cambridge: MIT Press, pp. 3-41.

_____ (1978), "A Monetary Approach to the Exchange Rate: Doctrinal Aspects and Empirical Evidence," in Frenkel, Jacob A. and Johnson, Harry G., eds., (1978), *The Economics of Exchange Rates* Reading, MA: Addison-Wesley.

_____ and Goldstein, Morris (1988), "Exchange Rate Volatility and Misalignment: Evaluating Some Proposals for Reform," in Federal Reserve Bank of Kansas City *Financial Market Volatility*, Jackson Hole, Wyoming, Aug., pp. 185-215.

_____ and Razin, Assaf (1987), "The Mundell-Fleming Model a Quarter Century Later." *IMF Staff Papers* 34, Dec., pp. 567-620.

_____ and Rodriguez, Carlos A. (1982), "Exchange Rate Dynamics and the Overshooting Hypothesis." IMF *Staff Papers* 29, March, pp. 1-30.

_____ and Mussa, Michael L. (1980), "The Efficiency of Foreign Exchange Markets and Measures of Turbulence." *American Economic Review: Papers and Proceedings* 70, May, pp. 374-381.

_____ and Levich, Richard M. (1979), "Covered Interest Arbitrage and Unexploited Profits? Reply." *Journal of Political Economy* 87, pp. 418-422.

_____ and Johnson, Harry G., eds., (1978), *The Economics of Exchange Rates* Reading, MA: Addison-Wesley.

_____ and Levich, Richard M. (1977), "Transactions Costs and Interest Arbitrage: Tranquil Versus Turbulent Periods." *Journal of Political Economy* 85, Dec. pp. 1209-1226.

_____ and Johnson, Harry G., eds., (1976), *The Monetary Approach to the Balance of Payments.* Toronto: University of Toronto Press.

Friedman, Benjamin M. (1984), "Lessons from the 1979-82 Monetary Policy Experiment." *American Economic Review: Papers and Proceedings* 74, May, pp. 382-387.

Friedman, Milton (1988), "Introduction," in Leo Melamed, ed., *The Merits of Flexible Exchange Rates* Fairfax, Virginia: George Mason University Press, pp. xix-xxv.

_____ (1984), "Lessons from the 1979-82 Monetary Policy Experiment." *American Economic Review: Papers and Proceedings* 74, May, pp. 397-400.

_____ (1953), "The Case for Flexible Exchange Rates," in *Essays in Positive Economics* Chicago: University of Chicago Press, pp. 157-203.

Funabashi, Yoichi (1988), *Managing the Dollar: From the Plaza to the Louvre* Washington DC: Institute for International Economics.

Giddy, Ian H. (1979), "Measuring the World Foreign Exchange Market." *Columbia Journal of World Business* Winter, pp. 36-48.

Gintis, Herbert (1982), "International Capital Markets and the Validity of National Macroeconomic Models." Unpublished, University of Massachusetts, Amherst.

Glick, Reuven and Hutchison, Michael (1990), "Does Exchange Rate Appreciation 'Deindustrialize' the Open Economy? A Critique of U.S. Evidence." *Economic Inquiry* 28 28, pp. 19-37.

Goldfeld, Stephen M. (1976), "The Case of the Missing Money." *Brookings Papers on Economic Activity* 3, pp. 683-730.

_____ (1973), "The Demand for Money Revisited." *Brookings Papers on Economic Activity* 3, pp. 577-637.

Goodhart, Charles (1988), "The Foreign Exchange Market:
A Random Walk with a Dragging Anchor." *Economica*
55, Nov, pp. 437-460.

Greider, William (1987), *The Secrets of the Temple: How
the Federal Reserve Runs the Country* New York:
Simon and Schuster.

Grossman, Sanford J. and Shiller, Robert J. (1981), "The
Determinants of the Variability of Stock Prices."
American Economic Review: Papers and Proceedings
71, May, pp. 222-227.

Guttentag, Jack M. and Herring, Richard J., "Disaster
Myopia in International Banking." Princeton
University *Essays in International Finance* no. 164,
Sept.

Hakkio, Craig S. (1986), "Interest Rates and Exchange
Rates-What is the Relationship?" Federal Reserve
Bank of Kansas City *Economic Review* Nov., pp. 33-43.

_____ (1985), "The Reaction of Exchange Rates to
Economic News." Federal Reserve Bank of Kansas City
Research Working Paper no. 85-01.

Hart, Oliver D. and Kreps, David M. (1986), "Price
Destabilizing Speculation." *Journal of Political Economy*
94, pp. 927-952.

Haynes, Stephen E. and Stone, Joe A. (1981), "On the
Mark: Comment." *American Economic Review* 71, Dec.,
pp. 1060-1067.

Helkie, William L. and Hooper, Peter (1988), "An
Empirical Analysis of the External Deficit, 1980-86," in
Bryant, Ralph C., Holtman, Gerald, Hooper, Peter, eds.,
*External Deficits and the Dollar: The Pit and the
Pendulum* Washington, DC: The Brookings Institution.

Hetzel, Robert (1986), "Monetary Policy in the Early
1980s." Federal Reserve Bank of Richmond *Economic
Review* March/April, pp. 20-31.

Hicks, John (1974), *The Crisis in Keynesian Economics*
New York: Basic Books.

Hillier, Brian (1986), *Macroeconomics: Models, Debates
and Developments* New York: Oxford University Press.

Hobsbawm, Eric (1987), *The Age of Empire, 1875-1914*

New York: Random House.

Hooper, Peter and Mann, Catherine L. (1989), "Exchange Rate Pass-Through in the 1980s: The Case of U.S. Imports of Manufactures." *Brookings Papers on Economic Activity* 1, pp. 297-329.

Horsefeld, J. Keith, ed. (1969), *The International Monetary Fund 1945-1965: Twenty Years of International Monetary Cooperation* vol. III: Documents, Washington DC: International Monetary Fund.

Huang, Rodger D. (1981), "The Monetary Approach to Exchange Rate in an Efficient Foreign Exchange Market: Tests Based on Volatility." *The Journal of Finance* 36, March, pp. 31-41.

Humpage, Owen F. (1986), "Exchange Market Intervention: The Channels of Influence." Federal Reserve Bank of Cleveland *Economic Review* 3, pp. 2-13.

Isard, Peter (1978), "Exchange Rate Determination: Survey of Popular Views and Recent Models." Princeton University *Princeton Studies in International Finance* no. 42, May.

_____ and Stekler, Lois (1985), "U.S. International Capital Flows and the Dollar." *Brookings Papers on Economic Activity* 1, pp. 219-229.

Kaldor, Nicholas (1987) "Limits on Growth." *Oxford Economic Papers* 38, pp. 187-198.

_____ (1960), "Speculation and Economic Activity," in *Essays in Economic Stability and Growth* London: Gerald Duckworth and Co. Ltd., pp. 17-58.

Katz, Eliaken (1982), "Money Supply Turbulence and Exchange Rate Turbulence: Some Empirical Results." *Journal of Macroeconomics* 4, Fall, pp. 483-488.

Kemp, Donald S. (1976), "The U.S. Dollar in International Markets: Mid-1970 to Mid-1976." Federal Reserve Bank of St. Louis *Review* 58, Aug., pp. 7-14.

Kemp, Murray C. (1963), "Speculation, Profitability, and Price Stability." *Review of Economics and Statistics* 45, pp. 185-189.

Keynes, John Maynard (1980a), *The Collected Writings of John Maynard Keynes* vol. XXV London: Cambridge University Press.

_____ (1980b) *The Collected Writings of John Maynard Keynes* vol. XXVI London: Cambridge University Press.

_____ (1964), *The General Theory of Employment, Interest, and Money* New York: Harcourt, Brace and World, Inc.

_____ (1920), *The Economic Consequences of the Peace* New York: Harcourt, Brace and Howe.

Khoury, Sarkis J. (1984), *Speculative Markets* New York: Macmillan.

Kimbrough, Kent P. (1983), "Prices, Output, and Exchange Rate Movements." *Journal of International Economics* 11, pp. 25-44.

Kindleberger, Charles P. (1988), "International Public Goods Without International Government," in *The International Economic Order: Essays on Financial Crisis and International Public Goods* Cambridge: MIT Press.

_____ (1988), "Is There Going to be a Depression," in *The International Economic Order: Essays on Financial Crisis and International Public Goods* Cambridge: MIT Press, pp. 3-15.

_____ (1986), *The World in Depression,1929-1939* Berkeley: University of California Press.

_____ (1978), *Manias, Panics, and Crashes: A History of Financial Crises* New York: Basic Books.

_____ (1966), "Flexible Exchange Rates," in *Europe and the Dollar* Cambridge: MIT Press, pp. 112-136.

Klitgaard, Tom (1983), "Are Markets Really Efficient?" Federal Reserve Bank of San Francisco *Weekly Letter* Sept. 30, pp. 1-4.

Kohlhagen, Steven W. (1982), "The Experience of Floating: The 1973-1979 Dollar," in Dreyer, Jacob S., Haberler, Gottfried, and Willett, Thomas, eds., *The International Monetary System: A Time of Turbulence* Washington DC: American Enterprise Institute, pp. 142-179.

_____ (1979), "The Identification of Destabilizing Foreign

Exchange Speculation." *Journal of International Economics* 9, pp. 321-340.

Kouri, Pentti J. K. (1976), "The Exchange Rate and the Balance of Payments in the Short Run and in the Long Run: A Monetary Approach." *Scandinavian Journal of Economics* vol. 78, no. 2, pp. 280-304.

Krause, Laurence A. (1989), *A Theoretical and Empirical Examination of Speculation in the Foreign Exchange Market: A Search for Speculative Bubbles* Ann Arbor, Michigan: University Microfilms International.

Krugman, Paul R. (1989), Exchange-Rate Instability Cambridge: MIT Press

_____ (1983), "Oil Shocks and Exchange Rate Dynamics," in Frenkel, Jacob A., ed., *Exchange Rates and International Macroeconomics* Chicago: University of Chicago Press, pp. 259-271.

Lessard, Donald R. and Williamson, John, eds. (1987), *Capital Flight and Third World Debt* Washington DC: Institute for international Economics.

Levich, Richard M. (1979), "On the Efficiency of Markets for Foreign Exchange," in Frankel, Jeffrey and Dornbusch, Rudiger, eds., *International Economic Policy: Theory and Evidence* Baltimore: Johns Hopkins University Press, pp. 246-269.

_____ (1978), "Further Results in the Efficiency of Markets for Foreign Exchange," in Federal Reserve Bank of Boston *Managed Exchange Rate Flexibility: The Recent Experience*, conference series no. 20, Oct., pp. 58-80.

MacDonald, Ronald (1988), *Floating Exchange Rates: Theory and Evidence*, London: Unwin Hyman, 1988.

Marris, Stephen N. (1985), "The Decline and Fall of the Dollar: Some Policy Issues." *Brookings Papers on Economic Activity* 1, pp. 237-249.

Marx, Karl (1974), *Capital* vol. I, London: Lawrence and Wishart.

McCormick, Frank (1979), "Covered Interest Arbitrage: Unexploited Profits? Comment." *Journal of Political Economy* 87, pp. 411-417.

McCulloch, Rachel (1983), "Unexpected Real Consequences of Floating Exchange Rates." Princeton University *Essays in International Finance* no. 153, Aug.

McKinnon, Ronald I. (1983), "Why Do Floating Rates Fail?" Hoover Institute *Working Papers in Economics* no. E-83-12, July.

_____ (1982), "Currency Substitution and Instability in the World Dollar Standard." *American Economic Review* 72, June, pp. 320-333.

_____ (1981), "The Exchange Rate and Macroeconomic Policy: Changing Postwar Perceptions." *Journal of Economic Literature* 19, pp. 531-557.

Meade, J. E. (1952), *The Balance of Payments* London: Oxford University Press.

Meese, Richard A. and Rogoff, Kenneth (1983), "Empirical Exchange Rate Models of the Seventies: Do They Fit Out of Sample?" *Journal of International Economics* 14, pp. 3-24.

Minsky, Hyman (1986), *Stabilizing an Unstable Economy* New Haven: Yale University Press.

_____ (1975), *John Maynard Keynes* New York: Columbia University Press.

Moffitt, Michael (1983a), *The World's Money* New York: Simon and Schuster.

_____ (1983b), "Global Monetary Mess." *New York Times* 29 July, p. 23.

Morgan Guaranty Trust (1986), "LDC Capital Flight." *World Financial Markets* Mar., pp. 13-15.

Mussa, Michael L. (1979), "Empirical Regularities in the Behavior of Exchange Rates and Theories of the Foreign Exchange Market," in Brunner, Karl and Meltzer, Allan H., eds., *Policies for Employment, Prices, and Exchange Rates* Carnegie-Rochester conference series in Public Policy, a supplement to the *Journal of Monetary Economics*, pp. 9-57.

_____ (1978), "The Balance of Payments, and Monetary and Fiscal Policy Under a Regime of Controlled Floating," in Frenkel, Jacob A. and Johnson, Harry G., eds., *The Economics of Exchange Rates* Reading, MA:

Addison-Wesley, pp. 47-65.

Nurkse, Ragnar (1944), *International Currency Experience: Lessons of the Inter-war Period* Princeton: League of Nations.

Obstfeld, Maurice (1985), "Floating Exchange Rates: Experience and Prospects." *Brookings Papers on Economic Activity* 2, pp. 368-450.

_____ (1982), "Can We Sterilize? Theory and Evidence." *American Economic Review: Papers and Proceedings* 72, May, pp. 45-50.

Okina, Kunio (1983), "Speculative Bubbles and Official Intervention." Unpublished, University of Chicago.

Palyi, Melchior (1972), *The Twilight of Gold* Chicago: Henry Regnery Company.

Parboni, Riccardo (1981), *The Dollar and its Rivals: Recession, Inflation, and International Finance* London: Verso.

Pippinger, John (1986), "Arbitrage and Efficient Markets Interpretations of Purchasing Power Parity." Federal Reserve Bank of San Francisco *Economic Review* Winter, pp. 31-47 .

Poole, William (1967a), "Speculative Prices as Random Walks: An Analysis of Ten Time Series of Flexible Exchange Rates." *Southern Economic Journal* 33, April, pp. 468-478.

_____ (1967b), "The Stability of the Canadian Flexible Exchange Rate." *Canadian Journal of Economics* 33, pp. 205-217.

Prakken, Joel L. (1979), "The Exchange Rate and Domestic Inflation." Federal Reserve Bank of New York *Quarterly Review* 4, Summer, pp. 49-55.

Quirk, Peter J. (1977), "Exchange Rate Policy in Japan: Leaning Against the Wind." IMF *Staff Papers* Nov., pp. 642-664.

Rapping, Leonard A. and Bennett, Stephen (1988), "Financial Deregulation, Speculation and the Interest Rate." in Leonard A. Rapping, *International Reorganization and American Economic Policy* New York: Harvester.

_____ and Pulley, Lawrence B. (1985), "Speculation, Deregulation and the Interest Rate." *American Economic Review: Papers and Proceedings* 75, May, pp. 108-113.

Rivera-Batiz, Francisco L. and Rivera-Batiz, Luis (1985), *International Finance and Open Economy Macroeconomics* New York: Macmillan.

Sachs, Jeffrey D. (1985), "The Dollar and the Policy Mix: 1985." *Brookings Papers on Economic Activity* 1, pp. 116-185.

Salant, Stephen W. and Henderson, Dale W. (1978), "Market Anticipations of Government Policies and the Price of Gold." *Journal of Political Economy* 86, pp. 627-648.

Samuelson, Paul A. (1980), *Economics* 11th ed., New York: McGraw-Hill.

Schadler, Susan (1977), "Sources of Exchange Rate Variability: Theory and Empirical Evidence." IMF *Staff Papers* July, pp. 253-296.

Schulmeister, Stephan (1983), "Exchange Rates, Prices, and Interest Rates: Reconsidering the Basic Relationships of Exchange Rate Determination." C. V. Starr Center for Applied Economics *Economic Research Reports* July.

Shafer, Jeffrey R. and Loopesko, Bonnie E. (1983), "Floating Exchange Rates After Ten Years." *Brookings Papers on Economic Activity* 1, pp. 1-70.

Shiller, Robert J. (1981a), "The Use of Volatility Measures in Assessing Market Efficiency." *Journal of Finance* 36, May, pp. 291-304.

_____ (1981b), "Do Stock Prices Move Too Much to be Justified by Subsequent Changes in Dividends?" *American Economic Review* 71, June, pp. 421-436.

Shonefield, Andrew (1976), "International Economic Relations of the Western World: An Overall View," in Shonefield, Andrew, ed., *International Economic Relations of the Western World: 1959-1971*, vol. I of *Politics and Trade* London: Oxford University Press.

Spero Edelman, Joan (1980), *The Failure of the Franklin*

National Bank New York: Columbia University Press.

Stein, Jerome L. (1962), "The Nature and Efficiency of the Foreign Exchange Market." Princeton University *Essays in International Finance* no. 40, Oct.

_____ (1961), "Destabilizing Activity Can be Profitable." *Review of Economic Statistics* 43, Aug., pp. 301-302.

Strange, Susan (1987), *Casino Capitalism* Oxford: Basil Blackwell.

Sweeney, Richard J. (1985), "Stabilizing or Destabilizing Speculation? Evidence from the Foreign Exchange Markets," in Arndt, Sven, Sweeney, Richard J., and Willett, Thomas D., eds., *Exchange Rates, Trade, and the U.S. Economy* Cambridge: American Enterprise Institute, pp. 107-123.

Sweezy, Paul M. and Magdoff, Harry (1987), "The Financial Explosion," in *Stagnation and the Financial Explosion* New York: Monthly Review Press, pp. 141-150.

Thurow, Lester C. (1985), "Exports and the Japanese Economy," in Joint Economic Committee, 99th Congress, *Japan's Economy and Trade With the United States* Washington DC: U.S. GPO, pp. 1-12.

Telser, Lester G. (1959), "A Theory of Speculation Relating Profitability and Stability." *Review of Economics and Statistics* 41, Aug., pp. 295-301.

Tobin, James (1978), "A Proposal for International Monetary Reform." *The Eastern Economic Journal* 4, July-Oct., pp. 153-159.

Von Furstenberg, George M. (1982), "New Estimates of the Demand for Non-Gold Reserves Under Floating Exchange Rates." *Journal of International Money and Finance* 1, pp. 81 - 95.

Willett, Thomas D. (1986), "Exchange Rate Volatility, International Trade, and Resource Allocation: A Perspective on Recent Literature." *Journal of International Money and Finance: Papers and Proceedings* 5, pp. 101-112.

_____ (1982), "The Causes and Effects of Exchange Rate Volatility," in Dreyer, Jacob S., Haberler, Gottfried, and

Willett, Thomas D., eds., *The International Monetary System: A Time of Turbulence* Washington DC: American Enterprise Institute, pp. 24-64.

_____ and Wihlborg, Clas (1990), "International Capital Flows, the Dollar, and U.S. Financial Policies," in Haraf, William and Willett, Thomas D., eds., *Monetary Policy in an Era of Change: The International Dilemma* (Washington DC: American Enterprise Institute, 1990), pp. 73-99.

_____, Khan, Waseem, and Hovanessian, Aida Der (1985), "Interest Rate Changes, Inflationary Expectations and Exchange Rate Overshooting: The Dollar-DM Rate," in Arndt, Sven W., Sweeney, Richard J., and Willett, Thomas D., eds., *Exchange Rates, Trade, and the U.S. Economy* Cambridge: American Enterprise Institute/Ballinger, pp. 49-71.

Williamson, John (1983), "The Exchange Rate System." *The Institute for International Economics* 5, Sept.

_____ (1981), "The Crawling Peg in Historical Perspective," in Williamson, John, ed., *Exchange Rate Rules* New York: St. Martin's Press.

_____ (1977), *The Failure of World Monetary Reform, 1971-1974* New York: New York University Press.

_____ (1972), "Another Case of Profitable Destabilizing Speculation." *Journal of International Economics* 2, pp. 77-84.

Wolfson, Martin H. (1986), *Financial Crises: The Postwar U.S. Experience* New York: M. E. Sharpe.

Wonnacott, Paul "U.S. Intervention in the Exchange Market for DM, 1977-80." Princeton University *Essays in International Finance* no. 51.

Yeager, Leland B., *International Monetary Relations* New York: Harper and Row, 1966.

Index

Ackley, G., 70
Adjustable peg exchange rate system, 5, 8, 29, 64-65, 77, 201, 265. *See also* Bretton Woods
Akhtar, M. A., 268
Aliber, R. Z., 51, 53, 196, 198, 233
Arendt, S. W., 187
Ayanian, R., 197-198

Backus, D., 192, 194, 195
Baker, J. A., 93
Balbach, A. B., 231
Bank for International Settlements, 93, 216, 224. *See also* BIS *Annual Report*
Bank of England, 2, 18, 205
Bank of Japan, 206, 222, 232
Banks, and foreign exchange market, 66-67, 68
Baumol, W. J., 31-32, 53
Begg, D. K. H., 54, 55
Belgium, 3-4
Bennett, S., 109
Bergsten, C. F., 244, 268, 269, 270
Berstein, E. M., 196
BIS *Annual Report*, 93, 108, 112, 113, 196, 233, 234
Blanchard, O. J., 36, 38-39, 54-55, 55, 56, 69, 108, 115
Block, F. L., 105, 106
Blumenthal, M., 90. *See also* Carter Administration
Branson, W., 165-178, 181, 195, 199
Bretton Woods System, and currency and financial arrangements, 62-65; and

currency overvaluation, 236-238; and currency speculation, 218; demise of, 7, 63-65, 75, 88, 104, 106, 185, 215; and exchange rates, 7-8, 14; key features of, 5, 105, 202; and macroeconomic performance, 247-249. *See also* adjustable peg
Brimmer, A., 87-88
British pound, 3, 4, 80, 115
Brown, B., 111
Bryant, R. C., 106
Buiter, W. H., 193-194
Bubbles, definition of, 13-14, 55, 59; economic and political effects of, 238-263; empirical evidence for, 44, 49-50, 76-105, 115, 181-185, 200-201; and financial markets, 36-39; and the foreign exchange market, 14-16, 34, 39-41; and government policies, 40-41, 93-94, 202, 215-230; irrationally of, 46-49; and policy remedies for, 265-267. *See also* destabilizing speculation
Budget deficits, and exchange rates, 23-24, 163, 165-170; and interest rates, 164-170, 178-179; U.S. and foreign, 176, 199-200, 235. *See also* fiscal policy
Bundesbank, 87-88, 92, 217, 221, 222, 227, 235

Canada, 121, 134, 158, 206,

291